Worship is grand Story enacted, not just told. It is the ⸱ writ large and passionately visioned. It is our tangled un-doings, hard choices, wrong turns, and second chances ⸱⸱ beauty and painstaking care. McFee gets all this deep in her bones, and her book is brilliant because of it. Clearly, she is one of the most masterful worship guides to appear in decades.

—SALLY MORGENTHALER, AUTHOR OF *WORSHIP EVANGELISM*

Marcia McFee has written an amazing "A-ha!" book on worship in a sea of "Ahh!" resources. "Ahh!" books confirm and carry on what you've always thought. Think Like a Filmmaker *is an "A-ha!" book that will introduce you to new approaches and fresh ways of thinking about worship design. Worship artists will not want to let it out of arm's reach.*

—LEONARD SWEET, BEST-SELLING AUTHOR, PROFESSOR (DREW UNIVERSITY, GEORGE FOX UNIVERSITY, TABOR COLLEGE), AND CHIEF CONTRIBUTOR TO *PREACHTHESTORY.COM*

The Church in the West needs all the encouragement it can get to re-evaluate its worship forms. There is no prescriptive form for how we all should worship. Marcia describes a stimulating creative process that we can all relate to. Best of all she describes a process for teams to collaborate across disciplines and skillsets. Any worship curator will find the worship events they design significantly enhanced with the practical help Marcia offers.

—MARK PIERSON, PASTOR, SPEAKER, WORSHIP CURATOR, AUTHOR OF *THE ART OF CURATING WORSHIP: RESHAPING THE ROLE OF WORSHIP LEADER*

Marcia McFee's use of the filmmaker model for the exploration of sensory-rich worship is a treasure of discourse, concepts, vocabulary, processes, exercises, procedures, illustrations, and online resources. She has hundreds of suggestions for ways to approach worship in a variety of congregations and settings. Possessing not only a substantive grasp of worship, McFee integrates it with the know-how that combines scholarship, art, and craft. The sustained excellence of this volume is simply mind-blowing.

—TEX SAMPLE, AUTHOR AND ROBERT B. AND KATHLEEN ROGERS PROFESSOR EMERITUS OF CHURCH AND SOCIETY, SAINT PAUL SCHOOL OF THEOLOGY

Lived liturgy happens when people—all the people—do the work of bringing our whole selves to the table, sitting together and passing on what we receive. Marcia invites us to ritual artistry—a "trellis" on which the expression of the people grows from the ground up, making room for more voices and for declaration that isn't just decoration.

—TRAVIS REED, FOUNDER & FILMMAKER, THE WORK OF THE PEOPLE

I consider this a new must-have book for pastoral leaders who are serious about helping worship go deeper and farther in the task of growing your congregation's spiritual life. I believe that the monotony of much of our worship (no matter the style) is contributing to the demise of many of our congregations. Marcia's experience in helping congregations create and experience meaningful and memorable worship for all kinds of people is distilled into this book. What a gift!

—THE REV. DR. ANN M. PHILBRICK, ASSOCIATE FOR CHURCH TRANSFORMATION FOR THE PRESBYTERIAN MISSION AGENCY (PCUSA).

Our favorite films "make us forget we're in a movie." Transported into other worlds via scripts, soundtracks and cinematography the power of story takes hold. And why should our worship gatherings be any less? Think Like a Filmmaker will empower worship teams to let go of the linear "three songs and a sermon"—uncover their own layers of divine creativity – and engage an entirely new way of designing worship.

—KIM MILLER, AUTHOR AND WORSHIP AND CAMPUS DESIGNER—GINGHAMSBURG CHURCH

We know a good movie when we see one, just like we know sensory-rich worship when we experience it. Here, the art of worship, especially the artistic lens of great worship design, is explored from angles both sensory and scientific, challenging the plugged-in, piecemeal approach of "insert hymn here" and "now we need a prayer." Think Like a Filmmaker offers a different take, believing worship can be, and should be, as sweeping and memorable as the best film you've ever seen. This book shows you how.

—THE REV. J. BENNETT GUESS, FORMER EXECUTIVE MINISTER, LOCAL CHURCH MINISTRIES, UNITED CHURCH OF CHRIST

The powerful medium of film and the alluring power of mystery go together, and Marcia McFee knows why and shows how in her one-of-a-kind book. She is in full command of the creative capacities inherent in the "lens" of film for the shaping of compelling worship proclamations in the 21st century. Those who design worship will find here abundant resources for shaping ultimately transformative experiences for congregations of all sorts and sizes.

—Dr. Bob Hill, Minister Emeritus, Community Christian Church, Kansas City, Missouri and host of "Religion on the Line" radio talk show

"Dr. Marcia McFee's vision and ideas are a gift to the global church. This is a must-read for worship planners challenged to connect the worshipper with the Divine in exciting and innovative ways. Packed with 'A-ha' moments, Think Like a Filmmaker provides insight about the theory and practice of worship. Its message is universal, making it an essential resource for every pastor. Once I started reading, I could not put it down.

—Sudarshana Devadhar, Bishop, Boston Episcopal Area (New England Conference) of the United Methodist Church

This is a desperately needed book for today's Church. Marcia offers real insight and sources of inspiration for those designing worship services. I challenge anyone to read this book and not find it filled with "A-ha!" moments. Beware – this book could seriously change your Sundays!

—Chris Loughlin, PictureWise Productions, former Executive Producer, BBC TV Religion and Ethics Department

Having taught worship for 27 years, I can't wait to use this book in class. Marcia McFee has identified some new dimensions of vital worship and clearly explained best practices for worship that will nurture faith and discipleship in the world. Many people who are yearning for ways to design worship that will be meaningful in our changing world will find help in this very interesting book.

—Ruth Duck, Emeritus Professor of Worship, Garrett-Evangelical Theological Seminary

Anyone who has a serious investment in the "big picture" of Christian worship's potential should read this book. I have worked and played beside Marcia in worship for many years, marveling at her vision and exquisite skill in leading meaningful and memorable liturgy. Now worship designers everywhere can rejoice that she has shared her wisdom, leading us with refreshing insight into the possibilities for vital, faithful worship in the 21st century church.

—MARK A. MILLER, ASSOCIATE PROFESSOR OF CHURCH
MUSIC, DREW THEOLOGICAL SCHOOL AND LECTURER
IN SACRED MUSIC, YALE DIVINITY SCHOOL

For those designing and leading worship for the first time or early in their ministry as well as those who have been designing and leading worship for years, Think Like a Filmmaker offers a new, if challenging, way to develop meaningful, dynamic, authentic and beautiful worship. Dr. McFee has provided a resource for churches of all types to utilize for the glory of God!

—SALLY DYCK, UNITED METHODIST RESIDENT
BISHOP OF THE CHICAGO AREA

In a world of noise pollution and sensory overstimulation, the Body of Christ often suffers in silence, frozen in old forms that once held life. Marcia McFee offers a vibrant vision of the arts in service of the gospel in this congregational-friendly text and on-line resources. She invites us to take up the task of being "ritual artists" and "story-dwellers" and there is a place for everyone in this new creation.

—HEATHER MURRAY ELKINS, PROFESSOR OF
WORSHIP, PREACHING, AND THE ARTS

Words are my stock-in-trade, but as a filmmaker, writer and ordained minister, I believe an over-reliance on "the words" in worship dilutes their very power by neglecting the visual-sensory context in which those words are received. Dr. Marcia McFee understands this paradox, and her book provides a provocative new lens for looking at communicating "the story"—not just the words—in worship more effectively and powerfully.

—THE REV. KATHLEEN LaCAMERA, FILMMAKER,
WRITER AND CHAPLAIN, UNITED KINGDOM

THINK LIKE A
FILMMAKER

Sensory-Rich Worship Design for Unforgettable Messages

STEP-BY-STEP HELP FOR WORSHIP PLANNING
FROM THE WORSHIP DESIGN STUDIO

Marcia McFee, Ph.D.

Trokay Press
Truckee, CA

Trokay Press
14757 Royal Way
Truckee, CA 96161

Author photo by Chris Nelson
Cover photo by Jeremy Fukunaga
Cover Figure and Interior photos by Alexandra Childs
Back matter photo by Jamie Steckelberg Scott
Book Design by 1106 Design
Editing by Tyler Nickl

ISBN: 978-0-9974978-0-9

Library of Congress Control Number: 2016905889

Distributed by IngramSpark

Printed in the United States of America

For the countless churches, pastors, and worship teams that,
week after week, strive to bring a liberating message to a hurting world
and then go out and live that message—
welcoming the stranger,
feeding the hungry,
clothing the naked,
sheltering the homeless,
and working tirelessly to free the oppressed—
all in the name of the One who is Love and Justice.

CONTENTS

ACKNOWLEDGEMENTS

As you will surmise from reading this book, I believe wholeheartedly in the need for collaboration in our art forms, in our worship, and in our work to make this world a better place for all people. This book is no exception, and it is only by vast numbers of collaborations over the last 20+ years of ritual artistry and ministry that I am able to offer you the knowledge and experience expressed here.

There are congregations all over this country who have been my teachers even as I was their "consultant." It is their passion for, and response to, life-giving, diverse, and transforming worship that urges me on in this ministry of teaching. I acknowledge their gift of simply showing up to workshops, retreats, and worship services and then feeding back to me their experience and wisdom. To the hundreds of churches that are now actively part of the Worship Design Studio, I am honored to walk alongside you in your ministry.

There are denominational leaders who continue to give me so many opportunities to keynote, teach, and design worship for regional, national and international gatherings where I am blessed to interact with people from many walks of life and contexts of ministry. These experiences have been invaluable and continue to stretch and challenge me to make worship "the work of the people"—all the people.

Educators and mentors throughout my life—from my early career in professional music, dance, and theater to later theological degrees—have colluded with the Spirit to create a stream of vocation whose flow I could not resist. Colleagues at the North American Academy of Liturgy keep my love for inquiry and research alive in the midst of this ministry of practical theology to which I am called.

And to the team of people without whom the scope of my work would not be possible: you inspire me, inform me, and add to my love and passion for ritual artistry. The number of Worship Design Studio guest experts grows, increasing the depth of wisdom available to local church pastors, staff, and volunteers who benefit from their work. Special thank you's to my amazing team, whose efforts keep the whole thing not only running but keep it fun and real for me: Jordan Decker, Director of Operations; Jenna Johnson, Projects Assistant and Social Media Coordinator; Mark Bowman, Events Coordinator and Registrar; Michelle Jones-Whitlock and Chuck Bell, Worship Design Studio Associates and Content Contributors; Dave Baker and GetUWired, Marketing; Brian Sheridan and Lance Brown at iComSolutions Group, Web Design, and Management.

The most unforgettable message I am privileged to know is that divine love is made tangible through the family, friends, and colleagues that comprise the blessing that is my life. Jordan, through your life and our relationship, I will always know that being truly who God has created us to be is the greatest act of courage and most precious gift we can give to the world.

INTRODUCTION

The camera pulls back to a wide shot and then sweeps over the landscape. The camera's moving perspective lifts us into the air like a bird in flight even though we are planted firmly in our movie theater seats. The musical score reaches goose-bump intensity, notes soaring not just in our ears but through our whole bodies. We have become part of the action—our own neurological Epcot Center-esque experience.

Now let your imagination cut to another scene. The music swells as a colorful procession enters the worship space. Dove-kites fly overhead, calling your eyes to the upward regions of the sanctuary architecture. Bells begin to peal in surround-sound from ringers in the balcony, and a single candle held aloft makes its entrance as the worship leader gestures for all to stand. In some ways it is a superfluous gesture—so ready are we to rise to new heights in this moment.

The art of filmmaking can offer accessible and valuable lessons to worship designers as we strive to bring the Greatest-Story-Ever-Told alive. Filmmakers practice what I call the "layering" of the senses in order to tell a story. They use narration and dialogue, but words are not the only—or at times even the primary—medium of communication. Music sets mood, tone, and context. Visuals, including color palettes, lighting contrast, panoramic, or close-up views, create deeply symbolic contributions to the sequence of events. Action, or "blocking," becomes carefully thought out because of its immense impact. And dialogue is compact and rich. These are the elements of deeply meaningful and memorable worship as well.

"Design" is what I intentionally call the process of worship planning because it alludes to the artistry involved in this endeavor. We take some pretty incredible stories and transformational messages, and we try again and again to bring them to life in deeply meaningful ways. The church today has begun to reclaim the power of the arts and to practice them in ever-more-complex ways. This is not just the latest worship trend to entice worshipers to church. Underlying the embrace of multiple art forms—what I call "sensory-rich" worship—as proclamation of the Word are some of the latest theories in effective communication, learning styles, and the science of memory and formation. "Unforgettable messages" are the result of taking our God-given diversity seriously, especially as it pertains to the myriad ways our bodies experience the world, take in and process information, and assimilate those messages into the fabric of our lives and behavior. This book will connect the strategies of sensory-rich communication to the tools we need as worship designers. It will also teach you a creative process for worship design analogous to a "production schedule" that can ease the stress that all pastors and volunteers feel ... because Sunday comes around every week like clockwork!

YOU ARE A RITUAL ARTIST

We are going to learn interesting and valuable lessons from artists in the field of motion pictures: directors, cinematographers, screenwriters, art directors, editors, and composers. What these folks know about creative processes and telling great stories will invigorate and streamline your task of preparing weekly worship. But we need to get one important thing clear before we begin so that you can see these analogies clearly:

You are also an artist … a ritual artist.

Not many people have ever said that about themselves. Perhaps both words feel a bit foreign to you. We often use the word "ritual" to connote worship that feels dried-up and rote. And we sometimes think that if we aren't Van Gogh or Nureyev, we dare not classify ourselves as "artists." But let me reframe each of those words.

By "ritual," I mean those things we do that help us know who we are. Those of you who drink coffee in the morning are engaging in a ritual because the act of drinking coffee is not just about the caffeine or the hot beverage; it signifies the beginning of your day. It may even be that moment of taking a deep breath before the busy-ness ensues. It has meaning beyond just the cup of joe in front of you. Worship is ritual because it contains both new and repeated elements that signify the spiritual journey of which we are a part. Ritual is something we actively participate in, and, therefore, we are formed by it. We are innately connected to others who participate in the ritual as well. When worship is meaningful and memorable (what I call "M-M-Good" worship), it is because we have connected the faith narrative with our own life stories through the combination of words, visuals, actions, and media of the ritual.

But someone had to put those elements together. This is where the artistry part comes in. It takes creativity and collaboration to combine the elements of human communication in such a way that we are drawn powerfully into the story with our whole selves. This is artistry. Those who choose the words, those who carry out and lead the melody and harmonies, and those who think about color and image must understand themselves as ritual artists.

Here is a definition of ritual that I keep before me to understand fully what I do as a ritual artist:

Christian ritual happens when engaged persons express and enact their deepest longings through repeated as well as innovated sensory-rich languages in such a way that the Spirit of the Living God is experienced and imprinted upon them so that they are convicted and sent into the world to go and do likewise as disciples of Jesus Christ.

More simply put, the mission of worship is to build up the Body of Christ for its work in the world through encounter with the Holy Living God. Such an awesome task requires a specific kind of artistry. Communicating seemingly ineffable concepts wrapped in mystery is the domain of artists. And whether you have ever thought of yourself as an artist, if you have answered the call (clergy and lay alike) to bring the Word of God to the people of God in speech, music, visual, dramatic or media expressions, you are a ritual artist.

My first career was in professional dance and musical theater. I was based in New York City and toured the world. It was a dream come true. But at the height of my career I encountered a line from Cecil Williams' book *I'm Alive* that said, "If your doin' doesn't dance with your sayin' you haven't chosen life."[1] And I knew my life would change. You see, my faith journey had always walked hand-in-hand with my love of the arts, from the time at 12 years old when I put a little cassette tape recorder in the front pew of First United Methodist Church, Adrian, Missouri, and had someone read from Isaiah over the music as I danced with "wings like eagles." That little rural church let me play keyboards, sing, dance, mime, and act my way through my childhood and adolescence. I knew all along that God had a call on my life that would come to fruition through my artistry.

Some of us came to this task from an arts background. Our love of a particular art form and our love of God brought us to an intersection of ritual and art. In the process, we found out that this task required us to be theologians—to dig deep into the rich texts and traditions in order to feed our art form in the context of worship. Others of us came to this task because our love of theology or mission or pastoral care guided us to vocational ministry. Along the way (perhaps in our first worship class at seminary), we realized we had to be public speakers, spiritual guides at crucial rites of passage and those who wed words, music, and visuals together week in and week out. In other words, we realized we had to be artists.

Whether you came from the artistry or ministry end of the spectrum, we are all in the same boat now. Ritual artists do not create visual art for the gallery. They create in order to engage a faith narrative through color and texture and line and dimension. Ritual artists do not create music for the concert hall. They describe encounter with the divine through crescendo and legato and phrase and pause. Ritual artists do not create poetry or prose for the page. They write for living, breathing bodies to hear and recite, whisper and shout, expressing life's range of joy and lament.

So even if you don't think of yourself as an artist, if you have chosen or written words for yourself and/or the congregation to say, music for them to sing, arranged poinsettias on the chancel area, played or sung a note, lowered the lights, clicked on a slide, or turned on a microphone, you are a ritual artist.

Why paint this effusive picture of worship, insisting that you claim this title of ritual artist? Because ritual artists know that in the moment of encounter between the congregation and the Word proclaimed, sung, seen, and felt, nothing less than the transformation of lives is possible. And when we understand the depth and importance of this task of worship preparation, we decide to make the move from phoning-it-in, plug-n-play, check-list worship planning to what I call "intentional design."

THINK LIKE A FILMMAKER—A LENS

Intentional design is a process by which all the ritual artists work in a collaborative manner, far enough in advance so that the worship of a community takes on the character of a particular spiritual journey within a set period of time. That's a fancy way of saying "Don't wait until the week before Advent to start thinking about what you will do for Advent." Most artists do their best work—whether it is a sermon, an anthem, a visual worship center, or projected media—when there is time to dream, ruminate, gather resources, and implement the art with as much excellence as possible. Then the art becomes not only a spiritual expression at the time of worship, but a spiritual journey in the preparation as well.

I have been teaching intentional design for worship to professionals in ministry and lay volunteers for more than twenty years. Over time, I have used many analogies to help people understand the creativity and processes required for intentional design. One of those analogies that is much-written-about by other authors is the comparison between worship and theater. And even though I came from professional theater in my first career, I never really felt like that analogy was communicative or accessible enough to get my points across about ritual artistry and intentional design. The analogy works well for some people who actually go to live theater, but a lot of people don't actually attend—whether because of cultural upbringing or access to funds to do so regularly. But just about everyone goes to the movies. This intrigued me.

I also had posed myself a question about eight years ago: "Who are the most provocative storytellers of our day?" The answer, "filmmakers," came easily to mind. Films in the 20th and 21st centuries come in many genres and most, whether comedy or drama or documentary, offer stories that help us see our world in a new way. Story has been the primary way humans have handed on information, taught lessons, evoked empathy, and formed cultural and moral viewpoints. Filmmakers search out stories to embody through their art form that will draw us into reflection and sometimes action. Sound familiar? Jesus certainly used story, metaphor, and analogy to invite his listeners to learn and even rethink their lives and relationships. The sacred texts that guide our faith are full of stories, characters, and plot twists. Ritual is the way those narratives intersect with our own stories through words, music, action, visual, and tangible environment and symbol.

So I began to investigate what it might be like to "think like a filmmaker" in relationship to my ritual artistry. Could the creative processes and teamwork necessary to tell stories in the form of movies be helpful to ritual artists? Could we glean knowledge by watching films and analyzing their art and techniques that could make us better storytellers and better able to draw people into an encounter with the "Greatest-Story-Ever-Told"?

I began to research the many filmmaking techniques, from cinematography to art direction, the scoring of music to the directing of actors. I began to talk to filmmakers about what they do and how they do it. Immediately, I began to learn many lessons that have infused the way I design and lead worship. And then I began to share those lessons in my workshops, retreats, and keynotes (www.marciamcfee.com). The instantaneous "a-ha!" was amazing. I could watch one four-minute film clip with a group, and we would discover multiple elements of communication that we could apply directly to worship design.

This book is about creating vital, engaging, sensory-rich worship that communicates unforgettable messages using the lessons I've learned from the artistry and technique of filmmakers and other theorists in the fields of science and communication. The filmmaker analogy is not that worship is like a movie or that worship design is like filmmaking or that going to movies is analogous to going to worship—although there are similarities. And this is not about how some movies are theological, although some are, and much has been written about that. It is not a study of filmmaking to any great extent. Rather, our goal here is to look through a new lens (pun intended) at how we communicate in worship and utilize some basic concepts that filmmakers use to make movies "work"—that keep us engaged and move us.

WHAT YOU WILL FIND IN THIS BOOK

It all starts with the story to be told. Chapter One helps us to think like a filmmaker as we conceptualize the story and how it will progress. We'll learn how to write synopses for the worship series—what a film-maker calls "loglines"—that will literally put the whole worship team on the same page and get people excited to begin the creative process of bringing the story alive.

Chapter Two addresses gathering and organizing the creative team. Every director knows that the vision comes to fruition only with good help. We'll talk about the various roles on a worship team, how to work well together, and strategies for a team process that avoids having "too many cooks in the kitchen."

The next five chapters are divided into the worship art forms as I delineate them in my Worship Design Studio online coaching website (www.worshipdesignstudio.com). My recommendation is that the whole team read this introduction and Chapters One and Two. Then individu-als could skip to the chapter(s) that deal with their particular art form (although I would recommend that visual and media artists read both of those chapters as well as verbal and dramatic artists reading both of those, too). Then the whole team will want to read chapters eight and nine. Ultimately, as time allows, the best results happen when all the ritual artists read each other's chapters because, to use the filmmaking analogy, what the art director does affects what lighting the cinematographer uses, which affects the camera angles, the actor placement, and the mood of the music. Collaboration is the name of the game, and the more each person knows about the artistry and technique of each team member, the more seamless and effective the collaboration will be. You may be reading this without any team in place yet or very few members currently helping with worship. Read the whole book, and use it to invite some folks to work with you.

Chapter Three explores thinking like an art director as we discern the visual arts and tangible symbols that will accompany the worship series. We'll learn about how space, line, and color affect our experience of the story. This chapter will help turn your HGTV enthusiasts into liturgical visual artists with an eye for visual installations that become deeply meaningful experiences for worshipers.

Chapter Four moves to the power of the words we choose to use in worship. When we think like screenwriters, we pay attention to concise verbal artistry in our liturgy and preaching as well as the role of verbal transitions throughout worship. We'll take a look at poetic structures for liturgy that can help anyone learn to write prayers and litanies.

Probably some of the most profound lessons I have learned from filmmakers have to do with the power of music, which is covered in Chapter Five. When we think like a film composer, we see the role of music expand from simply plugged-in hymns, songs, and anthems to an element that sets a tone and mood and moves the story along dynamically. Even if you have musicians with rudimentary skills, they can learn techniques that will help worship flow as a seamless whole and add dimension and drama to readings and movement. We'll also address various dynamics of music and look at how each one has a place in our spiritual formation. I highly recommend that pastors and music directors read this chapter as an entree to a discussion about enhancing their collaboration.

A cinematographer is one who helps to give the film focus through light and angle and image. Chapter Six delves into the media arts, which encompass everything from whether the lights are dim or bright in the worship space to projected graphics and whether or not we can hear well (i.e. sound/audio). Technology is great … when it works. Filmmakers say that individual elements of a film are at their best when we aren't aware of them—when they enhance and support the story itself. Hear, hear! But we'll also explore how projected media and sound effects can come to the forefront as artful carriers of the message itself.

The final art form I address is the dramatic arts. In the Worship Design Studio, this covers not only dance and drama itself but all ritual action such as sacraments, prayer stations, processions, and children in worship. When we think like a director of a film in Chapter Seven, we'll discover the power of vocal tone, pitch, and the kinesthetics of effective oratory and placement, or "blocking." And we'll learn best practices for training lay readers.

Now that we've looked at the many sensory elements of worship, we move to Chapter Eight, in which we will continue the process of the production of a worship series—the process of putting it all together. While we don't have the luxury of producing a pre-recorded, edited-to-the-hilt movie, thinking like an editor will help us as we begin finalizing the details of worship from script-writing to producing the worship guide (my term for bulletins), and doing cue-to-cue rehearsals that help everyone (especially leaders) have a worshipful experience without distraction. We'll pay attention to the whole structure of worship—the way all the pieces fit, flow, and move together.

Much goes into publicity for a movie even before it is finished in post-production. We can call it publicity or call it evangelism—it doesn't really matter. Getting the word out about the amazing spiritual journey that your church is about to embark upon for the next liturgical season is vitally important in this 21st-century world. From creating logos to "series trailers" we can learn much from the movie industry about offering a glimpse into the story that draws people into the experience, and Chapter Eight discusses this as well.

Finally, I'll address what we all deal with—reactions to worship and the evaluation process. Chapter Nine, "The Release and the Reviews," will help you navigate the dynamics of change and create a healthy environment in which to move forward with what you have learned in this book. All filmmakers deal with the subjectivity of movie critics and audiences. But like worship teams, if they lived in fear of bad reviews, they would never make a movie.

MORE THAN JUST A BOOK

Throughout this book, I will be referring you to the www.thinklikeafilmmaker.com, website where you will find links to more resources and opportunities to learn than I could fit in this book. I invite you to go there now and download the "Study Suggestions for Worship Teams" so that you can make the most out of this learning experience. In it, one of the first steps

Get the Study Guide at
thinklikeafilmmaker.com

is to watch a movie together, *Under the Tuscan Sun,* which will serve as our case study in this book. This is a film I have been using in my research and teaching as an example of many of the concepts about sensory-rich worship that I will share with you in this book. I chose it not because it was an award-winning or revolutionary film, but because it exemplifies a beautifully told story with a deeply human message. It uses metaphor and symbolism in powerful ways that show up in all the art forms—objects, colors, dialogue, music, gesture, and movement. It is a character piece. Diane Lane plays Frances, a successful writer whose husband has left her and who has writer's block. She is convinced by her dearest friend, played by Sandra Oh, to go on a package group tour of Italy to get her mind off the heartbreak and jumpstart a new adventure in life. On the tour and on a whim, Frances buys a broken-down villa in the Tuscan countryside near a small town. The rest of the film is about the renovation of the house that mirrors the renovation of her own spirit. Like the transformational narrative we embody in worship, this is a story of resurrection.

I suggest you watch the same movie after you've been through the first seven chapters of the book. You'll be astonished at what you notice that you didn't notice the first time! I should probably warn you now: you'll never watch a movie the same way again after reading this book. My spouse frequently laughs at me, saying, "Can't we just watch the movie instead of pausing it every ten minutes as you exclaim, 'Wow!!! Did you see how they …?'" Seriously though, thinking like a filmmaker has enriched my ritual artistry, and I know it will do that for you, too.

What I hope is that this book will help the ritual artists at your church have more spiritually deepening experiences, have more fun, more ease and more creativity in everything they do. We'll do this by giving you a common vocabulary for design and a clear process and timeline that everyone can count on for success. When this happens, being part of the worship team will become one of the most sought-after ways to live out discipleship at your church. And the vitality of worship at your church will then form disciples who are energized to make this world a better place. What could be better?

CHAPTER 1

CONCEPTUALIZING THE STORY

As long as we've been humans, we've been telling stories. The ancients even recorded their stories on the world around them, etching and painting the earth's surface with their symbols. We lived among our own stories, and the images embedded in them came alive as we used them to make sense of our place in the world—sharing information, preserving memories, and expressing dreams, beliefs, and fears. We spoke, sang, painted, acted, and danced our stories. We used all of our senses in order to create indelible memories so that the stories would be repeated and handed down through the ages.

"Story is everything," says documentary filmmaker Abigail Wright. "We are hardwired to understand stories. What are stories? They are sequences of events that help us to understand the tidal wave of sensations that come to us. They put order into our world. They tell us what to do, who we are, where we come from. Is there justice in the world? How do we die? All the important things of our life."[2] As humans began to seek deeper meaning about their world, their stories took on another role, communicating messages that could *bind together,* connecting people to each other and all the mystery of existence.

Those of us who design worship have the same task as our ancient ancestors. We must call on all of the senses through every expressive medium we have at our disposal. The stories handed down to us through our sacred texts come alive when we do. Our goal is to tell the most amazing Story—and the stories that point to that liberating message—in the most compelling ways that invite people to live with hope and conviction for the "good news" that we share.

But more than simply being story-tellers, we are invited to create an *experience* of the story—to invite the congregation to be "story-dwellers."[3] In his book *Powerful Persuasion*, theologian Tex Sample uses the terms "critical distance" and "critical immersion" to describe an important difference between modern and postmodern sensibilities in communication.[4] Audiences were once encouraged to "listen-from-afar," putting distance between themselves and the message they heard. Whether delivered in the lecture hall, beamed to radio and TV towers, or spoken from the pulpit, the message was something happening "out there" that the hearer could think on and evaluate without actively participating in. Things are different now. Communication styles have changed as audiences crave the opportunity to learn by experience. People now want to be immersed in the messages they receive rather than merely hear them. Advertisers focus more on the products' fit with consumers' lifestyles rather than on their specific benefits. Museums have moved to more sensory-rich experiences that immerse patrons in a moment in history or a far-off place such as the deep sea or outer space. Long airport corridors are filled with art, light shows, and soundscapes. Documentaries for film and television are moving away from simple "talking-head" expert shots to images and re-enactments that help us imagine what "being there" is like.[5]

Jon Boorstin, author of *Making Movies Work,* says filmmakers know that "people don't just want to watch a movie, they throw themselves into the experience—they want to lose themselves in what they're seeing."[6] Director Steven Spielberg tells the story of losing himself in his first movie-going experience as a young child. His father told him he was going to take him to "the greatest show on earth" and described the lion tamers and circus acts. Spielberg was ecstatic and waited the week out with anticipation. The day of the show, they stood in a very long line next to a red wall. Why weren't they seeing a tent, he wondered?

> "Finally we walked into a dimly lit room … and the ceiling looked like a church. It felt like a place of worship. The curtain opened, and the lights went down. A dimly lit image came on the screen, and suddenly I realized my father had lied to me, had betrayed me, and we were not going to see a circus—we were going to see a *movie* about a circus. I had never seen a movie before. The feeling of disappointment and regret and betrayal lasted only about 10 minutes, and then I became another victim of this tremendous drug called cinema. And I was no longer in a theater, in a seat, I wasn't aware of my surroundings, I was no longer in a church—it was a place of equal devotion and worship, however. I became part of an *experience*."[7]

When worship acts more like a meeting agenda of items to be completed, with little attention to the flow of the storytelling endeavor, it loses its power to move us. We keep our distance from the story, from *our* story—observers of the trappings of ritual rather than participants in an unfolding journey of discovery. Becoming immersed in a story means that we allow ourselves, for a while, to suspend the minutiae of our lives and take a step back to examine and reflect on the bigger picture—how we are living our lives, the choices we make, and how we relate to God and to each other. To be immersed is to allow an holistic engagement of cognition and emotion and physiological response. It puts us in touch with the depths of our selves, what we think and feel. It puts us in relationship with our companions on the journey through shared experience. Religion, after all, is derived from a Latin root that means *to bind together*. And as we allow ourselves to slip into time-out-of-time, we are so bound, closer to each other and to the divine.

Martin Scorsese has said, "I can … see great similarities between a church and a movie-house. Both are places for people to come together and share a common experience."[8] Of course, there is much more, we hope, to the interaction that happens as people worship together rather than just watch a movie together. But what goes on in an immersive experience of a story through film can also be akin to something we hope to achieve in our worshiping communities. Clive Marsh describes the way films often draw us in without us realizing the effects. "The complex way in which they move us, get us thinking, compel us to make links and draw contrasts with life-experience past and present indicates that films are doing something important to their viewers"—namely, inviting people into theological reflection.[9]

How much more could we invite people into deep theological reflection about our narratives of faith by immersing ourselves in the sights, sounds, color, and drama of the message? How can such sensory-rich storytelling invite more participatory worship? In this book, we will learn how all of the worship art forms can contribute to the storytelling endeavor, making sure that every element of worship moves us toward the expression of unforgettable messages.

UNFORGETTABLE MESSAGES

Anyone who has been to one of my workshops has heard me speak of "M-M-Good" worship—worship that is "meaningful and memorable." These are worship moments that, years later, we can still remember. Such moments go beyond their literal meanings as they kindle the embers of emotion we experienced when we first encountered them. The images and emotions of indelible memories are connected together in our brains with the messages conveyed through that experience.[10] We want the messages we proclaim in worship to be meaningful (the intersection of our life and faith story) and memorable (living beyond the time and place of worship) because these are the messages then by which we live our lives. They remain present to us, *reinforced* by our recollection of them and *reinforcing* certain values and behaviors.

But what gets noticed and remembered is different for different people. Life is a story that we are all interpreting differently based on our perspectives and proclivities. Ever hear your spouse describe your vacation to a friend and wonder, "Was I on the same vacation?" Or go to a movie with friends but afterwards realize that you all noticed very different things? We go through the world with our own special set of lenses. We notice different things based on how "tuned in" various parts of our brain are. We move through the world with different rhythms in our bodies. The great variety of human perspectives and personalities make crafting unforgettable messages all the more difficult.

Sensory-rich worship creates multiple paths by which to reach people. Everyone learns differently. When I ask people in my workshops to remember an "M-M-Good" worship moment that they encountered, whether 20 years ago or last week or anytime in between, the descriptions vary widely. Some remember a stirring image, some the quality of music. Others have an ear for language and metaphor, or a sensitivity to the group feeling in the room. The memories range from moments that were contemplative to rousing, from surprising to deeply centering. Which "M-M-Good" moments we remember depends greatly on the modes of worship that resonate with us most powerfully.

How each of us is "wired" affects what we notice and remember. According to cognition specialist Howard Gardner, all people can learn and communicate in many different styles, but each of us has special strengths. Some areas of our brains are more facile, or accomplished. His "Multiple Intelligences Theory"[11] changed the face of education some decades ago as he challenged the idea that those with verbal-linguistic intelligence were the "most" intelligent. Rather, the world presents all kinds of detail and stimuli to make sense of, and words are just one source. We all receive information in different ways. A sermon may be called the "meat" of the service for those who are more facile in their *verbal-linguistic* processes of the brain. But preachers, I'm sorry to tell you that not everyone comes for the sermon. Some people will more likely get the message in worship from the music because their brains are more tuned in to *musical-rhythmic* aspects of worship. And bonus points if the music actually has something to do with the message being preached that day! Some folks will be invited into the story in a deeper way if the visuals—colors, textures, objects, lighting—have set an environment that complements the message. This *visual-spatial* sensibility is piqued at those times when we give special attention to the space and diminished when the worship space looks the same week in and week out.

A *logical-mathematical* intelligence is going to see the connections between elements of the worship. They will notice and appreciate, for example, when the opening prayer uses imagery from the song we just sang and when the anthem clearly is an exclamation point on the very message just preached. Communion, going to prayer stations, touching water, or lighting candles will be meaningful and memorable to someone with a *bodily-kinesthetic* intelligence because, for them, actions do speak louder than words. And some people like a more *interpersonal* experience of warm interaction with others around them, while still others readily resonate with time for *intrapersonal* reflection, times of silence, and meditative singing.

To wrap our minds around this concept is to accept that if we want our messages to be "unforgettable" to most people, we are going to have to tell our stories with sensory-rich strategies. Those who study cognition say that "cells that fire together, wire together" in the brain. And the more cells that are firing off in various areas of the brain around any one message, the more likely we are to remember that message. If we proclaim the Word—not only with language but with music, visual environment, and physical action—then we will make lasting impacts on the lives of those we reach.

LAYERING

But it's not enough to simply have a little bit of everything at different times during the service. It would seem ludicrous to us if a movie's different elements were used without considering how they harmonize, if there were talking-head dialogue for a while, and then we listened to music for a bit, and then we watched some scenery in silence. Filmmakers know the power of these elements working in concert to offer an experience of the story. In any one moment of a film, intentional decisions are being made regarding color and hue that sets a "look," camera angles and lenses that offer an intimate or spacious feel, timing of dialogue that fits the pace of the story, and musical scoring to bring out the emotive landscape. This is a *layering* of the art forms that brings out a way of communicating a moment in the story that cannot be done by one art form alone.

Layering is how we experience everyday life. We combine sensory experiences to create moments. If you pace your exercise with music playing through earphones, or pair a beautiful centerpiece with a lovely dinner, or kiss your spouse as you say, "I love you," you are essentially creating a layered experience using multiple forms of expression at the same time. While I was writing a book on skiing as a spiritual practice, I got to spend a night riding in a snow-cat machine that grooms the snow on the mountain near my home. I was on slopes that I'd skied many times before in daylight. But being out there in the middle of the night, seeing that landscape through the headlights and moonlight, was mystical. Add to that enchanted landscape the fact that my guide enjoyed listening to movie soundtracks as she masterfully drove this huge machine up and down the steep inclines. My memory of that night is laced with the drama of orchestral scores that soared and pounded along with my heartbeat as we careened around the majestic pine tree-lined mountains. What could have been hours of tedious back-and-forth snow farming was turned into a grand experience that I remember with awe and wonder.

Let me take a moment, however, to say something very important. Designing worship with a sensibility for sensory-rich communication layered with multiple art forms does not mean that there is never a moment for simplicity. There is a time to soak in silent reflection and then have that silence broken by a single instrument playing a melody line softly and slowly. There is a time to simply hear a scripture read by a single voice without music underscoring the reading. But when we engage in intentional design, we are making the decision for that simplicity, well … intentionally.

Nor is sensory-rich worship confined to large worship spaces with lots of people. Picture a small community sitting in a chapel, immersed in a layered and sensory-rich moment. We see them surround a bowl of water, into which they drop pieces of dissolving paper with their regrets written upon them. All the while, they sing "I Will Change Your Name." A house-church or table-focused gathering can be sensory-rich simply in the way that we decide what color of tablecloth or how to arrange and light the room—is it dim and candlelit or bright and energetic? Is there a playlist of music going as people arrive? Worship design for a coffee house or jazz club will ask these same questions about environment, atmosphere, "feel," and order.

You might be asking yourself if sensory-rich worship is really "your style." The truth is, sensory-rich design can improve *any* style of worship service simply by helping you to improve what you already do. "Boring" worship is not about style. Friends, I've been doing worship consulting for long enough that I have seen "boring" in every style! Boring is about monotony, and it comes in many forms. Monotony happens when we don't take the time to be intentional about our worship, when we express every message in the same way, with the same energy, in the same order, with the same surroundings. I had a reporter ask me in an interview, "What do you think is the biggest problem in worship in our day?" Well, that's a pretty big question, so I thought carefully about it. And what I said then, and continue to say, is "Worship that has flatlined." When a worship experience in Lent feels the same as one during the Easter season, we are in trouble. The story has lost its power because we have forgotten to express the depth and heights and particularity of an amazing narrative of life and faith. It takes real talent to take our faith narrative and make it boring—but we can do it! Have you read the stories of our sacred texts lately? Far from boring, my friends. But the monotony (lack of intentionality, diversity, and nuance) with which we treat our stories would bankrupt a film company pretty darn quick. The critics would rage, the audiences wouldn't go, and … well … you get the point. No matter your style, layering can help you create unforgettable messages.

As we will talk about in the next chapter, "layering" requires teamwork and a timeline for collaboration. And the first thing that must happen is for the whole team to have a sense of the story that is being told. Let's move to a look at the beginning of the creative process—defining the story.

THE WORSHIP SERIES—HELPING US SEE DEEPER

Sharpening our perception of and relationship to life is part of what we do in worship. Engaging in a "deeper seeing"—a deeper engagement with God and the story of faith by creating a "time-out-of-time" experience of the story—offers us the opportunity to home in, to dive deep into the waters of reflection, be moved by our experience, and then take that in our bones out into the "real time" of our world, where we can apply that "seeing" to our lives. Clive Marsh likens "deeper seeing" to both worship and cinema because "film watching at its best not only trains sight. It makes use of sight and emotional involvement to make a person more critical of what they see and experience." In both activities, we learn to interpret what we experience, engaging our "visual, emotional, moral, and cognitive ways of seeing."[12]

Depth of vision takes time and a different perspective. It used to be that scientists touted only repetition as the mother of memory. But more recently, innovation was added to that equation. When we say, "Wow! I never thought of it that way before!" we have just had an experience that we now know is more likely to sear itself into memory. Repetition and innovation are partners in meaningful and memorable expressions of the story. Both are about *deepening* our experience of what we already have—something reinforced and something differently introduced. This is why I'm a firm believer that we must attend to the messages of our faith in intentional ways over periods of time—in what I call "worship series." In a series of services that are purposefully connected, we can experience the ingredients of worship in ways not possible if we're only stringing together "one-hit-wonders" Sunday after Sunday. Repetition and innovation can walk hand in hand for deeper engagement and memory-making. Yes, there will occasionally be those services that are not part of a series (especially in churches where worship does not happen weekly) and the same sensory-rich principles and processes will apply to giving those occasional worship experiences all you've got. But let's focus right now on moving through the year in a setting of weekly worship.

Why create worship series? Songs have verses. Books have chapters. Movies have scenes and sequels. The logic is that we move from one verse, chapter, scene, or sequel to the next because we want to deepen our experience of a story or idea. So it is with the spiritual journey called worship series. Step into an art gallery at a curated show of an artist's work, and you will probably see series of paintings that are all different but share a common theme. Artists have told me that this is a commonly desired format—the series—and that seeing variations on a theme is effective. You may have heard of Picasso's "blue period" from 1901 to 1904, when he painted all works in shades of blue and blue-green—now considered some of his most popular work. Designing worship is also about choosing a "hue" for a period of time, investigating a particular perspective for a while. When we have the opportunity to deepen our spiritual journeys, we deepen our lives.

In the Worship Design Studio (www.worshipdesignstudio.com), I have been creating worship series for churches to use for many years now. Churches who move to using series on a regular basis report what I have long suspected—there are so many advantages to this approach:

Worship series help us embark on a *communal* spiritual journey. I had a conversation with a preacher (well, a Bishop, no less) not long ago over lunch about planning thematically. He was wondering why this was necessary rather than just being able to preach whatever inspired him that day. I'm glad he asked me that because I'd never put the answer in quite the way I did that day. Initially, I told him, "Well, you can" (because that's what you generally tell a Bishop!). But then I asked him to consider this: besides making it pretty difficult to collaborate with a team of ritual artists to bring the story alive in other ways besides the sermon, his suggested method makes the whole congregation captive to the particular spiritual journey of one person ... the preacher. Commentary on the *community's spiritual journey,* rather than simply their own, is the role of the preacher. This is not to say that the unique talents and inspiration of leaders doesn't matter. The method that I teach in the Worship Design Studio of thematic series planning depends first on the discernment of a Visionary (what I call pastors/preachers in the Worship Design Studio) as they shepherd the congregation. But if we design with the context of that congregation in mind, with their spiritual needs and challenges in mind, with an openness to the inspiring Spirit and even the input of others in the community about topics to address, we can be faithful stewards of a communal journey.

Planning worship series is not antithetical to following the liturgical year or lectionary. Within any year, any set of texts, there will be many options of perspectives and thematic pathways to take. Good leadership involves discerning what will be the most poignant for this year, in this particular community. A Visionary's job is to have their fingers on the pulse in such a way that, much like a teacher who develops a lesson plan based on the needs of the class, they can offer their gifts of proclamation within a context of connection to a community, not just their own spiritual wanderings.

Worship series help us remember and reinforce messages over time. Cognitive scientists have long touted the advantages of repetition for making memory. As I already said, "cells that fire together, wire together!" The more our synapses literally connect around the same thing over and over, the more those things become "common knowledge" or "second nature."

One reason that worship series are effective is because we get to revisit the main message or underlying truths again and again instead of every worship experience being a totally new message. Exploring a theological concept or an aspect of our faith narrative over several weeks "steeps" us in a set of symbols and metaphors that get more and more solidified in our vocabulary over time. The message in a series changes and deepens each week. Singing "Nothing Can Trouble" over six weeks has an effect on us when that song springs up in our heads during the week when things get stressful. A U-turn sign used as a logo in a worship series about turning our lives around gains a layer of meaning when we see one out in the world. You get the idea.

Worship series are a container for the familiar *and* the new. We get the "oh yeah!" factor ("that feels familiar") because we repeat what I call "thread items" over the course of several weeks. A new sung refrain that bookends our prayer time might be new on the first Sunday, but by the 3rd and 4th Sunday, that new refrain is sinking comfortably into the "that feels holy" part of our brains and hearts. Then, at the beginning of the next series, we get some fresh elements particular to a new series. This is the "a-ha!" factor ("wow, I never thought of it that way") neuroscience says is equally important to making something memorable. If we follow this practice of both "oh yeah" and "a-ha!" our congregations start to trust changes in worship more, knowing that their leaders hold the familiar and the new as equally important partners in our spiritual formation.

Worship series help the worship team not get burned out doing sensory-rich and creative worship. Creating sensory-rich worship for a different message week after week is near impossible. It cannot be sustained. But purposeful repetition can make the most of the resources you dedicate to it and can save time over the course of a worship series. If you are designing an "altarscape" (another word for visual worship center) for a series, you can put more time and attention into the creation of it because it will be up for a while. Some music within a series will be "thread items" (repeated elements such as an invocation song or prayer song), making rehearsal for musicians more doable and offering more lead time to learn new things. If you use media, the same "palette" for background visuals on slides can be used so you aren't starting from scratch every week.

Worship series act as an "on-ramp" for new sojourners. The use of a thematic series over time creates anticipation before the series if we utilize "coming soon" communications (like movie trailers) and creates a "buzz" during the series as people talk about what they are experiencing and invite others to join in the journey. "We've got this amazing series going on about how anyone can turn their lives around" is a much more natural kind of "evangelism" for many folks rather than simply, "come to church with me." How many times have you passed over a movie, a book, or a restaurant until you hear great recommendations?

The beginning of a series gives people an "on-ramp" of sorts into your community's spiritual journey.

Creating series may be old hat to some of you. However, you may have called them "sermon series." I like the more inclusive term "worship series" because it reinforces the idea that the whole of worship is proclamation of the message and encounter with God—not just the sermon. An overarching series message can unite the words we speak with the songs we sing, the images we see and the actions we do, and that unity deepens and transforms the manner in which we experience the Holy.

DISCERNING THE DIRECTION

By now you've begun to glimpse the power of sensory-rich worship series to share the compelling stories of our Gospel message. But how do you begin? The first step for a screenwriter is to fall in love with a story and then cast the vision of that story in such a way that they can actually get the film produced. The first step for a Visionary (pastor) in the creative process of bringing a worship series to fruition is much the same: fall in love with a particular aspect of the faith story, discern how it intersects powerfully with our context—our lives, our community, and our world—and then cast that vision to the rest of the team so everyone can begin to brainstorm about how to bring the story to tangible, inspirational form. We'll go through the whole production timeline in the next chapter. But let's spend some time on the first steps here because it all begins with story.

Screenwriter and teacher Allen Palmer says that the story is the most important place to start because it is the vehicle through which we deal with one core universal human truth: life is hard.[13] Inspired by the famous mythologist Joseph Campbell, Palmer says we look for these three things when we go to the movies: 1) to expand our emotional bandwidth — to feel sensations that we rarely experience in our normal lives; 2) to reconnect with our higher selves — to be reminded of what humans are capable of, in terms of both good and evil, and to alter course if we're steering more towards the latter than the former; 3) to be reminded we're not alone—that, by the collective reaction of others in the audience, we realize that we are not the only ones wrestling with life.[14] In each of these points, we see story intersecting with context. Stories are maps to the oceans of human meaning and feeling; we seek out stories in order to understand and navigate those waters in our own lives just a bit more confidently.

So one of the first things to do when discerning the vision of the spiritual journey the community will take in upcoming worship series is to spend some time with questions. What does the congregation come to worship thinking about, worried about, dealing with? What is your prayer for this congregation in this year? What has transpired in this community's recent (or not-so-recent) past that affects how we are with each other and in ministry? What has transpired in our world that has an effect on people's spiritual well-being and journey? What Word is needing to be heard in this congregation? A comforting word? A challenging word? An inspiring word? A radically transforming word? All or some of the above? In what order?

These questions set the stage for our discernment and creativity. The scriptures are full of the very same thing—words of comfort, healing, challenge, inspiration, and transformation—to communities that needed to hear it, wrestle with it, interpret it, and act on it. The role of the Visionary in the worship design process at this moment is to discern the "frames" through which the Holy will do its work. This work is highly creative, and creative processes are best served by structure. The framework of the liturgical year is an incredible structure in which to answer the questions of our lives. When I lead worship teams through this discernment process at the beginning of my worship planning retreats, I begin with some of the major themes of the liturgical year as a guide. The liturgical year takes us on a journey through the story of faith and its messages, each important stop on that journey intersecting with our fundamental human longing. What are the central questions of our lives that intersect the narrative of Good News?

For examples of series for the liturgical year from the Worship Design Studio, go to thinklikeafilmmaker.com

The *Advent/Christmas* story evokes our yearning for the presence of the mysterious, something "beyond," something more, something planted and born within us. A provocative question to begin our visioning for the story in that season could be "what will the Spirit birth in this church?" *Epiphany* and the Sundays after it are usually filled with scriptural stories of people discovering who Jesus is as he teaches, heals, and draws people into a different way of being with each other and thinking about God. Illumination, discovery, knowledge, and relationship are part of our human story, and so asking questions about "where is greater understanding, relationship, and discipleship needed in our church?" can offer insight in this time frame. *Lent* was originally developed as a time of preparation for baptism and later gained a reputation as a time for deep reflection on the direction and behavior of one's own life, our yearning to be fully known and accepted. "What are the deep questions?" or "What will it take to get real with ourselves, with each other and with God?" are questions that offer rich possibilities for the Lenten journey.

Holy Week in the Christian year is a crucible of the joy and sorrow of human life. It is a story that exposes our yearning for comfort in suffering, for making sense of the pain of life, and for the cry of "justice!" in a world still host to abuse and oppression. "How can we be more present to the suffering of others?" *Easter* is perhaps the human longing above all—to know that life exists in the midst of, and beyond, death, that resurrection—starting over—can happen for us even during our lifetime. "What would it be like to really live as Easter People—living without fear of death? How would we live our lives differently day in and day out?"

The *Easter Season* offers seven weeks to continue to celebrate life and love. To break out of the hold that depression, stress, oppression, hate, and fear have on us seems a far stretch at times, and, yet, here is a season where we can ask "What holds us back from daring to dance our dance fully?" and "What could the world gain by our living wholeheartedly?" The Easter season, with its culmination at *Pentecost*, offers an opportunity to focus on shedding the shackles that diminish our church's capacity for unabashed passion and doing real good in the world. "Can we allow ourselves to claim the Spirit's movement in our lives?"

Finally, we come to *Ordinary Time*—a good half of the year. This is where the narrative of the life of Jesus does not necessarily dictate the flow of the story, but rather how we as the Body of Christ are living out that story—which leaves us with a myriad of possibilities for spiritual journeys. The term "ordinary" as it is used in *Ordinary Time* comes from "ordinal" or "numbered"—not the opposite of "extraordinary." But it is worth exploring that metaphor for the stories we will portray through this time of year. Our lives' most profound experiences often happen to us while we sit squat in the middle of everyday life. *Ordinary Time* can still prompt us to seek God's extraordinary presence as we ask "How can this church affirm and strengthen its purpose, find common purpose, and be empowered?"

Find out more about each liturgical season and other structures at thinklikeafilmmaker.com.

Essentially, we are like a filmmaker who strives to find a new angle to bring life to the common human themes of our lives that happen over and over. Because "over and over" is what we deal with. Inevitably,

Christmas comes *every year!* Easter comes every year, and we must find powerful ways to connect to that story yet again. Gratefully, the story comes into a new moment in history, into a new context of circumstances every year, and the answer to the questions posed above are different. One year the "angle" for Lent may be a series called "Ready for a Change" because the congregation is dealing with a lot of change, and taking stock of the direction of our lives would speak most profoundly. Another year it may be that the pace of the congregation feels like a rat-race, and a theme like "Busy: Reconnecting to an Unhurried God" would call the community into making more room for God during the liturgical season. As we revisit the liturgical year every annual cycle, we hear the same narrative differently, and we tease out new ways of looking at it and experiencing it.

Planning requires some real focused time on the part of the Visionary. Whether you are beginning with a set of lectionary texts as your starting point or carefully considering what parts of the scriptural narrative will speak to a desired emphasis, this takes study, prayer, and a willingness to be open to inspiration. Some people will want to do this alone. Others will want the company of others as a sounding board. No matter how you do it, the point is to see this time as *essential* to the entire process. I recommend blocking out a two- or three-day retreat twice a year to map out directions for worship series (in August/September for Advent through Pentecost and in January/February to map out series for Ordinary Time) and hold that time as sacred. Be accountable to it in the same way you are accountable to show up on Sunday mornings. It isn't a luxury—the rest of your creative process and the work of the entire team depends upon this first step.

Go to
thinklikeafilmmaker.com
for more tips for the
Visionary Retreat.

PITCHING THE STORY

Once the idea for the angle of the story is decided, it is time to "pitch" it the team. While we do not have to worry, as screenwriters do, about pitching it to producers and funders, we still can gain so much for the creative process and the "buy in" of our worship arts team and congregation by following a technique called "writing a logline." A logline is a brief bit of writing that distills the essence of the message of a movie. It is the main concept or the premise and answers the question "so what is your film about?" The logline for our case-study, *Under the Tuscan Sun,* is this:

> *When Frances Mayes learns her husband is cheating on her from a writer whom she gave a bad review, her life is turned upside down. In an attempt to bring her out of a deep depression, her best friend, Patti, encourages Frances to take a tour of Italy. During the trip, the new divorcée impulsively decides to purchase a rural Tuscan villa and struggles to start her life anew amid colorful local characters, including the handsome Marcello.*

In this short description, we discover the context, the setting, and the character's dilemma and purpose. It communicates enough to intrigue us and help us decide where the story is going and whether we want to tag along. This, actually, is the post-production logline most likely developed for advertising purposes. But screenwriters will use loglines for several purposes before the production—to pitch the idea to producers, to test its marketability (whether it is compelling), to make sure it is simple and clear enough to fit into a 1.5–2 hour window of time, and to keep themselves on track as they are writing the full story.[15]

The screenwriter and director for *Under the Tuscan Sun* were one and the same person—Audrey Wells. She based her script on Frances Mayes' autobiography because Mayes' story explored the human drama of heartbreak, renewal, and the eternal power of love.[16] With these underlying themes in mind, Audrey augmented the actual storyline to include minor characters besides the heroine who would also experience their own heartbreaks—with some references more subtle than others. Besides Frances' own divorce, we see a young couple's agony over the cultural and class barriers between them, a grandmother's heartbreak over the death of a lifelong love, a woman's deep disappointment in her partner's rejection of parenthood. The result is a tapestry of experience that holds the movie together thematically in various subplots, providing a structure that is analogous to the way a worship series can explore the same theme via different avenues over several weeks. Early in the creative process, loglines clarify main themes and trajectories that the screenwriter must keep in mind as later decisions are made for characters and storylines.

Many years ago, even before I heard of loglines, I began to write what I call "synopses" for my worship series—one for the entire series and then one for each week of the series. My mentor in this was my friend Howard Hanger, celebrant at Jubilee Community Church in Asheville, North Carolina. He describes the benefits of writing synopses for a whole series in this way:

> I do it for the people … I want to do everything I can to encourage people to participate. So I started creating "Seeds for Celebration" [his synopses] so that people could contribute their gifts based on seeing a little bit about the themes that were coming up and the scriptures associated with them. Not only does it prepare me—it makes my homily writing

so much easier—but it sets it up so that the people can truly be part of it.[17]

As I have used synopses over the years, the benefits have multiplied from what I first learned from Howard. Writing synopses is one of the most important disciplines for inviting, exciting, and involving other staff and volunteers as part of the worship design process. Taking the time to communicate clearly the trajectory for the spiritual journey as a whole (the series) and then every stop on that journey (each week) makes it possible for others to begin to contribute ideas that are useful and right on point. It is simply not enough to say to a musician, "I follow the lectionary" as a so-called guide for them to choose music. There are so many directions and threads of thought through any text, let alone the four texts of the Revised Common Lectionary. It is impossible to know where someone would be going without more specific explanation. Usually that kind of direction means that a preacher has not yet done their own homework and has decided to wing it and hope the music fits.

I often use the synopsis for each week at the beginning of each worship experience—what I call a "threshold moment." It serves to set the tone and the mood, and introduces the theme, inviting folks to the spiritual journey (more about that in Chapter Eight). And as Howard mentioned, writing a synopsis also helps preachers to define the scope of the message for the day, helps them to remember the essence of the message weeks or even months after the visioning retreat, and also enables preachers to be creative in how they contribute to that message. Some preachers feel hesitant to corner themselves into something months or weeks before they will

See a video of a threshold moment using a synopsis at thinklikeafilmmaker.com.

actually preach. But like good jazz music, the best creativity happens within structure, and preachers report to me that once they start this discipline of writing synopses, they begin to enjoy the structure and are grateful for how it jumpstarts the weekly sermon preparation process.

When screenwriters pitch their ideas with a logline, they are helping the producers get excited about the story, and the producers in turn are able to clearly communicate the film idea to the next several people they must recruit. Funding must be found, an entire team of professionals has to be hired, and actors must be cast. Similarly, the worship series synopsis can also provide good language to get the word out about the series. As I mentioned above when we discussed the benefits of creating in series, creating series "trailers" (like movie trailers) and creating invitational postcards for mailing or images for social media are easy to do when team members working on getting the word out have a few sentences about the theme to use in their work. One of the things I ask myself after writing my synopses is this, "If I came to the home page of our church website and saw this description, would it feel like a meaningful spiritual journey to be on? Would I want to know more? Would I come to worship?"

Find out how to make your website more "guest centered" at thinklikeafilmmaker.com.

Here is a synopsis for a worship series called *"Risky Business"* that I created based on the Narrative Lectionary texts for Epiphany and the Sundays following.

> ***Theme scripture excerpt:*** *"All who want to save their lives will lose them. But all who lose their lives because of me and because of the good news will save them." —Mark 8:34-35*

> ***Synopsis:*** *If Jesus had lived in our day, the risk-assessment folks would surely have rejected his application for life insurance. Time*

and again, he put himself in positions of risk—saying things that upset the rule-keepers, eating with people not fit for good company, and putting himself in harm's way as he rubbed elbows with the sick and unclean. It seems the message was that the reign of God requires a bit of risky business. Are we willing to take risks for love and justice? What price do we pay by playing it safe?

In this synopsis, I help people see how the series title (of course a play on the title of a popular movie which has perhaps piqued the interest of some people) applies to the scriptural journey, I allude to several of the stories we will encounter, and I ask a couple of provocative questions that suggest how this series will relate to our lives and discipleship. During my own Visionary Retreat, I would go through the liturgical calendar, think about the worship series I'd program, and try at least to come up with titles and synopses for every worship experience (yes, a title for the service, rather than a sermon title). Sometimes the synopses will be more like sketches than finished loglines. I may go back and tweak and flush out the synopses closer to the beginning of production time for the series, but at least I give it a start during the retreat. Here is a sample of one of the weekly synopses from this series. The title of the service is *"Not So Untouchable."*

> ***Scripture excerpts:*** *"Because she had heard about Jesus, she came up behind him in the crowd and touched his clothes. She was thinking, If I can just touch his clothes, I'll be healed.... He responded, 'Daughter, your faith has healed you; go in peace, healed from your disease' … While Jesus was still speaking with her, messengers came from the synagogue leader's house, saying to Jairus, 'Your daughter has died. Why bother the teacher any longer?' But Jesus overheard*

their report and said to the synagogue leader, 'Don't be afraid; just keep trusting.' —Mark 5:21-43

Synopsis: *Jesus' risky behavior continues. All tied up in his healing ministry is the fact that he is around a whole lot of sick and hurting people. Rather than separate himself, he walks right into the midst of crowds who have gathered with hopes that their suffering will end. A woman who has spent twelve years separated from humanity because of her condition risks coming close and daring to touch the Healer. A Jewish leader risks his reputation in order to seek healing for his daughter. Had not any one of these people, including Jesus, taken a risk and crossed boundaries that kept them apart, healing and wholeness would not have happened. Where are we called to cross boundaries in order to bind up the brokenness of this world?*

This is just one of six weekly synopses for this series. Yes, it is an investment of time to create these but, as screenwriter Allen Palmer counsels new writers, "writing the logline up front could save you years … Typically, screenwriters sweat for months or years over a screenplay, going through endless drafts, major revisions, and minor refinements. Only when the script is 'finished,' and even then only at the request of the producer, will they write the logline. This is arse about … The logline—write it early, and write it often." Of course, our cost is not lost years or thousands of dollars when a storyline loses its focus, but it can cost quite a bit. One important cost to consider is the frustration of a worship arts team who are not quite sure where they are going. The bottom line is this: the

See the rest of the synopses for this series at thinklikeafilmmaker.com.

work of the rest of the team cannot begin without the vision in place. Even if your natural tendencies may be for last-minute planning (you enjoy the rush and pressure of a deadline), *your* deadlines will need to consider the good stewardship of your "people resources"—your team.

I once consulted with a church that was doing amazing sensory-rich worship. I wondered, frankly, why they needed my help. The first day I arrived, I was cornered by the entire team … minus the senior pastor. They said, "You have to help us! We love volunteering our time and are passionate about what we do, but we have no idea what we are working on for Sunday's worship until Wednesday—week in and week out!" These wonderful, creative, and dedicated folks were about to quit something they loved doing because the pressure of last-minute scrambling was taking all the fun out of it.

Doing this prep work up-front can save preachers lots of moments of staring at a blank page in the sermon process saying, "Now what was I thinking and where was I going with this?" Howard talks about his experience, still after years of writing synopses, "I devote some time. I sit down a month before I want to have them out there, and it usually takes me three days of writing [note: he is doing one whole quarter of a year at a time]. I immerse myself and sometimes I think, 'Oh, I'm so sick of doing this,' but, by God, I'm going to get it done, and when it is finished I am so relieved because I am set! I've laid the groundwork for the community to participate—for liturgy to be truly a 'work of the people.'" While it may, at this moment, feel like this process adds much more time to your current worship design process, what you will find is that front-loading this creativity early on will make the rest of the process much easier, more satisfying, and more effective and that it is a love-offering to the rest of the team.

CASTING THE VISION

The last part of establishing the story is to choose what I call an "anchor image." If you (the Visionary) are a more visual-spatial person, you will probably begin with this process and then write your synopses. If you are more of a verbal-linguistic person, you may be tempted to skip this part. Don't. An anchor image is a key metaphor related to the message. We will talk much more in detail about the power of symbol in Chapter Three, but for now it suffices to say that providing the team with a visual idea that expresses the core of the worship series message is a real gift. It can become fodder for the visual arts, media arts, ritual action or even a logo for the series.

My suggestion for discovering an anchor image is to come up with a few "keywords" that express your theme. For the "Risky Business" theme, I came up with the word "risk," of course. But putting that into photograph library search engines online didn't produce much of anything. And putting "risky business" just came up with lots of photos of Tom Cruise! So I tried words like "on the edge," "daring," "daredevil," and found images of people on the ledges of mountaintops. This was the visceral feeling I wanted to convey to my design team as they began to search for resources for the series. Being at the edge of the unknown and daring to risk flight by jumping into an expanded understanding of "Who is my neighbor?" is the action Jesus is nudging us toward. Getting out of our comfort zone is scary. Finding an image to express this message to the team at the beginning of the design process was a way of helping to cast the vision and ensuring the team caught my drift.

Visionaries, once you have your title, your scriptures, your synopses, and your anchor image you are ready to include the whole team in the next step of the creative process. You are providing a strong, clear and inspirational start that will reap many rewards. You have steeped yourself in the story to be proclaimed, and it is ready to be expressed through all the senses. Now we can begin to imagine how the message will be profoundly experienced in the worshiping community.

CHAPTER 2

GATHERING THE TEAM

When asked what he likes best about being a director, Ron Howard replied, "The director gets to play with everybody!"[18] Teamwork is the name of the game in filmmaking, and it can make or break the experience of creating a film. No one person can do it alone—it takes a group of people with a shared vision cast by a director they trust to lead the creative process through a production timeline. So it is with sensory-rich expressions of worship. Yes, more simple forms of the techniques I'm teaching here can be done with just a couple of people. But ultimately, you will want to expand the number of folks who are involved in worship design. My motto has always been, "If liturgy literally means 'work of the people,' then let's put the people to work!" Director of *Under the Tuscan Sun* Audrey Wells relates with delight the participation of the folks living in the little Italian town where they filmed.[19] The scenes in the piazza are filled with people who actually walk through that piazza daily. The food in the dinner scenes was cooked by the local restaurant. The movie theater featured in a scene is the same one where these same people would eventually watch themselves in the final Hollywood product. The story was told not only with famous actors and out-of-town celebrities and crews, it was populated by the local people themselves.

Participation in worship can come in many ways. Of course, for most congregants, it will be in the act of worship itself. Worship becomes entertainment if the people are not active participants in the worship of God. However, the more people you engage in your worship design and leadership, the more they know about worship and therefore appreciate about worship. Your congregants' increased attention to worship design creates excitement in them as they anticipate the inspirational storytelling of upcoming services, just as the Italian townspeople's anticipation and appreciation for *Under the Tuscan Sun* was piqued by their participation in the film just as much as the actors' and crews' appreciation of the storyline was enhanced by their interaction with the people of that place. This is a wonderful analogy for the symbiotic relationship we hope to cultivate between leaders and congregations.

As we've established, sensory-rich worship consists of including what we see, hear, and do as proclamation. This approach is important because proclaiming the message in all these modes will reach more people who learn and communicate in a diversity of ways while creating for everyone a more lasting memory of the message expressed. Over the years I have used the "Three V's" as a barometer for whether I'm including all the senses. The *verbal* is everything we hear—words, music, sound effects, silence. This will involve the verbal, musical, media, and dramatic ritual artists. The *visual* is everything we see—color, objects, lighting, and the way we are configured in the space in relation to each other, to leaders and to our tangible symbols. The visual, media, and dramatic ritual artists will be engaged in this category. The *visceral* aspects of worship have to do with our actions—communion, baptism, prayer stations, postures, movement of objects, leaders, and people in the space. Verbal, visual, and dramatic ritual artists will be concerned with this aspect. As you can see, there is a good bit of cross-over because any one moment in worship may be layered with various expressive arts that must work together. Collaboration and creative process is key to the success of the whole.

Ron Howard continues in the interview: "Most human endeavors depend on a methodical consideration of all the possibilities and then preparation and execution … [In making movies] you are facing the possibility of complete public humiliation, you are putting yourself up for judgement. As a result there must be trust … In a creative process you can get that pretty fast."[20] We may not be worried about complete public humiliation (although we'll talk about the risks involved in worship change in Chapter Nine, "The Reviews"). We can, however, take a lesson from Howard's statement about how a concrete and methodical creative process can establish trust. A reliable creative process will foster trust among not only the team but also among the congregation, who increase their trust in the worship design team when they begin to experience the rewards of enhanced worship through advanced planning strategies. Before we get to my "plan together and plan ahead" strategies and timeline for design, let's take a closer look at the makeup of the team itself.

TEAM MEMBER ROLES

For most churches, the days of getting people to commit to a year-long "committee" are over. People are busy and hesitant to say, "Yes" to a long-range commitment. And highly creative people—the ones most likely to bring great energy to a design team—are usually booked to the hilt with exciting projects. We have to be creative in the ways we offer opportunities to be involved, or we will get the same people, and usually very few people, all the time.

Tiers of commitment are one way to deal with this. There will be people who are able to help out at some times of the year more than others. There will be people who can help out only occasionally, but they have specific skills that the team will need. There will be some who are willing to spend a Saturday afternoon helping out with some guided grunt work but don't have time in their lives to put in any more effort than that.

A *core team* member is someone who is a permanent member of the team. This may include staff whose job is to work on worship (pastoral, musical, technical—depending on the size of your church), and the core team can include people who want to be involved all year round and have the time to do so (these people are akin to choir members who offer their gifts all year with perhaps a break here and there). A *series team* member is someone who is able to work through the whole creative process on *one* series or liturgical season. Then they sit out for a while and rotate back into the team for a series when they have some more time. *Extended team* members are those that have specific skills or time frames to help out on occasional tasks such as building something (a handy-person), coming to a brainstorming party (a geologist for a theme about "deep wells") or

See my interview with Stacy Hood about the youth program she developed at thinklikeafilmmaker.com.

helping to keep track of songs for license purposes (a librarian). When we think outside of the box about ways to involve people, we heighten the possibilities and excitement for involvement. Another way to extend and grow future participation is to create an internship program for the youth of your congregation to be trained and to contribute.

Films require a vast number of people in multiple departments to pull off the artistic vision and all its supporting details. Let's take a look at some of those roles[21] and how they might inform our own attention to the kinds of team members we need for sensory-rich worship design.

The *director* of a film is analogous to what I'm calling a Visionary—the pastor(s) of the congregation. The overall concept starts with their discernment, as we talked about in the last chapter. The "buck stops" with the director of a film as they work with all the artists to create a cohesive expression of the message. Someone has to have their finger on the pulse of the whole. When artists work in "silos" without a common direction or connection to each other, we are less likely to see each part synthesizing seamlessly. Worship design is not a democratic process. A film director needs the creative input from the whole team, and there are moments in the production timeline when the team works collectively. But there must also be a Visionary who is able to steer the team down a common river of intent. As I said in the last chapter, when the Visionary casts a clear vision at the beginning of the process, guiding the team will not take a lot of effort. This is crucial to lowering the stress of working with a team.

The *screenwriter*, as we have already seen, has responsibility for the story's verbal form. The pastors have responsibilities related to this at the beginning of the process but in worship, unlike film, most of the writing of liturgy and sermon preparation will be done later in the process. The word-smithing role can be shared with members of the team who love verbal-linguistic communication. Being part of a think-tank reflection group for the preacher(s), searching for readings, poetry, and liturgy—or, better yet, writing their own—can be a stimulating and creative outlet for these folks. A *casting director* works closely with the director to cast the film and assists with the organization and administration of actors. Someone who is part of the verbal arts team who loves to call people on the phone is the perfect person to carry out the task of finding and scheduling readers or other volunteers once the worship scripts are finished.

A film *producer* and production department associated with that role (unit production manager, assistant directors, script supervisors, production assistants) take care of the details and logistics. From coordinating and facilitating preparations to create efficiency between departments, organizing rehearsals and shoots, supervising and communicating to cast and crew, and ensuring continuity from beginning to end, these professionals think about the whole process so the artistic teams can focus on their unique contributions. One of the most important things I have learned as I've worked with pastors who are just beginning to do sensory-rich worship is that if you don't have help with managing the details, you become more a "manager" than a Visionary (for example, dealing with last-minute substitutions when a reader doesn't show up, or scrambling right before worship for the lighter, or worrying if the volunteer at the light switch will remember their cue). This can take the depth right out of your role and leave you frazzled at just the moment you need to be centered. So I've begun to talk to teams about the importance of having a Series Team Leader. This is a person (or preferably a couple of people who can switch off from series to series) who really enjoys managing the details of tasks, scheduling the group, and keeping the communication flowing. This is not someone who does it all—this is just someone who makes sure it is all getting done by various members of the team and can be "in the wings" taking care of last-minute instructions and hiccups. We will pursue this in more depth in Chapter Eight as we deal with the editing and production part of the worship design process.

The *production designer* and *art director* oversee the overall design, or "look," of the film—they deal with anything that will appear before the camera. Their team consists of the set designer, costume, hair, makeup, property manager, and set decorators. In worship design, the visual arts team is instrumental in helping to create a "look," an environment, a color scheme and symbol/object choices for the worship series. This is a role that is often at the forefront early in the process so that all the team members can visualize and feel how the essence of the message will be embodied in the space. The early focus on visual elements is true of films as well, as the art department researches what the visual concept of the film will be before it even begins to shoot. Once the "ethos" or palette and visual design is decided, the visual arts team will collaborate with media and dramatic arts to make sure the arrangement of the space, the symbolic objects, even clothing and vestment choices are cared for intentionally.

The *cinematographer*, or director of photography, is the camera and lighting supervisor on the film production and has responsibility for camera operators, gaffers and electricians, sound operators and grips. They work with the director to bring the story to life through the focus and perspective of the viewer. They will decide camera angles and movement and filters. Understanding how the audience sees is part of this role. Media arts teams in our worship design are not just about images and words on projection screens in worship. Even if your church isn't using projected media yet, you will still have a media arts team. Media artists are those whose role is to make sure that "how" the congregation sees (lighting) and hears (sound) is attended to carefully. For those churches that do use projected media, deciding where the congregation's focus will be directed requires media artists to discern the timing, movement, and flow of projected images and other visuals. They will ask questions about whether a still photograph or a moving video image is the right choice during any given moment in order to enhance what is going on rather than distract from it. They will also create montages of still or moving images that are themselves proclamation of the message and will work closely with the music artists for timing in, out, and perhaps during a visual Word. In churches that stream their services or provide live camera feeds to screens in worship, the media arts team will be making artistic choices about camera shots that will deeply affect the ways that the congregation or viewers at home experience the service.

The *composer* on a film is an artist whose work cannot be underrated. Music is the emotional coloring of the film. It provides continuity, pacing, and timing. The main purpose of music in a film is to further the story and immerse us deeper in it. Those whose purview is the musical arts in worship are tasked with these same responsibilities. Their choices for congregational, choral, instrumental, and ensemble music can either invite us deeper into the experience of the story or take us out into "left field." As we will discuss in depth in Chapter Five, instrumentalists in worship also have the ability to provide continuity as we move from one worship element to the next. As film composers sculpt the energy of the film, they are keeping the (unseen) audience ever in mind, knowing when to ramp up the intensity and when to change the tone and feel of the moment to draw viewers in. Being "in tune" with and actively sculpting the energy of the congregation are essential skills for song leaders who want to invite worshipers into more meaningful engagement.

The *sound designer* of a film deals with the overall mix of the film sound—not just music, but also added sound effects that enhance the experience of the story aurally. Media artists will also contribute to sensory-rich worship as they search for sounds that can enhance a sense of "place" in the story, such as wind or waves or storms.

The *editors* on a film are part of the post-production staff and work with the director to assemble the film. We won't consider the editing and script-writing phase of the worship design process as "post-production," but this moment in worship design does have much in common with the tasks an editor of a film carries out. This is when decisions are made about what will be included based on the worship team's overall vision. Some good ideas will have to be cut because there just isn't room, resources, or reason for them to appear in the finished product. These kinds of decisions must be made with just a core group—sometimes just the pastor, music director, and series team leader. Decisions about order, repeated elements, and timing make a difference for both editors of film and editors of a worship script.

All roles are equally important, and establishing communication between all of the arts is essential during the creative process. I've already mentioned the concept of "layering" where multiple art forms may be contributing to the same moment in worship. Imagine this: the dramatic arts team may have conceived of congregational movement to prayer stations to light candles during prayer time for a Lent series called "Watch and Pray." The visual arts team will need to place those tables around the sanctuary and cover them with fabric in the "hue" of the series palette, buy tea light candles and tapers for people to light with and hand to the next person. Musicians will need to decide the mood and content of the music for that time period. Verbal artists will need to think carefully about the invitation and instructions to the congregation so that all happens smoothly and without anxiety, and they will need to prepare a concluding prayer for the end of that element. Media artists may want to video some of the candles flickering beforehand to put in a loop for the screens during that time. This is but one example of the kind of teamwork that a layered, sensory-rich moment of worship can require. It may seem daunting when you lay it all out like this, but when the design process is in place and everyone knows their roles and responsibilities, working together to create an experience like this one can be exhilarating for a team. Being part of a worship arts team can be one of the richest discipleship group opportunities in a church. It involves study of the sacred texts, theological inquiry, creativity, teamwork, and the satisfaction of immersing one's beloved community in an experience of our faith narrative. What a gift.

One of the biggest benefits of intentional worship design in a team setting is that every detail is cared for in such a way that nothing distracts from the message and everything points to the message, making it more unforgettable. The director of a film knows that without the team, there will be no movie—they literally cannot do it all (at least not anything bigger than a student film project). Pastors *can* do it all—Sunday will come around, people will show up, and something will happen. But one of two things will happen if you stick to "lone ranger planning" (no matter the size of your church). First, you'll burn out quickly trying to do sensory-rich worship without at least a little help, and you'll either be looking for an easier job or drop all the other pastoral duties associated with the gig. Or, second, you will fall into a rut of "same ole, same ole" because you don't have time to give it more than that. What do you have to lose? It will take some time to build a team if you don't have one now. But, step by step, you will enhance one element at a time. Perhaps first you find an HGTV (Home and Garden Television) addict with a passion and an eye for arranging things in your congregation who can help you choose some fabric and items for prayer stations for the season of Lent. Then perhaps you make time to work with your part-time accompanist to play softly under a poem you will read during your sermon. Then just maybe you will write some synopses and gather some fun and creative people just to brainstorm with you one evening about the next series over a potluck. A choir member comes forward to help you search for hymns for the next series. As you do this together, perhaps you find a piece that would work great as a "theme song" to be repeated each week as a sung introduction and then played instrumentally as the light is recessed out at the end. Bit by bit, you will find people who can be trained to "see" like ritual artists and begin to collaborate with you to contribute their vitality and excitement, bringing the story alive.

The "production" timeline

I don't want you to get nervous about the word "production." A few decades ago, when the contemporary worship movement began making

For my two cents about whether "to clap or not to clap" see thinklikeafimmaker.com.

headway into heretofore traditional churches, the controversy about "worship is not a performance or a production" began to take a lot of our energy. I'm not sure it did us any favors because I think it was a bit misguided, or at least we weren't talking about the right things in the right way. It's important to ensure that congregations are engaged and participating, not simply spectators for "the professionals" who do the work of worship while lost in their own little world (and by the way, I've seen this in every style of worship as well). That indeed should have been the crux of the conversation. But we instead got too sidetracked about things like whether or not congregations should clap after musical offerings.

The other way that this conversation set us back a bit was how it made us hesitant to actually discuss helpful processes of planning and collaboration that would enhance the quality of worship—like planning ahead and even *rehearsing!* We make these efforts, not so that worship can be *slick*, but to serve the message well, so that the congregation is not distracted by uncared-for execution of the storytelling that takes them out of their worshipful experience. To *perform* is to "give form." Simply that. And the form we want to give our worshipful expressions should be the form that communicates in the most powerful way possible. That might just take some preparation and collaboration—especially if we believe sensory-rich communication is one of the most powerful ways to communicate.

So yes, I am going to unabashedly call this a "production timeline" for sensory-rich worship. Without a clear creative process that holds us all accountable and provides something we can count on, teamwork can be pretty frustrating and won't last long. Most of us who went to seminary did not learn a creative process or production timeline for planning worship. We may have learned to fill in the blanks with the basic elements of a worship service, but as a guest lecturer in many seminaries in my career, I know that what you can actually teach in one semester of worship (if you are lucky to have even that these days) is limited. A theological and historical foundation is essential in training ministry professionals, and so the nitty-gritty, how-you-do-it is often left to learning as you go. There are exceptions. But don't despair if this sounds like you. Like everything else, it will take some getting used to, but a more efficient way of doing something can always be learned and will improve your life and ministry immeasurably.

We've already talked about the various roles of the team, and the next five chapters will expand on the skills specific to each part of the worship team. So let's lay an important ground rule about planning *together* that will serve the timeline we are about to see. I've already said that designing worship as a team is not a democratic process. There must be a Visionary guiding and making crucial decisions, just like the director of a film. Here is another important fact—including a team as part of the design process means that we will end up with more ideas than we can use—that is the gift of the "community of imaginations." A team must realize that not all ideas will make it past the cutting-room floor. And that needs to be understood and accepted by everyone. There can be "too many cooks in the kitchen," which ends up being a recipe for unnecessary power struggles and hurt feelings that jeopardize the team concept. So here is my number-one rule for successful teamwork: When there are *decisions* to be made (discerning the vision at the beginning of the process and later in the editing stage), there are *less people involved*. When there are *no decisions* to be made (brainstorming, resource-gathering, and task management), there are *more people involved*. When everyone has a clear understanding of their role, they can trust that doing their part in stirring up ideas has been a gift, whether or not their particular idea is utilized in the end.

The production timeline that I have been teaching for years is based on these two principles: plan together and plan ahead. The organization of time spent is different than what many pastors were taught—the monthly committee meeting augmented with weekly check-ins. It is different because we are going to follow the timeline of the structure of the series' progression (such as the liturgical year), rather than a regular schedule based on the secular calendar. Monthly meetings might work when you are planning one Sunday at a time, but when you are planning series, we treat the timeline based on the timing of the series. It is more akin to the production schedule for a "project" such as film production—we begin to see each series as the creative project, and the timing of our efforts are aligned with the most efficient way to complete the work before the "launch." It will feel unfamiliar at first and perhaps will seem like you are spending more time on worship. The reality is that you've simply moved the planning effort in your schedule to take advantage of what we know about creativity—immersion, rather than dispersion, of energy and time creates faster results. And your planning occurs further in advance of the beginning of the series, drawing on something else we know about creativity in teams—it is much more fun when there is less pressure. We have time to consider our best ideas, not just the first thing we think of.

This model grew out of my work as a Minister of Worship Arts, my research into creative processes, and then over 20 years of working as a consultant with churches all over the country. This timeline brings together the best practices from all those that I experimented with and saw working for others. Most churches I have worked with tweak the model in some way to fit their context, working styles, and personalities. My suggestion, however, is to start here and find out along the way where you need to adjust.

Get an infographic of this process at thinklikeafilmmaker.com.

1. Naming the direction—Most of what happens in this first part of the creative process was discussed in the last chapter. The Visionary makes time to retreat at least twice a year to do long-range planning. They will either go alone, if that is their best way of immersing themselves and making decisions, or they will take a core team with them if they enjoy bouncing ideas off of others. The most important thing a congregation can do is support these retreats through funds and making sure all needs of the church and its members will be cared for during the retreat—creating a sacred and uninterrupted time for the Visionary to do this important groundwork. The question for this part of the process is "What will be the most poignant, meaningful, and memorable direction for this year, this community, at this time in our spiritual journey?" They will come out of the retreat process with a series title, synopsis (2–4 sentence description), and *anchor image* (visual/metaphorical representation of the theme) for each series as well as titles and beginnings of synopses for every week of each series (I call each service a *frame*). They might even have some ideas for music, visuals or media that will repeat throughout the series (this is called a *thread item)*. This initial work will be shared with the core and series team when they get back so that everyone can begin to let these themes ruminate in their hearts and minds. One of the most productive parts of a creative process—and one that many skip over because they haven't started early enough—is the time to let ideas "steep" in the back of our minds.

One part of the process can actually begin to happen right away after the Visionary Retreat: publicity. With this much information already discerned, preliminary work can begin on logos, ideas for postcards, series video trailers, etc. You won't need those concretely finished until the creative process for each particular series begins, but you'll have a big head-start on work to get the word out.

About ten weeks prior to the start of the series, the Visionary will pull out the series information they created at the retreat and over the next two weeks, tweak it, fill out the weekly synopses, and prepare to present the concept, the main message, the journey, to the whole team at what I call a "brainstorming party."

2. Brainstorming party/retreat—This gathering—eight weeks before the series begins—can be as short as an evening of brainstorming, or it can be a day-long retreat over several hours if you want to get more concrete work done. Thinking back to our rule about successful teamwork, this is a part of the process when no decisions are being made so we want "all hands on deck." The core team (those working on worship all year), the series team (those who are working on just this series), and any extended team members (those who are just great idea-generators and can commit to helping with only this brainstorming process or people whose expertise can offer something specific related to the theme) should be there. If you are using the day-long retreat option, you might have extended team members present only for the first part of the day when the "dreaming" is happening, and then pare down to the core/series team for the afternoon as you begin to hone the ideas into some working proposals.

Here is a sample outline for a Brainstorming Party:

Gathering—Have the party at someone's home who has a large-enough gathering space for the number of people you imagine. If you do this at the church, it immediately feels more like a "committee meeting" than a party. Have food that is easy to eat sitting on couches or standing, and make sure it is ready to eat soon after the appointed gathering time. The energy of the group will tank if you wait, or if you sit at a formal table, and it will be more difficult to generate creativity. Be sure there is upbeat music as people arrive. This sets a tone of energetic movement. Find places in the house to put large pieces of paper from a Post-It pad with markers by each one. There will be one for each worship experience (the "frames") and one for general ideas. Write those headings on the papers. I like to tape the synopsis for that week at the top (print it out in large font). As people gather and get food, have someone act as a host, making sure everyone knows everyone.

Pitching the Vision—Don't let the energy in the room drop or wait too long after people are finished eating. In fact, if the space is conducive, you could start working after everyone has gotten food and are settled in the gathering space (family room, living room, den, basement rec area, etc). The Visionary begins to pitch the vision for the series. They can have copies of what I call an "inspiration page" (the series title, theme scripture, series synopsis, and anchor image photos) to hand out there, or they could have sent those by e-mail beforehand. This is a moment to give folks a "feel" for the series and is the first moment the team will be immersed in it. Make it worshipful! I like to show photos on projected media and play or sing a song or instrumental that reflects the theme (religious or secular). I speak the synopsis I've written and lift up a spoken prayer. Then I offer some context by explaining why this line of thought inspired me for the series/season, perhaps sharing something interesting

I discovered during my study of the sacred texts. Then I go through all the titles for each "frame" (service), giving a summation of the synopses I have written (I like to send those out ahead of time as well so people are already primed and I don't have to read all the synopses verbatim but instead simply describe each one). This should not take a long time. Just prime the pump so you have time to hear from the team members and the energy continues to crackle in the group.

Immediate Feedback—Take about 15 minutes to invite folks' brief responses to what has been offered. What does it stir in you? Does something leap immediately to mind? Can you relate? Are there questions about the essence of the message? If someone has been invited because of their expertise (like a geologist for a theme called "Deep Well"), this would be the time to ask them to share what comes up from their perspective. The person who invites and coordinates discussion does not necessarily have to be the Visionary. There are some folks who are great at facilitating group brainstorming, and they would take the reins at this point.

Brainstorming Warm-up—We are about to go into an idea-generating time. Because we've been eating and sitting for a bit, we need to get bodies (and therefore, minds) moving so that the ideas flow easily.

For my rules for brainstorming and more warm-up exercises, go to thinklikeafilmmaker.com.

Invite people to stand and then go over the "rules for brainstorming" (like "all ideas are welcome, even the seemingly silly or impossible" and "no decisions will be made tonight, so anything is possible!"). Then do a fun exercise to get people talking and thinking, like getting in partners and making up a story one word at a time, bouncing between partners or "babbling"—giving partners a word to riff off of for 30 seconds each. This warm-up exercise does not have to pertain immediately to the theme but just needs to get people's creative juices flowing.

Idea Explosion—This happens in three configurations: individually, in pairs or small groups, and then among the whole group. Introverts and extroverts process differently, and so we want to mix up our methods of getting ideas out. First, turn on some energy-generating music that has a rhythm to it (not too overbearing but enough to create a buzz in the room). For about 10–15 minutes (you'll have to gauge the length, depending on the size of your group), invite people to go to the large post-its and record anything that comes to mind. This can be just phrases or questions, or it can be concrete ideas for any of the worship arts for each frame/service. It can be descriptions of visual images they imagine, words, ritual actions, or song ideas. Anything goes! When you see the activity slowing in the room, bring the music to a stop. Divide people into smaller groups (I usually do this according to how many pieces of paper are posted), and place them at the papers around the room. Give the groups a couple of minutes at each one (like round robin) to look at what people have written on the papers and to add more if they want as they talk to each other about what is popping out at them from the ideas already gathered. Either put the music back on very low or not at all. We want people talking to each other in their pairings or groups. When that is finished, invite the whole group to assemble together, but keep them standing (of course, unless some folks need to sit). Standing keeps the energy buzzing and the comments brief! Ask folks, "What ideas did you see or contribute that have you jumping up and down saying, 'Yes!'"? This is a way to feel out what I call "energy surges"—ideas that are deeply resonating with the group. Pay attention to the group's reactions, what is called their "paraverbals" like "Me too!" or "Oh, yeah!" Someone on the core team should be taking notes of this portion of the process.

Closing—The final exercise is to hand out a piece of paper and pen to each person and invite them to find a place to sit and write quietly for five minutes. Invite them to simply write a reflection about the theme.

You may describe this as writing what your heart is telling you at the moment. There are no rules about what should come out, no expectations that they will share or not share what they write. Depending on the familiarity, comfort level, and time frame of the group, you can choose to share these with each other, reading aloud in the large group after the five minutes or just invite people to leave them in a basket if they are comfortable sharing them privately. These can be used as inspiration during the creative process. Gather for a prayer of thanksgiving for the group's volunteered time and effort, and ask for guidance for the rest of the preparations. Then ... eat dessert!

For a Brainstorming Retreat Day, do the same exact things listed above in the morning. Then in the afternoon, divide up into artist groups (visual, verbal, musical, media, dramatic) to begin thinking more concretely about ideas for each service and ideas for "thread items" (things that will repeat throughout the season). Making lists of ideas is the goal—remember this is still a time when no concrete decisions have to be made. Don't stop with the first good idea. You have time to explore. Musicians may get inspired to find or write a musical theme, and the visual team starts to make some preliminary sketches. The dramatic arts team may look closely at the scriptures and synopses and dream about choral readings, dramatic presentations, or ritual actions. Verbal arts folks may spend the afternoon exploring the biblical and theological implications of each frame. Every 30 minutes (set a timer), come back together in a stand-up circle (to keep it brief), and have each break-out group give a description of what they are working on or what has come up. This is essential because with sensory-rich worship, you will find ways that the ideas collaborate and feed on each other. The last step to a full-day Brainstorming Retreat is to wrap up with to-do's for further research over the next month (step 3 below).

A note about churches that have multiple services of different styles: the brainstorming process is about fleshing out the main concepts of the theme and throwing out some "what if" ideas for any of the art forms. You may find it helpful to spend some time working all together on the theme, since it will be the same for all services. But then, when you begin to throw out ideas and resources, you may want to, if you are a larger church with separate teams working on separate services, split out into separate working groups so that your time is more pointedly directed toward specific contexts. But I highly recommend that you be all together for some time so that everyone is really on board with the "essence of the message"—both for the overarching series and for each week. The community is still one church on a spiritual journey together no matter what time or worship space individuals frequent.

3. Brainstorming and resource-gathering—Creativity experts tell us that blasts of energy are good for idea-making, such as the Brainstorming Party. But time can also be our friend when it comes to envisioning more. The next four weeks are spent researching and gathering possible resources for the series. This is done by the whole team. The more ideas, the better. There's time enough to allow many "right answers" to come along. Each worship arts sub-group can gather together at least once in person to check in and share/generate ideas. However, this is not the decision-making time. In other words, while many ideas are generated, no part of the worship team should become completely attached to one idea at the expense of not explor-

See how the WDS Brainstorming App can help ignite and streamline this process at thinklikeafilmmaker.com.

ing several options. Only when all the possibilities are gathered together from all the artists will we begin to see ways that they will merge and "layer" together for sensory-rich communication.

This part of the process is about discovery. I love to research. And so if I'm brainstorming about a series called "My God is a Rock," I'm going to begin to find out information about the geology in our area. This is what I call "metaphoraging" (foraging for metaphors). This information might come from the internet, or I might seek out a conversation with an expert in the congregation or community. I live in Tahoe. I have found out that the rock around here is formed both by ancient explosive volcanoes as well as slow-moving glacial ice. Isn't that a bit like our experience of God? Sometimes we are inspired by big, dramatic "a-ha!" moments, and, at other times, spirituality comes through diligent, relentless practice. This might spur me to an idea about using lava rock and smooth river rocks at some point in the series as part of the visual arts or in some sort of ritual action response. As I make discoveries, I add them to the list. Even when an idea seems far-fetched or downright crazy, it is important to capture it. You may dream of creating a big stone labyrinth in the churchyard for the series. Even if you can't imagine how to get this done, it doesn't mean that someone else might not see a way to do it. Now is not the time to listen to what I call the "VOJ" (Voice of Judgment) that says, "We could never do that!" Dream big! And even if you are a musical artist and you had this idea for a labyrinth, capture it even though it may be out of the purview of your particular art form (you may also hear a small ensemble playing outside as people walk the labyrinth). The truth is that as the team gets more and more used to the concept of sensory-rich worship, they will all start thinking automatically in terms of "layers," and so everyone needs to feel free to express ideas, no matter the medium.

In fact, brainstorming and resource-gathering during this time period is sometimes just about making lists. How many "rock" songs can you list? "My God is a Rock in a Weary Land," "Lead Me to the Rock," "Rock of Ages," etc., etc. Sometimes it is just about going through song title indexes, looking at scads of Creative Commons License photos online of rocks, rocks, rocks to find some really great ones. Sometimes it is about combing books for poems about rocks, the earth, etc. Again, this is not a time for editing. The purpose of this part of the process is to provide enough fodder so that when it does come time to choose resources, we can make good choices with a balance of familiar and new.

4. Production Week: Writing Scripts—Four weeks before the series begins is what I call "production week." This is when all the idea-generating comes to a close, the resource-gathering of the whole team over the previous month is reported, and the rubber hits the road. This is decision time and so involves fewer people, perhaps just the Visionary, music director, and series team leader. During production week, *all the scripts for every week of the series are completed.* One of the first things that will happen is to decide on "thread" items that will act as continuity throughout the series. Some songs will repeat (themes songs, prayer, and benediction songs), and some ritual actions will repeat (our example of going to light candles at prayer stations). Some congregational spoken responses will be the same throughout. Thread items will get copied to all the scripts, and then the elements that will vary every week get filled in. This process actually makes it easier than you might imagine to finish all scripts at one time.

Chapter Eight will go into detail about this process so I won't say much more here … except one thing. This is a very important shift in the way worship is usually designed. This does not mean sermons are written or worship guides (bulletins) are printed—those are the only things that wait for the week-by-week schedule dur-ing the series. But everything else is put into writ-ing so that we know exactly what we are doing and what needs to get done during the next three weeks before the series launch. As you calendar your year with these production dates, those involved in the script-writing will need to create more time in their schedule during this week for the work on worship than in other weeks.

For example scripts, go to thinklikeafilmmaker.com.

5. Task Management—There are three weeks until the series launch. Because we know exactly how many readers we need each week, what visual items we need, what every word to every song is, etc., we now move into the "git 'er done" mode (my Midwest and Texas roots are showing). The decisions have already been made, so we can get the whole team on board to help. I'm actually going to say that again because this is where many pastors get off-track. They try to do too much themselves, and, again, that is a major reason for burn-out. So here goes: *there are no decisions to be made (the scripts describe everything!) so we get the whole team on board to help.* Preparations for all services are made. Rehearsals happen, trips to the fabric store or hardware store happen. Media slides are made (yes, for all the services). Readers, communion servers, ushers, acolytes are scheduled. Worship Guides are created (but not yet printed). Special items are ordered (like customized seed packets for a theme on growing our trust in God). There are people who will help out with this part of the process who aren't part of the initial brainstorming and creating—they love to just have a concrete task and carry it out.

6. The Final Countdown—Final preparations happen the week before the first Sunday of the series. Chapter Eight will help you step by step through this process. The cue-to-cue rehearsal is a practice taken from my theater background and has proven to be *the most essential element to making worship flow* as a spiritual journey from beginning to end. Because there will be some thread elements that will repeat (or slightly morph) week to week throughout the series, the first cue-to-cue rehearsal with key leaders will take more time than the weekly ones that happen during the rest of the series.

Here is what I'm hoping you are seeing at this point: what we have done is take the creative process that many people *try to do in its entirety* week in and week out, 52 weeks a year, and spread it out to create more ease and less last-minute stress while inviting all members of the team to bring the fullness of their artistry to our immersive worship. It honors the way our brains work most efficiently and creatively, and it spreads the work load out to various people with various gifts. When we try to create one-hit-wonders week in and week out (weekly worship planning model), we never get the time to fine-tune that sermon or carry out great ideas that come to us because we simply don't have time to carry them out.

THE TEAM COVENANT

Including more people in the work of worship design is a faithful thing to do. If only one or two people are always planning how the story will be told, then the whole community is cut off from the breadth of the "community of imaginations." Imagine a beautiful piece of sculpture on a table in the center of the room. Then imagine your congregation in a single-file circle at the perimeter of the room completely encircling the sculpture. If one person in that circle described the sculpture from their vantage point, we would have only that one perspective. But if someone on the other side of the room also described it, we would have yet another view. If every person were to describe the sculpture from their particular place, the whole community would end up with a fuller picture of the sculpture from many angles and perspectives. So it is with the faith narrative. We are community because there are advantages to belonging, and one of those advantages is the gift of seeing things in ways we never would have seen on our own. To invite more people into the process of dreaming, designing, and carrying out the storytelling endeavor is to expand the community's experience of that story.

But community can also be messy. Teamwork can be weakened by many things. Filmmakers know about this. Stories abound about "divas" on the set or miscommunication between departments that cost weeks of delays and millions of dollars. Some people end up vowing never to work for "that" director or actor again.[22] Film teams have a harder time than worship teams simply because of they are exponentially larger and their timeline is longer. One film production author says that film crews and studios are more likely to think of themselves as individuals rather than invest in the creation of a strong team because too many things can go wrong if there isn't a strong structure in place for connecting team members. "In order for a team to function properly, a common ground between the needs of the individual, the team identity, and the objective must be found. Without this, the possibility for team breakups and task failure will always be high."[23]

While worship teams won't have "contracts," it is important to have good agreements and structures for our working relationships so that we clearly know what is ultimately important. All teams need concrete statements to help them function in the best possible way. Here is a Worship Team Covenant that I helped develop in consultation with a worship team that was in need of some "attitude-adjustments." It became a way to begin a conversation about a needed culture change within the group (and the church). Use it as a springboard to create your own.

What does teamwork require?

1. Willing heart and openness to the process
2. Covenant with the team—each part is important, and the whole is as important as each part
3. Flexibility—creativity in collaboration involves give and take
4. Enthusiasm—the gift of your positive energy and willingness to go beyond the minimum is the best gift of all
5. Appreciation—we all value and express our gratitude to one another on a regular basis

Our team covenant:

Designing worship for the community is an honor and a responsibility. Each soul who enters these doors deserves our best energy and our best effort. In order to offer this gift, we covenant to do these things:

- We will communicate clearly through agreed-upon channels.
- We will be as faithful to the timeline as humanly possible.

- We will offer our best enthusiasm and energy for the good of the team.
- We will honor each person's role and remember that each part of the team is only as good as the whole of the team together.
- We will honor the process of creativity, knowing that more ideas will be generated than possible to include and we will keep in mind that the vision for the whole might require that not all ideas can be included. We also know that the Visionaries and Core Team honor and appreciate all ideas, whether they are ultimately utilized or not.
- We will pray for one another, asking God's spirit to infuse our creativity and our collaboration.

Our filmmaking analogy applies to our "plan together and plan ahead" strategy outlined in this chapter. When multiple artists are working on one scene together, there's no way they could bring their best if the director told them what she or he wanted just days or weeks ahead of shooting. Art directors could think of a terrific prop from an historical era but would never have time to find it. Actors would be struggling to bring quality to their performances, not having had time to digest what inflections to bring to their lines. Cinematographers would have no plan of action for the right perspectives, having had little time to steep in the story. Planning together and planning ahead is simply good stewardship of people's time and energy. It creates excitement in the team and anticipation for the congregation. It helps us to bring our very best efforts for bringing the Word alive in unforgettable ways.

CHAPTER 3

THINK LIKE AN ART DIRECTOR:
VISUAL ARTS IN WORSHIP

The visual arts have had a long and, sometimes, difficult, career in the life of the church. Once the primary way for illiterate people to learn the faith narrative, visual images suffered a devaluation during the Reformation—with some people considering the focus on images to be idolatrous. Much of this was backlash as the Protestant church tried to separate itself from what it considered the abuses of the Roman Catholic tradition, including what many thought was an obsession with iconography and statues. This also coincided with the move to prominence of word-centered communication as the printing press made it more possible for the masses to become more literate and the Enlightenment era brought the idea that the best way to God was through more cognitive means.

But, as we discussed in chapter one, images provided the very first recorded expression of our stories, and modern science has since learned the important role of imagery in even the most logical of brain functions. In 21st-century expressions of worship, churches are embracing once again the power of visual arts in meaningful and memorable worship. There are so many exciting aspects of what a visual arts team can consider in their work. We aren't talking about what color the paraments are for the liturgical season. That was a nice, gentle step back into the use of color by Protestants, somewhat fueled by the rise of liturgical-supply stores. Rather, like the art director of a film who considers the context, the settings, the visual "palette" and the symbolism and functionality of props, we must deal with the total picture, including the space in which we worship, the colors and textures that will express each worship series message most powerfully and the objects and symbols that evoke that message.

THE SPACE

Being immersed in the story requires attention to every aspect of the environment of the space itself. The art director on a film is essential to the whole "feel" of the movie. Jon Boorstin explains, "If the art director does the job well, his [or her] environments are a metaphor for the actions and emotions of the story." He goes on to say that "people love to be taken to a place that's like nothing they've seen before."[24] Our job as ritual artists is to take people to places in their imagination and hearts by presenting the same space they've worshiped in for years in a different way—one that propels them deeper into the story.

When we enter a space, we get an immediate "hit"—a visceral snapshot of what we imagine will happen here. Several factors contribute to how a space feels. Color, light, architecture, and spatial relationship communicate energy dynamics. We perceive and react to light waves, movement of architectural lines, the "heat" or "cool" of color, and the arrangement of seating which forecasts the kind of relationships and movements which will take place in a worship space. Spaces, says liturgical theologian Rainer Volp, are "texts" with many levels of meaning. We have the ability to "read" space through the response of our bodies to the space.

> Even blind people can read spaces, and not merely by touch: they feel and sense, for example, whether spaces are lofty or

low, whether they stifle sound or let it resound, whether they are close or airy, oppressive or open. Faced with space, no one is illiterate. Each of us is a body and, as a body, responds to the body of that space. This is more than a vague sensitivity. It is a reading of space, a reading by means of which we define situations and thereby, in some sense, our very selves.[25]

The space itself has a dynamic that shapes the way in which speech, action, and music are performed, received, and interpreted. Art directors on a film are the "second-most-important thing in a film" says Chris Allen Tant. "The acting will make the film, but the art direction makes the actors."[26] In other words, the space where the action happens, words spoken, and music sung will make a difference for how we take in those messages. Liturgical theologian James White explains,

Church architecture not only reflects the ways Christians worship, but architecture also shapes worship or, not uncommonly, misshapes it … In the first place, the building helps define the meaning of worship for those gathered inside it. Try to preach against triumphalism in a baroque church! Try to teach the priesthood of all believers with a deep gothic chancel never occupied by any but ordained clergy![27]

When I am consulting with a church, one of the first things I want to know is what the worship space looks and feels like. When I walk around the space and begin to comment about the lines, ceiling height, sight lines, colors, and textures, people often say to me, "I really haven't looked carefully at our space for a long time. It's just there, and I don't really notice the effect it has very often." The worship space is the container in which everything happens. Unfortunately, we don't get to pick special locations for every series like a film director would, so we have to know our space well and find out what we can do in it to create differences in "the look"—and therefore, the "feel"—that brings us closer to the story.

I want to encourage you to lead your whole worship team in examining your space carefully—even and especially if most of you have been worshiping there for years. Start with the size and scale of your space. *Scale* is one of the "building blocks" in designing religious space, says Fr. Richard S. Vosko, a liturgical consultant on architectural projects.[28] In much of church architecture, historically as well as recently, *height* and *light* conveys "spiritual uplift." Diffused light in these lofty spaces "evokes the ethereal qualities of meditation." Large structures with lots of glass are described as radiating an "openness towards the world outside."[29] On the other hand, spaces that are not so lofty create more of a sense of intimacy and allow more focus on the community. In some spaces, "solid walls provide a sense of protection and thus solitude," and grotto or cave-like environments give a strong sense of interiority.[30] In these cases *depth, texture,* and *darkness* provide an entirely different bodily response when we walk into them.

What feeling does the scale in your worship space evoke? If you have a big, airy space with high ceilings and you have a series where you want the community to be more aware of each other or create a more intimate feel, how will you do that, or vice versa? (I'll give you some ideas later in the chapter for that question.) How is the inherent (permanent) paint or wood color affecting the mood? What about the lighting? What is the balance of natural and artificial light, and what control do you have over that balance? Is that lighting warm or cold in hue? Is there enough, and is that lighting flexible (we'll dive deeper into this in the Media Arts chapter)?

What *lines* are prominent in the space? Are the walls large and flat, with little definition, or are there windows, stained glass, molding and paneling that create line and shapes? If the only thing you are doing visually is to hang rectangular banners on walls with a lot of already boxy architectural molding, you may need to consider *non-linear* swaths of cloth to cut through the lines and create a more fluid feel occasionally.

Next, notice the "furniture" placement in the room. Pathways for movement and seating arrangement dramatically affect the experience of worshipers. The often-used configuration of straight rows of chairs or pews can convey a *firm* ordering of space and the sense that the only worthwhile view is toward the front, limiting our ability to see each other and sense the community as a whole. Other configurations such as diagonal aisles or labrynth-like pathways into a worship space engage worshipers in a *fluid* sense of space.[31] Circular, antiphonal (congregants facing one another) or three-sided arrangements of seating wrapped around a focal point such as the font or altar/table create a sense of *intimacy*, unity, and connectedness between people.[32] Different *levels* and *barriers* of a space, especially those between worship leaders and participants, affect the flow of energy in worship.[33] Do you have openness between the chancel and people, or do things "up front" feel distant? What can you change about the space's layout? Is there room to create worship centers or side tables for ritual action, or was the space designed mostly for sitting and listening or standing in place occasionally? How is your space contributing to or restricting a sense of community and movement? What are the sight lines of all participants, including from the choir loft and chancel? Can leaders and congregants see each other even when seated?

What is clear is that "the built environment affects us in real, predictable, physiological ways."[34] Space really can be "read." Consider your own worship space. What does it "say" about the Christian community who worships there—is it hierarchical or communal—and what do you *want* the space to say about that? Art directors for film know that answering such questions first will guide their later decisions about the location or set design for a scene. Establishing a film's "ethos," the overall concept for the film's look, is one of the very first things that must happen in pre-production.

THE ETHOS

To talk of "ethos" is to understand the character, the feeling, the distinctive nature of the message that is being proclaimed. Is this season a time when the color scheme and lighting may be more meditative and colors subdued in deep blues or grays with the textures more rough or stark? Or are we in a message of abundance and hope that begs for an explosion of bright colors and light, effusive and not-so-contained cascading flowers? Even if you are simply in charge of choosing fabric to swath the table, pulpit, font, etc., for the season, your choice will affect how people coming into the sanctuary will feel.

Color is emotion. Color can make a room feel cold or warm, cheery or dreary. And this will affect the way people experience the message. Nancy Chinn, well-known liturgical artist, says, "Our spirits respond to color combinations and harmonies with mood."[35] The experience of color is, at its basic physiological level, associated with interpreting light waves of varying wavelengths. The fact that we see the world in color means that we come to associate meaning and emotion with experiences of color. Therefore, entrance into a worship space and experience of that space's color scheme will immediately conjure up a mood, or sense, that literally "colors" our perception of what will happen there. Although psychological perception of color may differ depending on cultural differences or personal preference, "due to the biological bases of our color vision, there is a high degree of universality in the use of color terms across cultures and languages." We have physiological responses to particular wavelengths that affect the rhythms of our bodies such as heart rate, blood pressure, respiration, and eyeblink frequency. In this sense, the presence of "warm" or "cool" color schemes (the most universal effects of color) can either speed up our biological rhythms and give a more energetic feel (in the case of "warm" colors such as magenta, red, orange, yellow, and yellow-green) or slow those frequencies down (as in the case of "cool" colors such as violet, blue, light blue, cyan, and sea green) for a more meditative atmosphere.[36] Intimacy or distance can also be created by the color itself. "Warm colors tend to 'move toward you' while cool colors tend to 'move away from you,'"[37] creating an atmosphere that feels "cold" or "warm."

Besides color, Chinn discusses six other elements of visual design for worship, each affecting us in different ways. She says that one of the most significant visual experiences we have is the experience of *light* and *dark.* The use of illumination and shadow, bright and deep colors and the contrasts between, or going from one to the other, can create places of "mystery" and create a changing dynamic of energy. *Transparency* and *opacity* can hint at hidden realities or create that hiddenness. Sheer fabric suspended above that moves with air currents and the movements of the people beneath it creates fluidity. *Pattern*, which produces visual rhythm, creates order out of discrete elements— "an experience of power over chaos. It brings peace and a sense of completion." *Texture* shows that "life is varied and variegated." Shiny is not always "holy" (as most mass-produced paraments would seem to convey), but rough or dull textures can speak of a sacred complexity and diversity of life and more fully evoke the essence of a particular time of the liturgical year. *Scale* of art takes its cue from the scale of the architecture in order to have adequate impact and expression, although the ability to take photographs of the visual art in the space and project close-ups on screens now allows us a wider range of scale. Art also contains the element of *movement*, whether that is the literal movement of a piece of fabric, the addition or subtraction of pieces of the art during one worship experience or over the course of several ritual events, or simply the movement implied "in the gesture of the lines," which "prevents visual art from being static."[38]

In our mantra of "plan together and plan ahead," the subject of the overall feel for a series is one that the whole team must have even before the resource-gathering stage of the creative process. This will make a difference for the kinds of resources you look for or create. Visual artists can really be the ones to help a worship team engage in this discussion because you know the importance of having a "palette" to work with. Author of *The Art Direction Handbook*[39] Michael Rizzo describes how the art department becomes the center of visual source materials for the entire production. This is a time to steep your psyche in the story and its message. This will be aided by as much information about the message that you can get about the messages of the series. Film and commercial art director Judy Rhee says, "the more information I have from the story, writer, and director, the more I have to work with. The backstory always helps to support the visual narrative."[40] When designing for a liturgical season such as Advent, it is really important that we don't just rely on a description of the season itself, but the particular angle or message that the pastor(s) will highlight this year. Yes, we will probably have an Advent wreath, but how might it be different because of this year's thematic focus? You may decide to hang a very large wreath from the ceiling and hang lighted lanterns from it this year because the theme is "Light for the Path." Our work of worship design always considers the intersection of our traditions and new ways of experiencing those traditions.

In pre-production, art directors of film line their walls, surrounding themselves with images that show colors, textures, objects, and metaphors that evoke the messages within the film. I like to collect images and ideas on *Pinterest* boards that the whole team can access so we can easily share ideas—as well as the "sticky-note wall" in our Worship Design Studio Design App. One of the easiest ways to find people to help out the visual arts team is to put out a call for Pinterest and HGTV junkies!

This process of collecting ideas will be second nature to them and a whole lot of fun as well. During the brainstorming/resource-gathering stages of the worship production timeline, you will want to gather lots of ideas before settling on one and keep checking in with the pastors to make sure you are on the same page about the message.

See Worship Design Studio Pinterest boards at thinklikeafilmmaker.com.

THE SYMBOLS

The tangible symbols in our midst are a hot point for a lot of churches. Actually, I should say the "objects" are a hot point because problems occur when objects get detached from their symbolic meaning. We hold beliefs about what should or shouldn't be on the table, what candlesticks (given "in memory of") we must use forevermore, and why it would be absolute sacrilege to get rid of that modesty rail in the chancel that hides the choir members, who wear long robes anyway! Actually, it is no wonder we have problems over our worship "stuff," considering how attached we get to a lot of tangible items in our lives. And usually this attachment isn't about the actual objects at all. Anger over changing the candlesticks isn't about the candlesticks, for instance; usually someone is grieving that most of the congregation no longer remembers "Aunt Betty," stalwart saint of the church, whose name appears on the plaque. Losing the candlesticks means losing an era. Our problem is that we've forgotten the religious meaning and spiritual depth that liturgical objects offer. And when symbols lose their deeper meaning, we will attach *any* meaning to them. The candlesticks come to represent our attachment to Aunt Betty and a bygone era, not to the Light of Christ that shines in our midst (we will talk more about the "politics of change" in Chapter Nine).

Reclaiming the power of symbol is one way visual artists can help the whole congregation. We can educate about the deeper meaning of our traditional and permanent symbols in the space (including "furniture" like the font, pulpit, and table) as well as introduce ordinary objects from everyday life that can hold symbolic meaning for a worship series. I call these "anchor images." Before we get to that, let's go a little deeper into how symbols function.

Symbol (from the Greek word *symbolein*, meaning "to throw together") acts to fit together the element serving as symbol and the context in which it resides. An element is not a symbol without context. It is this fitting together that makes it symbol (or, in the linguistic term, metaphor).[41] For instance, water used in the rite of baptism is the element of water "thrown together" with the context in which the water resides. In our everyday lives, we know water as sustenance for life as it quenches our thirst, as bath for washing clean, as well as associating all the bodies of water we love such as oceans, lakes, and rivers. That is thrown together with the faith narrative when we bring water into the context of worship—the water of liberation through the Red Sea, the water of birth, death, and resurrection, the water of the baptism of Jesus, and the baptismal water which connects the community of saints of the church living and past. It does what symbols do—it points beyond itself to something much more.

Secondly, symbol functions to "crystallize." It makes the abstract "most real" by making it more tangible. Ritual scholar Mary Collins likens symbols to electric transformers.[42] Huge amounts of energy come over the wires that would blow up our houses if we tried to use it in this form. But when it goes through a transformer, it becomes usable. The water crystallizes and communicates such a mysterious concept as renewal, forgiveness and the power of the Holy Spirit—concepts that might be difficult for us to grasp were it not for our understanding of how water refreshes, washes clean, and gives us life. Making big concepts concrete is a huge gift to the congregation as we grapple with the mysteries of our faith.

Let me use another example. When I was about to turn 40 years old, I wanted to do something I thought I would never do in my entire lifetime as a kind of rite of passage. There were two things I thought I would never do: skydive and get a tattoo. I was not about to jump out of an airplane. So I decided to get a tattoo. I actually love watching the TV shows about tattoo artists because I love hearing the stories about why people are getting their particular tattoos. There is always a story behind it, and the artwork serves as a symbol of that story. I decided to get the words "peace" and "passion" in Chinese calligraphy. I use those words in closing all my letters and e-mail communication and when I give a benediction in worship. They have come to be a symbol of my relationships and ministry. My father had also just remarried a woman with Chinese heritage, so I asked her to write out the words. Thus the tattoo also became a symbol of that new relationship. Add to that its timing on my 40th birthday, and that tattoo is now full of much more meaning than just ink in my leg. There are multiple meanings to good symbols. The term we use to describe this is that symbols are "multivalent." They will mean different things to different people, based on our experience.

Even though the first example (of water and baptism) is a very traditional part of our faith narrative and the second example (the tattoo) is much more "ordinary," they both function the same. As humans, we are "meaning mongers," and our brains are wired to find meaning by throwing seemingly dissimilar things together. This enriches our life and, well, makes us human. And so, as worship designers—and this goes not only for visual artists but for the whole team—we are what I call "metaphoragers!" We forage for metaphors.

To get a "Metaphoraging" exercise to do with the whole worship team, go to thinklikeafilmmaker.com.

ANCHOR IMAGES—METAPHORAGING

Metaphoraging comes in handy as we search for symbols that will help messages be unforgettable. One of my favorite "M-M-Good" moments of all time in worship (those moments we will never forget) was from a worship series at a church I attended while doing my Ph.D. It was a series about Jesus as a boundary-breaker. He seemed in the habit of ignoring social norms in order to be in relationship with folks. One Sunday the focus was on his table practices—he seemed to make it a habit of having meals with the so-called "wrong" people. At the end of her sermon, the pastor rolled out a piece of plastic yellow "Caution" ribbon like you see at construction sites and crime scenes that says "Do Not Cross." She placed it on the floor just at the mouth of the aisle, in front of the communion table and when we came to receive communion that day, we had to cross over it, asking ourselves what boundaries we were willing to cross out of our comfort zones in order to be with those not like us. That caution tape was an ordinary object that became a powerful symbol that keeps reminding me again and again of that message every time I see it out in the world.

An "anchor image" for a series will be a symbol that can speak powerfully of the underlying message and help it stick with us in indelible ways. Were I to re-create that series again, perhaps calling it "Crossing Boundaries," I would use that caution ribbon as an anchor image and use it in different ways each frame of the series. Perhaps on a Sunday when we are talking about Jesus' prophetic messages to folks who maybe didn't really want to hear it, I would wrap a piece of the "caution" ribbon around the pulpit. An anchor image needs to be able to be interpreted in a variety of ways—to be multivalent—so that it can point to the variety of meanings of the main message that will be teased out each week of the series.

Art directors are experts at using symbols, and they use this technique of letting the symbols show up in different ways throughout a film. Rizzo says that visual concepts in a film are "shorthand for longer explanation; it abbreviates words into symbols, metaphors." Visual concepts are "an image that defines the central idea of a movie."[43] In our case-study film,

Under the Tuscan Sun, there are several times that we encounter a bucket hanging from a faucet protruding out of a wall. The first time, there is nothing coming out of the faucet. Later in the film, when work on the house is moving along and Frances is writing again, we see the bucket dripping. This bucket actually gets the "last word" of the film as Frances watches it gush water in a torrent onto the floor. This metaphor is never verbally acknowledged in the film. There is absolutely no dialogue about it. It quietly symbolizes and reflects the main character's journey from a dry and thirsty state of mind to a heart that overflows with the love and community she experiences at the end of the movie. And we don't need a verbal explanation to "get it." It gets to proclaim that message in its own way—as a visual that changes over the course of the movie.

Imagine that you are doing a worship series called "More Light." Perhaps the overarching series message highlights prayer for enlightenment in the dim corners of the world where hate, greed, and violence are threatening to destroy people. The anchor image for this is somewhat obvious—light. That anchor image could bring its own version of the message simply by adding more and more light—candles, strings of white lights, lanterns, etc. to the worship space each week.

Sometimes the anchor image won't be as obvious, or the obvious choice might be too literal. In the Worship Design Studio series, "Busy: Reconnecting to an Unhurried God," we might think conveying "busy" with lots of clutter around the space would be the way to go or perhaps we think about putting clocks all over the space. Actually for me these two ideas are a bit too literal for the tangible visuals in the space. I would leave the metaphors of how our spaces and time of our lives are too cluttered to be spiritually satisfying for the verbal art forms, and I would certainly think of using ticking clocks as sound media in a creative way and projected images of Salvador Dali's famous melting clocks on the screens. Dramatic arts might even think of having people turn off their phones or take off their watches as a ritual action at prayer time.

But for the tangible visuals, I might do something more abstract and beautiful that evokes the opposite of "busy"—offering a sense of sim-

See more anchor images used in Worship Design Studio series at thinklikeafilmmaker.com.

plicity and space—perhaps utilizing the Japanese art of flower arranging (*ikebana*) for the season rather than the effusive floral arrangements usually used. This art form is intentional about the beauty of the open spaces created between the materials used. There are times when we want to guide people's attention to the symbol when they might not automatically get it. They might not be aware of this kind of flower arranging, and so the visual arts team might invite the preacher to use it as a metaphor in the sermon, a worship leader as an introduction to a song or prayer, or have a simple note about it in the worship guide.

VISUAL INSTALLATIONS

Visual installations for a series can happen in many ways. The most commonly used form is an arrangement situated in the center of the chancel (whether you call it an "altar" or a "table") that incorporates colors, textures, fabrics, and objects that symbolize the message along with traditional symbols such as a cross, Bible, candle(s), communion ware, etc. But visual installations can also be off-center—to one side of the chancel, in a corner of the sanctuary, at the entrance to the sanctuary, or in "stations" all around the room.

There are two schools of thought about the central table that, for some traditions, is called an altar, for others a communion table, or simply "the table." One school of thought is that you shouldn't mess with it—that there is an historical precedent for a "fair white linen cloth" as the only adornment, especially when the table is being used for communion. Some communities believe there is something sacred and unchangeable about a table with a brass cross in the center back with an open Bible in front of it and two brass candlesticks on either side.

Another school of thought does not feel beholden to these conventions, seeing them as time-captured cultural interpretations. Given an intentional discernment that understands the liturgical function of that table, the proponents of this school of thought believe that the materials used in this visual installation at the table can bring a deeper engagement with the symbols when they creatively interpret the message through variation from series to series.

You can probably guess where I land in this discussion. Any adornment of worship space is culturally conceived and changed over time. If brass candlesticks were somehow "sanctioned" by God for exclusive use, communities where brass is not available or affordable would be "in violation" of God's "commands." This is not an accurate or ethical approach to human relationships with God, I believe. Humans have always used the materials at their disposal to bring their best offering to their holy spaces. When visual installations draw us powerfully into the story, they become proclaimers of that story—especially for congregants who rely on a more visual-spatial intelligence to connect with the message.

But we do have to acknowledge that when the cross/Bible/candle combination described above has been the visual setting for the table for decades, there will be some resistance to changing that, whether because of a time-captured idea of what is "holy," an attachment to "those" particular candlesticks because they are a memorial gift, or simply that our brains kind of freak out a bit for a while when something changes (again, there's much more to be said about this in Chapter Nine). So if your community has not been using a variety of visual materials, you will want to perhaps start with an "off-center" visual installation to one side of the chancel or on the floor level at the mouth of a center aisle or in the corners of the room, until people get used to (and grow to love) the Word proclaimed through visual arts.

Prayer stations have also become much more widely used as new generations of worshipers hearken back to a more interactive style of worship reminiscent of "side altars" of the medieval era. Mark Pierson coined the term "curator" for worship designers who are attentive to the environment of the whole of the space, those who often set up several places around the worship space for people to go and engage in an activity. The term "station" comes from the Latin *statio*, meaning "to stare" or "to stand"—a place to stop for a while. Pierson says "the purpose of stations is to provide a worshiping community with a variety of options for interacting with the biblical story or theme being presented in the worship event."[44] You might visit several stations, engaging each in a different way, such as lighting a candle for hope in one corner, writing the name of someone in need of prayer on a "prayer wall" in another corner, sitting and contemplating near a small babbling fountain somewhere else, and adding a piece of glass to a mosaic in yet another area. Or a worship series may require only doing the same action at one or more stations every week, offering a meditative repetition that deepens the experience. What stations do—especially for churches that do not practice communion every week—is to expand the possibilities for active forms of prayer. People who are bodily-kinesthetic intelligences will thank you whenever this happens.

Here are a couple of "tips" from years of creating stational worship experiences: 1) Always have "stewards" of the space who can bring the activity to someone in their seat whose mobility does not allow them to move easily to the stations; and 2) be sure to have enough stations so that people are not standing in long lines. My rule for churches of smaller or medium size is no more than 25 persons per station (for very large gatherings such as conferences, the rule is no more than 50 per station and know that the time for the activity will need to be longer— this goes for numbers of communion servers as well). So divide your average attendance by these numbers and that's how many stations you will need to keep the traffic flowing. This number will also differ depending on how long it takes for people to actually engage in the activity at a station.

Worship Design Studio guest expert Todd Pick says that there are several ingredients to keep in mind when creating a visual installation with a table as the "base," whether it is up front or elsewhere in the room. Again, *scale* is one of the first considerations. Can the

See more tips on avoiding "liturgical disasters" at thinklikeafilmmaker.com.

materials and objects in the installation (Todd calls this "holy hardware") be seen by people in the congregation—especially if it is an installation people will not get any closer to than their place in their seat? This will depend upon the size of your space, of course. A packaged Advent wreath set bought from a church supplier may have taper candles that are not large enough to make a statement, and so you may opt to use larger pillar candles in a much larger wreath stand that you construct yourselves.

The *topography* of the visual installation is another useful consideration. What this means is that we can create *levels* on which to build the landscape of the installation. If we put everything on one level—the

See an excerpt from my interview with Todd at thinklikeafilmmaker.com.

surface of the table—it becomes static because our gaze will be flat. A visual artist's "tool kit" will need to have various-size boxes or stands to aid in raising various objects to different levels. The materials used for these "lifts" don't matter since you will most likely cover them with fabric—just make sure they are sturdy enough to hold what you are putting on them. Let's imagine you are doing a series on the book of Jeremiah, and the visual installation for the series will utilize pottery (a prominent image in this biblical story). As you are searching for pottery for two visual installations in the front corners of the sanctuary, you will keep in mind the scale but also *height* of the pieces of pottery you use to help with creating levels. In the front corner of the sanctuary, you might even get as tall as putting the highest pottery vase on a stool on top of the table because you have a wall as the backdrop and no one needs to see around or over the installation.

Of course *color palette* is important, as we've already talked about at the beginning of this chapter. But Todd encourages us to use a combination of hues within a color family rather than using all one color in fabrics and objects, etc. This also goes for *textures and patterns*. While we don't want to use patterned fabric with specific images too detailed to have an impact, abstract patterns of color in fabric offer textures that can be combined with solid colors for a more interesting and fuller look, and they can add movement, too. Texture comes into play in various candle containers like glass hurricanes or even the texture within a pillar candle itself. The question always goes back to "what feel does this series message have, and is this contributing to it, or am I just drawn to it because it is pretty?" I recently worked with a theme for Transfiguration, and the overall message was to "let your light shine." Appropriate materials had shiny qualities and even mirrored textures that bedazzled the space as light was projected onto it.

The overall feel also becomes a question as we consider what *natural* floral or plant items we might use. Many churches have a tradition of weekly bouquets of flowers, often underwritten by contributions from members in memory of someone or celebration of some event in their lives. This was a wonderful way to bring at least some color and visual interest into the sanctuary. But as you begin to be more holistic about the visual environment of the sanctuary and how it relates to the theme, you may discern that fresh flowers are not the best choice in a Lent series called "Wilderness Wanderings." Rather, more stark natural items such as reeds and bare branches may communicate the story in a more powerful way. We have to be careful and incremental in changing our traditions, but eventually you may be able to shift the gift money into the visual arts budget while still acknowledging the gift in the weekly worship guide.

It may seem odd to think of creating "movement" in a visual installation, but Todd teaches that *asymmetry* and *odd numbers* of objects will help our gaze move in our encounter of it. Anything even and symmetrical (like those two brass candlesticks with a cross in the center) will capture our gaze in a static way, and we'll stop actively engaging with it because our eye loses interest. For example, three candles at different levels cascading from left to right, top to bottom will guide our eyes right down to the bowl of water sitting on the table at the base of that diagonal, visual line.

Lighting can enhance our visual installations by creating more light and shadow in crevices of fabric, for example, creating reflections off of shiny or watery surfaces and generally helping to create focal points in the installation. Small under-cabinet spot lights are great tools. I also keep some battery-operated night-fishing headlamps available to use when there isn't a handy electrical outlet around.

Visual installations can also create unique interpretations for the "furniture" of worship itself. Perhaps a series called "A Place at the Table" that focuses on the theology of communion for a time will invite ideas about replacing the usual communion table with a kitchen table, a dining-room table, a picnic table or a fellowship-hall table that is used in the weekly food program for homeless persons. The use of these tables brings an opportunity for the verbal artists (preachers, worship leaders) to tease out various meanings of communion, from "family" metaphors to "fellowship" and feeding a hungry world. Perhaps a late-night Easter Vigil service calls for setting aside the usual baptismal font and creating a stand with a hole in the top to shine a light up through a glass bowl of water so the reflections of water dance on the ceiling.

See our gallery of images that demonstrate these design concepts at thinklikeafilmmer.com.

Visual installations can also be *environmental*. Rather than focusing on what can be created with a table as the base, we can think about visuals much the same way a movie theater installs "surround sound." For instance, in the Worship Design Studio worship series "Gifts of the Dark Wood," the anchor image is a path through the difficult times in our lives—the "dark wood" moments and how we can find gifts of the spirit even there. Churches who used this series during Lent sent me many photos of the way they took our suggestion to collect bare branches, place them in containers around the walls of the worship space, and uplight them from the floor to create shadows on the walls. One church even created stone-looking drawings on their floor to create a path that meanders in the space. From large spaces to small chapels, these photos show great ingenuity in creating a sense of "place" through these simple techniques. I'll talk much more about creating environments through the Media Arts in Chapter Six. Visual artists will be collaborators with media folks in these larger-scale installations.

Large churches that have a more flexible (and in many cases, generic) and contemporary space are going to great lengths to create entire "set designs" for worship series using the same principles of establishing the "feel" of the message—what designer Kim Miller at Ginghamsburg Church calls the "vibe"[45]—and then creating an environment that will immerse people into a visual world that supports the Word.[46] Kim likes to describe her method of finding materials for these installations as creating from "mud and spit." Budgets for visual installations don't have to be large. There are so many creative ways to borrow, find free materials, and repurpose basic pieces (those things that are like "the little black dress" that works in lots of ways depending on how you accessorize). I've pulled large items out of a junk pile in a back alley for a visual installation symbolizing seeing life in the midst of death and placed more and more flowers springing from the junk for each service. I've had people bring personal, ordinary glass pitchers they use in their kitchens filled with water from home to pour into a common vessel for a reaffirmation of baptism and month of focusing on "the water of life." I've invited people to bring candles from home at the beginning of a worship series on the "burning passion" for mission and discipleship and had the youth group learn how to make candles out of chunks of all the wax so that each person could go home at the end of the series with a candle made from a common mixture. One of my favorite things to do is to let folks know that certain pieces are for sale at the end of a series (for instance, the pottery pieces I mentioned above), and this literally recycles the money initially spent. I've never been left with anything because people attach a special meaning to objects that are used in service to a wonderful message, and they can't wait to install it in their own homes! Are you getting the point that having a small visual arts budget can sometimes offer more, not less, opportunities for incorporating the visual arts?

MOVING VISUALS AND DROP-LINE SYSTEMS

"Beyond banners" is the title I have used ever since I began to teach workshops about visuals in worship. I don't have anything against banners *per se,* but for too long our focus on how to enhance the sanctuary visually has stayed in the realm of two-dimensional art forms that are essentially over-sized bulletin covers on the walls. Color and fabric can be used in many ways besides flat on the wall. Banners and objects can be processed into, around, and out of the space, creating a kinesthetic experience for the congregation even as they watch them. We have something called "mirror neurons" that give our bodies the actual internal experience of the movement that we are observing. Especially in worship spaces that do not allow much congregational movement around the space, this can be a great gift to the dynamics of a moment. Ribbons cascading from

See photos of processional items at thinklikeafilmmaker.com.

processional poles made of PVC topped with round foam board disks can offer drama, literally "stirring" up the air with movement and energy to match a grand hymn or rhythmic global song.

A set of 8 to 12 "T-poles" made of PVC or strong dowel with fabric or ribbons hanging from them can help define space. I told you earlier that I would suggest a way to make a cavernous space more intimate for a smaller crowd. This is it. Place these T-poles in stands from one side of the sanctuary to the other in a row of pews as far back as you want people to sit. These create a "false back," and people must sit forward of them. You still have a "back row" for people who just can't imagine coming to church without sitting on the back row, but it is now just closer to the front! You can also do this in a big gymnasium space to define a smaller portion of the room so that you don't feel like people are swallowed up by a space that is too big and generic.

Installing a drop-line system (permanent pulleys in architectural arches or other structures made of simple eye-hooks and fishing line) can help you bring color and texture in fabrics hung and draped in the air space above the chancel and above the heads of the congregation. Worship Design Studio guest expert Alexandra Childs (whose mentor was Nancy Chinn) has installed these in many spaces. Essentially, she engineers a system of pulley-like hardware (actually much simpler than pulleys) that are permanently installed so that churches can change out hangings without getting up into the rafters again, simply lowering the hooks and lines to the floor, attaching new materials, and hoisting them into the air. Using the air space is not something many of us have thought of, but, once you see it, you'll want to do it if the architecture in your ceiling is conducive at all to installing these drop-lines. The most exciting aspect of extending the color of visuals into the air of the entire sanctuary is that it extends the energy to the whole of the space and helps people feel immersed in the experience of worship.

See examples and find out more about installing your own drop-line system at thinklikeafilmmaker.com.

VISUAL HOMILETICS

Finally, visual artists, I want to introduce you to "visual homiletics"— a new term coined by Worship Design Studio guest expert Ted Lyddon

Hatten. Ted is ordained clergy who also is a trained visual artist. He combines his belief in the power of the arts with his call to proclaim the narrative of our faith and of our lives. "Homiletics" is the art of preaching. Ted extends homiletics to also consider how visual experience has a unique ability to deepen our encounter with the message and with each other—the work of visual artists, he says, can actually *be* a kind of preaching, and can spark communal conversations inspired by the visual art. Ted explains,

> Seeing is an act of interpretation. When you see something … you immediately begin to make associations, and you make sense of it. And so visual homiletics takes that visual experience of "I'm interpreting what I'm seeing" and uses it specifically aimed toward a sacred text or towards a moment. And so I approach it in the same way that I do other types of preaching: doing my exegesis, finding out what was going on in the story, and finding out the context, and then looking at our context and trying to see where some of those connections are.[47]

An example of Ted's visual homiletics comes from a project we collaborated on at the General Conference of the United Methodist Church in 2012. The theme of the conference had to do with the Great Commission—making disciples for the transformation of the world. Ted used many elements such as sand, rocks, shredded paper, mustard seed, and broken glass to create an artistic visual representation of the globe each day. One day he created a butterfly (a symbol of resurrection) whose wing markings were the continents of the world, but one wing was broken. On this particular day, the worship experience was a memorial service for Bishops of the church who had died since the last General Conference. "What happens when life

See photos of
Ted's work at
thinklikeafilmmaker.com.

is broken?" he asked. One of the main ingredients he used in the visual installation was myrrh. In his artist statement, he described its practical use, which leads to the deeper symbolism relating to life and faith.

> [Myrrh] is a resin, similar to sap—so picture a small little scrubby tree that grows in rocky soil—that when that tree is wounded, it secretes this resin. And the purpose of that is simply to restore wholeness. It doesn't carry nutrients for the plant like sap does, but it's like blood clotting. It staunches the wound of the plant. So if this substance is to restore wholeness, integrity to the plant, I think that speaks volumes about its use as a burial spice and that ritual of trying to restore wholeness when we are broken, broken in ways that we cannot repair. How can we then try to seek wholeness in that context?[48]

Ted's art form and the way he uses materials is incredibly complex and beautiful and particular to him. But the idea of visuals as homiletics—as a vehicle for the community to reflect theologically—can be done in more simple ways. Arranging fall leaves in concentric circles around a candle with the names of loved ones lost written on them for an All Saints' service can be an entree to a conversation about the cycle of life and the place of letting go in that cycle. Shattered plates on a disheveled table can spark a conversation about disappointing family situations juxtaposed with Jesus' last supper with his family of disciples. The possibilities are endless when we begin to think more broadly about the ways visual arts can be a powerful witness and catalyst.

COLLABORATORS

I hope this chapter has given you some ideas, some theory about the way that visual storytelling affects us, and, most of all, has inspired you to want to learn more. One last word is that all ritual artists have to be collaborators. Not only will you collaborate with the pastoral staff as you seek to understand more about the message for the series, but you will also be working with all the other artists as visuals get "layered" into other expressions. In fact, you may have an idea for a specific song that would be perfect for the prayer stations you are assembling. Be sure to communicate that to the Music Arts team members. They may be creating a musical underscore to accompany a procession of some visual elements into the space and will contact you to find out how long that needs to be. Verbal artists will need to hear from you about visual symbolism that they can include in their work. And those on the Dramatic Arts team that are caring for communion happening in a special way will need to check in with you to coordinate making sure the elements of communion are highlighted, accessible to the presider, and clearly seen in the visual installation for the central table that week.

We do not create for the art gallery or for the simple adornment of space like home decoration (which is why I refrain from saying we are "decorating" the worship space). Remember that your work is more akin to the purpose of an art director for film. When you "think like an art director" as a member of the larger production team, everything you do must support the main purpose of the whole team—to further the faith story, to inspire deep and faithful response from the congregation, and to change lives. You are an artist in service to transformation. What a blessed task!

Chapter 4

Think Like a Screenwriter:
Verbal Arts in Worship

When I was in college, I played the role of Eliza Doolittle in the musical *My Fair Lady*. One of my favorite songs to sing began with Eliza blasting Higgins and Pickering about their incessant running-on-of-the-mouth. "Words, words, words, I'm so sick of words! I get words all day through first from him, then from you, is that all you blighters can do?!" She finally pleads with them not to *tell* her in words, but to *show* her by their actions. As a Missouri gal from a little town in the "Show Me" state, I liked that argument. The ironic and comical thing about that song is that it is a "banter" song, with words tumbling out of Eliza's mouth in a rush!

But "show me" would also be good advice for our worship. We Protestants have given words the center of our attention ever since the Reformation when, at the same time in history, the printing press created much excitement about this form of communication newly accessible to the masses. We've even sometimes gone so far as to call the sermon the "meat" of the service with everything else the "preliminaries."

In our postmodern age of reclaiming sensory-rich communication, "wordsmithing" takes on vital importance, although we might wonder what role substantive verbiage has in our society these days. From "sound bites" in advertising to carefully crafted oration in political speeches, we wonder if we can say something of substance and hold our congregation's limited attention spans. Francis of Assisi is credited with this quote, "Preach the Gospel and when necessary, use words." There's a tension between "talking the talk" and "walking the walk." We do need words for our worship, but we need to shift our thinking from words *versus* visuals and action to verbal forms in the hospitable company of all the arts in worship. While a film begins as a screenplay—essentially words on a page—a screenwriter knows that the words are not carrying the whole weight of communication like a book does. The majority of words on the pages of a screenplay are not always the actual dialogue but also the descriptions of settings, scenes, movement and action. As we "think like a screenwriter" in our verbal artistry, we too must imagine much more than just *what* is said, but *how* it is said, by whom and where, with what dynamic, in the midst of what other sounds, and with what action into and out of the dialogue.

Verbal artists are those who carefully consider the verbal effects at play in our worship. These people on the team include not only preachers but also those who may be writing liturgy, choosing liturgy from various resources, leaders who provide verbal transitions from one element of worship to the next as well as those who format the words we use on the page or the screen. Those who love words and wordsmithing will relish the opportunity to be involved in this part of the worship team.

But terrific "wordsmithing" is about more than just a flourish for language. Screenwriter Allen Palmer says,

> While the best screenwriters tend also to be great wordsmiths, I don't think that we are fundamentally in the word business. Words are not the end product. It's not enough that what you put on the page sounds good to your ear. The words ultimately are only there to serve a higher goal. What is that goal? … to move the audience.[49]

WORDS ARE SYMBOLIC

In screenwriting for films, similar to writing for worship, we are not writing for the written page that will be read by folks in their own good time. We are writing words that will be spoken and then vanish in the next moment. We are writing for optimum *hearing* that doesn't stop at the ear but enters and changes the heart. And, in worship, we are writing words for living, breathing bodies to speak aloud. Words become living symbols embodied in the gathered community.

Liturgical theologian Don Saliers has had a great influence on my own belief in sensory-rich communication. He advocates for worship "come to its senses."[50] The human languages mediated by the senses are the only languages which we have to experience God. To be attuned to the senses is to be attuned to God. To fully engage human language with all our senses is to enter more fully into the action of worship and thus to be more fully formed by it. There are three problems inherent in Protestant practice that have to do with "words, words, words." The first is the problem of "Word alone"—a dependence on text and speech to the exclusion of other human languages like those we use to create sensory-rich elements of worship. This is an over-exaggeration of the "word alone" legacy of the Reformers to the exclusion of the vast array of human languages. The complexity needed to fully articulate the Gospel goes beyond the text, linking meaning with our experience through not only words but also visual, auditory, tactile, and kinesthetic symbolic forms.

But, ironically, we also have the problem of "not enough Word." Biblical minimalism experienced in churches with a practice of engaging with only one selection of sacred text within a worship experience means that what Saliers calls the "great chains of imagery"[51] created in the relationship between texts, prayers, gestures, and visual symbols are limited because of our exposure to so few texts. Our sacramental practices suffer when we fail to use rich verbal imagery to tease out the variety of theological meanings associated with them. Communion becomes a singular focus on forgiveness of sins rather than mining the depths of imagery evoking right relationship with our neighbors, economic justice, and great thanksgiving for God's action in all of creation and human history. Without the deep and rich recitation of water imagery used throughout the scriptures, baptism is relegated to a kind of "christening"—a simple naming—practiced without a sense of the liberation, cleansing, death-to-life, and community-grafting connections in this powerful sign-act. This diminishes the "multilayered" capacity of symbol.

And thirdly, Protestant practice ails from "too many words." Overly didactic explanation leaves very little room for cultivating symbolic imagination and the congregation's own interpretive skills. Words take up so much room that there is little time and space left for the mysterious nature of symbols to draw us back to them time and again to discover the "more" to be found there.

As verbal artists, we can constantly check our worship against these three "word" problems. Are we working closely with all the art forms so that words are not carrying the whole weight of the message? Have worshipers entered the story through what Saliers calls a "matrix of words *and* sign-acts" from the beginning of worship?[52] Do our words mine the depths of imagery from our sacred texts so that the connections between the narrative and our world are many and diverse? Or is our worship filled with too many words, especially words that fail to engage our imaginations?

THE EXPERIENCE OF WORDS

That words in worship are experienced orally (speaking) and aurally (hearing), sometimes without the time to read or re-read them, means we must continually edit for clarity, rhythm, and ease of cognition as we write. Filmmakers pay great attention to the economy of words—editing can happen on the set at any moment. Directors and actors can feel when the pace of a scene is belabored by too many words and they are in danger of losing their own connection with the story, not to mention losing the audience. "The quickest way to deaden the audience's impulse to join in is to tell too much, and it is remarkable how little can be too much … Exposition that is crystal clear on the page baffles on-screen."[53] We often pile words into the mouths of worshipers. And especially when we are requiring them to speak them in unison, we are asking a lot. They must read the words correctly, read them in a rhythm with other people, and comprehend the words simultaneously! Many times I will come to the end of a long unison prayer or litany and wonder, "What did we just say?" Take a look at this Call to Worship in a litany format used at a church I where I was consulting:

> ONE: This is the Lord's Day, the day of wonder and grace.
> **ALL: This is the day to worship the One who calls us here.**
> ONE: This is the Lord's Day, the day we are given joy and peace.
> **ALL: This is the day promised to us, the day of healing and renewal.**
> ONE: This is the Lord's Day, and it has come just in time!
> **ALL: This is the day we gather with hope, with faith, with love!**

Actually, this is a good length, and doesn't require too many words. But let's experiment with making it participatory for all generations. If our verbal participation always requires the skill of reading, we aren't being inclusive of those who don't read yet and those whose eyesight might not be up to it. As the leader, I would begin this revision with the instruction, "Your response is 'This is the Lord's Day!' Try that once with me, **'This is the Lord's Day!'"** Then I would continue:

ONE: This is the day to worship the One who calls us here,
the day of wonder and grace!

ALL: **This is the Lord's Day!**

ONE: This is the day promised to us, the day of healing and
renewal, the day we are given joy and peace.

ALL: **This is the Lord's Day!**

ONE: This is the day we gather with hope, with faith, with
love—and it has come just in time!

ALL: **This is the Lord's Day!**

The cognitive heavy-lifting is happening while we as a congregation are just doing one thing—listening to the leader. The congregation provides the verbal, rhythmic exclamation point. Because it is repetitive, the congregation doesn't need to have their heads in a page, and it is accessible to anyone who can lift their voice. This is also how I adapt "liturgy" for more informal or "contemporary" worship. I don't think we have to throw the baby out with the bathwater—there's no reason a more informal service can't have any "liturgy." If we are using the first version of this litany in a more "traditional" service, I would use the second form without any words in a worship guide or a screen for the more "contemporary" service. I wouldn't even announce it as a "Call to Worship." It most probably would happen between songs or right before a welcome. It would feel more spontaneous for that setting, and we would still get to have that same verbal artistry at both services.

WORDS ARE VISUAL

Education expert Marlene LeFever says that, by the 6th grade, only two out of every ten students learns primarily through auditory means while there are four who are more visual learners and four who will learn best by doing—they are tactile-kinesthetic learners.[54] What does this say about our ability to reach people in worship? Just hearing words will touch a very small percentage of people *if* those words are not imagistic (painting vivid pictures with our words) and if they do not offer us movement in our imaginations as we encounter them.

Our brains think in images. When you have a thought, you aren't seeing words on a page in your imagination, right? The scene is played out in images. As you read a book or hear a story, your imagination is immediately translating concepts into concrete scenes. So the more concrete our verbal "imagery," the more readily solidified into our sense memory are the concepts we proclaim. Does this make sense? Even "making sense" is a phrase based on how we turn concepts into sensory experiences!

So liturgy must be concise and full of imagery. It is more like poetry than prose. It is more like carefully crafted film dialogue, where every moment counts. What we create for liturgy and preaching is a "palette" of symbolic, vivid, imagistic verbal expression. Let's play with an example I created as a Call to Confession for Palm Sunday. Before I began to write, I imagined a palette of colors, so to speak, that came from the context of the story of Jesus' entrance into Jerusalem. The palette includes not just bright, celebratory colors of the parade, but also the fact that participating in this parade was an incredible risk to Jesus and his followers. They knew that this parade was flying in the face of the powers that be. At one gate of the city is Jesus proclaiming allegiance to "the name of the Lord"—to the kingdom of God's justice—and at the opposite gate of the city is Herod's entourage with the message of allegiance to the "kingdom of Herod" (the Roman empire). This is a palette that includes the murky, deep "colors" of fear and uncertainty. Standing at the gate and making a decision to march is the image that I settled on as a metaphor for our confession on this day. So the first lines became "Holy God, we stand at the gate, hesitant and uncertain. At times we are unwilling to answer your invitation; slow to take steps into the journey toward your reign. Forgive us, we pray …"

WORDS HAVE TO MOVE

As important as setting the scene through concrete imagery, liturgy also has to move. If I had included all the historical information from the paragraph above in the beginning of the prayer, it would have been laborious, and besides, that language is not addressed to God (prayer). That information is best left for the art form called the sermon, where images have time to be expanded and explored, opened and examined. Too much *in-formation* in liturgy makes it didactic and static rather than facilitating *trans-formation*. Sometimes liturgy and prayer becomes a "mini-sermon," one of my particular pet peeves. Think poetry! We simply introduce an image so that it can go somewhere—we stand at the gate—the threshold of every bold decision we've ever had to make as followers of Jesus—and then we get to the point. "Forgive us." We do this because it is from that point that we can move and be moved. We petition God in no uncertain terms. "Help us… Grant us the courage to join you in the procession …" Let's take a look at the movement of the whole prayer.

**Many: Holy God, we stand at the gate, hesitant and uncertain
                about joining the parade.
           At times we are unwilling to answer your invitation;
                slow to take steps into the journey
                     toward your Reign.
           Forgive us, we pray.
           Help us to embrace the joy and the pain
                that comes of following you,
                     of loving others,
                     of accepting ourselves.
           Grant us the courage to join you in the procession;
                the selflessness to lay our cloaks before you;
                the freedom to lift our palms to your glory;
                and the knowledge that by your grace
                     we are forgiven. Amen.**

One: Hear this good news! The procession is ever moving forward.
             We can join at any moment. The invitation still stands!
             In the name of Jesus Christ, you are forgiven!

Many: In the name of Jesus Christ, you are forgiven!
             Glory to God! Amen!

Notice the format of the prayer on the page. This is a poetic form rather than paragraph form. We often print unison prayer like this:

O God, we stand at the gate, hesitant and uncertain. At times we are unwilling to answer your invitation; slow to take steps into the journey toward your Reign. Forgive us, we pray. Help us to embrace the joy and the pain that comes of following you, of loving others, of accepting ourselves. Grant us the courage to join you in the procession... [etc.]

While this may save worship guide (bulletin) space, it is a sacrifice. What you sacrifice is understanding—actually taking in the word imagery as it flies by. The first poetic form has one idea per line, with subsets of ideas indented, so our brains can take in the meaning of this prayer more easily. Our eyes use the visual format as part of the clues about what we are expressing. In fact, we can also pray this together more easily as we follow the natural pauses created by the lines. We get to *feel* the rhythm and movement as part of the meaning of the prayer—the encounter with God—rather than our attention being taken up with the struggle of staying together in unison. Even worse is using ALL CAPS TO INDICATE UNISON SPEAKING. Our eyes use letters' difference in height to instantly recognize words on a page. When you place everything in all caps, you take away this shortcut, making cognition even slower.

I want to encourage you to write words for worship in poetic format. What happens as we do this is that we are forced to see the poetic rhythm of the phrasing, and we will notice more easily when the phrase is getting long or overburdened. And as you are writing, I invite you to read it aloud. No matter what the form of the words are that we create—prayers, litanies, verbal transitions, instructions, preaching, or blessing—all words have to be tried out aloud to see *how* they sound and which words trip up the tongue. Too often we never get to this editing stage, and we don't know how clumsy it is to say the words until they are coming out of our mouths, or the mouth of a reader or entire congregation. By then it's too late, and the power of the message has suffered.

As I was writing this Call to Confession for Palm Sunday, the verbal metaphor of being at the gate readying for the parade called to my mind a specific place in the sanctuary—the back of the center aisle, where the Palm Sunday procession would happen. I felt like we needed to see ourselves hesitating at that gate before we could really let loose with our "Alleluia's" and the resulting parade of palms. This imagining began to create a shape for the service, a place in the Order of Worship and a posture for the congregation while saying it. They would have to be oriented toward the "gate," standing and facing the back. If we couldn't get everyone back there actually in the narthex waiting to come in (this is one of the advantages for small churches), at least the leader acts as our representative and stands in that place on behalf of all of us. And when the words "Glory to God! Amen!" are spoken, then we immediately have much joyous energy bursting forth down the aisle. As I'm writing the prayer in the worship script, I would write what I see in my mind's eye in the form of a *rubric* (the word for a liturgical instruction)—*"music comes in immediately after the 'Amen!'"*

This kind of "blocking" will be discussed further in Chapter Seven, "Think Like a Director: The Dramatic Arts." But I wanted to mention it here because, as you begin to think organically in a sensory-rich way, writing liturgy will begin to inherently conjure up images of not only what words will be said, but how, where, and by whom they will be said.

THE VERBAL TRANSITION

Structure is the friend of creativity. It provides a container that helps us organize and move content along in the storytelling process. It keeps us on point, it gives us a goal, and it keeps us from rambling. And structural choices can give a series a particular "voice" or "feel."

> What distinguishes screenwriting from other forms of fiction is this compelling need for compactness, for concision … much of the advantage of visual storytelling is that it compresses so effectively. At its best, compression creates a compelling density. Every moment, every story beat does double duty or more … screenwriting is structure.[55]

One of the fascinating structures utilized in *Under the Tuscan Sun's* screenplay is the movement between actor dialogue and a voice-over narration by the main character Frances, played by Diane Lane. This happens several times during the film and is a structure that moves the story along and deepens our connection to the content. One of my favorite scenes is the moment just after actor Sandra Oh's character, Molly, has her baby. Diane Lane picks up the baby and says, "What's her name, Mol?" She hears and repeats the name, "Alessandra," with a wonderful breathiness that contributes to the importance of the moment. As she takes the baby across the room to the window, the voice-over narration says, "In Italian, to give birth—*dare a la luce*—means 'to give to the light.'" Diane Lane opens the window with the baby in her arms, looks at the sunrise, and says, "welcome to the light."

The filmmakers in this instance are offering us a poignant symbol—the connection of birth to exposure to the light. In order to express it, they have the scene occurring at sunrise and create the revelation of light as the window is opened. But, as viewers, if we did not know about the beautiful meaning of the Italian phrase for giving birth, this amazing symbol would not have been as powerful. The narration enables us to enter the story more deeply.

One of the most important contributions of the verbal artist is one that doesn't get a lot of attention in books about writing liturgy or worship leadership—the art of the *verbal introduction or transition*—a kind of narration. Knowing when to guide a congregation more deeply into a moment by offering a "signpost" is a gift that can help worship feel like a spiritual journey. At my retreat for worship designers and leaders each year, we spend time thinking about who we understand ourselves to be as a leader. One of the models I have for myself is that of worship leader as a kind of spiritual director. A spiritual director doesn't do all the talking and certainly is not there to tell you exactly what spiritual journey you should be experiencing. But a spiritual director does, occasionally, help us notice aspects of the journey we might miss without their guidance. Thinking of verbal transitions in this way can deepen our spiritual leadership by moving us away from simply being "bureaucrats of the agenda," with perfunctory comments like "let us turn to page thus-and-such and sing …" Instead, we might say, "*Dumiyah* means 'silence' in Hebrew. As we sing this simple chant[56] using this word from our Jewish roots, I invite you to breathe deeply before each phrase, and, when the music fades, continue simply to breathe in a time of extended silence, knowing God is present with each breath." This verbal transition includes a way to move more deeply into the experience by knowing more about the words of the song, and it provided suggested guidance for how to experience that meaning in the silence after it. Notice that the instructions were carefully crafted so that they were more spiritually rich than didactic.

We can often do more harm than good by over-explaining what is about to happen. For example, I created a layered sequence for an experience of the 23rd Psalm that combined the song "Shepherd Me, O God" with inviting the congregation to whisper aloud, on their own time, the scripture passage between verses 2 and 3. The people sing only the song refrain, and a soloist sings the verses, allowing both participation and deep meditative "soaking" time for the congregation. I carefully thought through any instructions the people would need to know in order to participate confidently. I decided to print the musical refrain that they would sing in the worship guide, along with the scripture they would whisper. This would eliminate the need to explain to them that they should turn to "this page" in a hymnal and "this other page" in the pew Bible. I also did not need to say that they would sing only the refrain because that is all they have in front of them. And I decided to simply say, "I invite you to whisper aloud, on your own time, the 23rd Psalm that is before you" just before they did it—after the 2nd verse was sung—rather than explain it beforehand. And I begin to do so into the microphone right after I issue the invitation, which models it for them and gets them going (I then back off the microphone since folks will be saying it in their own rhythm). This facilitates a flow inside the experience rather than a whole lot of explanation that doesn't make sense before we start: "We are going to sing a song you've never sung before. You will sing the refrain and a soloist will sing the verses. After the refrain after verse 2, you will recite the Psalm aloud, but whispering, on your own time." Oh my! The congregation is anxious and closed down before we even get to the experience. It is vitally important to think through, write out, and practice all instructions to make sure that we are using only the most necessary, concise, and clear wording. Especially when

See a video of this layered sequence at thinklikeafilmmaker.com.

leading the congregation in something new or "out of the box," making sure they feel confident while not taking them out of the worship "vibe" is crucial to building trust for other new experiences.

Verbal transitions can help us weave ritual actions in the midst of a song. Recently I used a song that says "Deep in our hearts, there is a common vision, deep in our hearts, there is a common song." There are four verses. I told the pianist that after the third verse I was going to invite the congregation to engage with each other. We devised a plan for the piano to continue softly under this verbal transition into the activity: "I invite you to turn to your neighbor and find out what you have in common with them." This was especially important in this worship experience because it was a conference on innovation and collaboration filled with a diversity of people, most of whom didn't know one another. The piano underneath helped keep the energy flowing under the activity, and, as the hub-bub began to dissipate, we swung right back into the last verse.

Just as important as discerning the right moments for these kinds of guided verbal offerings is to also know when *no* verbal introduction or transition is needed. Sometimes I can discern this as I'm writing my script, and sometimes I figure it out in the cue-to-cue rehearsal.

To see a worship script with verbal transitions included, go to thinklikeafilmmaker.com.

And sometimes, the spirit strikes in the midst of worship. What I will tell you, however, is that I wasn't always comfortable trusting that I could just make it up in the moment. When I first began to lead worship, I would write out every verbal transition word for word. My theater background taught me not to read it right off the page, but at least I had thought through it very intentionally, plotting exactly the economy of words that would express everything I needed to say *and no more*. This an excellent practice, especially if you tend to ramble off-the-cuff. If intentional focus on verbal transitions is new to you, I highly recommend that when your worship script is finished, go back and make sure that you write in all verbal transitions and instructions.

WRITING LITURGY

The words we say in worship take many "forms." I believe anyone can write words for worship if they have a good structure to work with. I have seen many people in my workshops amazed at their first attempt at writing a prayer or litany. They are able to do it because I give them a structure—almost a formula—and they simply bring their own words to it. Here is an example of a structure for an opening prayer, often called a "collect prayer."

1. Name for God
2. Tell what God does that makes that name appropriate
3. Make a petition or request of God
4. Why we make the request; what is the desired outcome ("so that …")?
5. Words of praise

I created a worship series in the Worship Design Studio for the Easter Season, called "Resurrection Stories." Each week someone who has a "turned-my-life-around" story gives a testimony to the resurrection they experienced in their life. In this example, on a Sunday when a recovering alcoholic gave their testimony, a prayer utilizing the structure of a *collect* prayer wove themes from the Psalm for the day ("I lift up my eyes to the hills—from where will my help come?") and a Hebrew text ("you led them … to give them light on their way") with some language that comes out of the twelve-step program that helped to turn around the life of our speaker.

1. God, our Help and Guide,
2. Time and again we find ourselves struggling, only to discover that you have never left our side.
3. Walk with us this day, one step at a time—especially when the same mistakes repeat themselves in our lives—so that we may discover the paths you have for us.
4. We give you thanks for second, third, and fourth chances to know you, follow you, be loved by you. Amen.

In this example, the structure of the prayer provides a container in which to play with the subject matter so that the prayer underscores the message of the day. For someone active in a twelve-step program, hearing the words "one step at a time" would probably have sunk deep into their hearts, making the message even more unforgettable. As I think about how this prayer might be *layered,* the song "Lead Me, Guide Me" comes to mind. It is a short refrain that could be sung just before and after the prayer, with the piano continuing to play softly underneath the reading of the prayer. Bookending a prayer with congregational song is a powerful device because the music allows time to settle into a prayerful mindset and then continue to reflect and let the imagery of the prayer sink in afterwards. And when the words of the music summarize the theme of the prayer ("let me walk each day with thee"), the message is reinforced. A song may come to mind as you write a prayer, but if not, send it to one of the music team for a suggestion. This is the joy of collaboration!

The first step in the structure of the prayer above was *naming God.* Writing liturgy invites us to expand our vocabulary so that we awaken to the plethora of ways the Divine is active in our lives. When we use the same metaphors over and over again, we rob our congregations of the rich poetic tradition of the Bible. Indeed, descriptors and names for God number in the hundreds in our sacred texts, such as "Liberator," "Covenant-Maker," "Well of Living Water," "Refuge and Strength." When we begin a prayer,

"Gracious and Loving God," we are assigning attributes that help us know more deeply and specifically the character of God and, by extension, who we believe we are called to be as *imago Dei*—made in the image of God. We, too, are called to be gracious and loving. Metaphors are all we have to describe the mystery that is God. Even "Father" is a metaphor, assigning a human attribute to God. If we use this anthro-pomorphic term as the only descriptor of the holy in our corporate prayer, it gives us only a partial image of the vast characteristics of the unnameable God and a very partial view of who among us is capable of taking on the characteristics of the holy for the sake of the world. A rich and varied use of language matters deeply as we seek to communicate the fullness of our relationship with God.

For an exercise to expand names for God, see thinklikeafilmmaker.com.

One of the best ways I know to expand and diversify my vocabulary is through a "clustering" exercise. When I begin to write liturgy for a worship series, I will do this first so that I have a lot of words to work with. Clustering helps push me to think of concrete symbolic imagery related to the message. I begin with the anchor image or main word or phrase related to the theme. For instance, "vine and branches" was the anchor image for a series of worship services based on our connec-tion as the family of God. I placed "vine and branches" in a circle in the middle of a blank page. Then I drew four circles on spokes from the center and challenged myself to come up with four words that would describe or relate the main message. I came up with "vineyard," "family tree," "gardener," and "connection." From each of those four circles, I created three or four more spokes and continued to expand the descriptive words. Before long, I had several concrete verbal images that I could use in my writing of prayers, litanies, and verbal transitions: fruit of the vine, winding vine, bearing fruit, a place at the table, relations, kin-folk/kin-dom, woven, grafted, nurture, sustenance, covenant, etc.

This is actually a wonderful exercise to include at the Brainstorming Party because not only verbal artists but all ritual artists can use these as keywords as they search for resources.

An example of using the words produced through a clustering exercise is the communion prayer I wrote for the worship series I described above, "We Are Family." Writing communion liturgy is one of my favorite acts of verbal artistry. When the repeated elements of our worship are infused with language specific to the message, we get to experience both the message and the ritual action in fresh ways. There are people who dread communion because of what they describe as a "long and boring prayer." As I've said in a previous chapter, "boring" is about monotony. Utilizing the same words in the same way no matter the focus of the service or series can make the prayer seem rote and detached from the message. But even the most "book-oriented" traditions—where words are prescribed—change the wording for ritual action based on the liturgical season or observance. And even the most extemporaneous traditions that have no words prescribed for presiders of communion can benefit from considering a structure within which to be creative.

I utilize an ancient structure (the Hippolytus prayer from c. 200 CE) that has become an ecumenical standard. It is a beautiful structure, incorporating the story of God's saving acts—past, present and future—through a movement from God the Creator, to Jesus' life, ministry, death, and resurrection and concluding with a petition for the Spirit to act in and through the meal and the gathered community. Here is how some of the verbiage I gleaned from my clustering exercise came out in the prayer:

All are invited to this feast
prepared in the vineyard of Christ's love.
Grafted to the Holy One and to one another as one family
let us come without need of reservation
for a place has been prepared for each of us!

The Gardener toiled,
and with soil, sand, water and wind
fashioned a place of beauty and called it good.
Winding the Vine of Life through all,
the Gardener crafted love in the form of human flesh
and breathed into us a measure of life and passion both
tender and strong.
Promising to nurture us always,
the Holy One reaches out constantly with life-giving sustenance.

[Sanctus—"Holy, holy, holy …" etc.]

Blessed is your Son who came to gather folks up
and re-name them *kinfolk* one to another—
part of the same family tree.
Who came to call us to righteous *relations*
in the most unlikely of combinations.
Who came to say "relative, your wellbeing is *relative* to my wellbeing."

On the night in which he gave himself up for love and justice,
He sat down at the table with those that had become family.
At that table were those who adored him and those
that would betray him.
He knew this. And he gave bread to all anyway.
"Take, eat; this is my body which is given for you.
Do this in remembrance of me."

When the supper was over, he took the cup,
invited all to drink from this cup of love, this cup of suffering—
the sign of the covenant of relationship.
"Whenever you gather as family around tables,

whenever you strive to overcome the adversity
of being human together,
whenever you need to remember I am always with you, do this."

[Memorial Acclamation—"Christ has died, Christ has risen …" etc.]
Look upon this your Holy Vine, O God, and pour out
your Spirit upon us.
Weave your lifeblood in and among us
as we partake of these gifts of bread and fruit of the vine.
Make them bear for us fruit in our lives and our ministries.
Make us one in our connection to you
until Christ comes and lays that heavenly feast finally
in the vineyard of this world.

See a photo of the clustering exercise and this entire prayer at thinklikeafilmmaker.com.

As you can see, the verbal imagery that I brainstormed in the clustering exercise helped me contextualize this communion prayer within the "We Are Family" series message. The sermon just before communion touched on the blessings *and* difficulties of being family, and this also showed up in the prayer (this information would have been gleaned from the synopsis for this service). I can tell you that when the community spoke the words of this prayer in worship, I saw heads nod when we got to the line, "relative, your well-being is relative to my wellbeing," as the message sank in further. And when the prayer recalled the night Jesus was at the table with his loved ones for the last time, the story hit home as we remembered that he broke bread with all of them—devotees and traitors alike. Family is messy business for just about all of us. Connecting our experience of not-so-perfect family with Jesus' experience creates an unforgettable connection that will come to mind at those not-so-comfortable family-table moments in the future.

When I am being creative within the structure of something as familiar to folks as communion liturgy, I try to balance the new with the familiar. I left some of the sections of the prayer "as is"—the *Preface*, *Sanctus* and *Memorial Acclamation*—so that the congregation would have something that still feels tied to the tradition. As I will reiterate throughout this book, "creativity" does not mean starting from scratch or throwing everything out. Indeed, it is precisely the juxtaposition between the familiar and the new that can bring delight and awaken our senses to a new perspective. It also helps the congregation get both that sense of "a-ha!" and "oh yeah" that is so important to inscribing the experience on our memory.

This combination of repetition and new material can also be established within a series to provide a sense of continuity as verbal "threads." In my Lent series, "Gifts of the Dark Wood," the Prayer of Confession each week was in litany form with the same response line for the people. Additionally, parts of the leader lines were also repeated. Here is a portion of two Sundays ("The Gift of Uncertainty" and "The Gift of Emptiness") for your comparison:

Leader: For giving fear too much face-time,
People: Forgive and restore us, O God.
Leader: For digging in rather than going with the flow,
People: Forgive and restore us, O God.
Leader: For holding on too tight when what we need to do is let go,
People: Forgive and restore us, O God.
Silent prayers ...
Leader: Hear these words of assurance:
God dwells with us, no matter how sure or unsure we are.
God is not uncertain about whether or not we are worthy of love.
God is with you, forgiving and restoring you to wholeheartedness.
People: Thanks be to God! Amen!

And the next Sunday ...

Leader: For filling up our lives with little room for You,
People: Forgive and restore us, O God.
Leader: For worry that outlasts trust,
People: Forgive and restore us, O God.
Leader: For choosing being right over being in relationship,
People: Forgive and restore us, O God.
Silent prayers ...
Leader: Hear these words of assurance:
God chooses relationship over perfection.
Who you are is "loved by God."
God is with you, forgiving and restoring you to wholeheartedness.
People: Thanks be to God! Amen!

Once I have created a structure that I like for a written piece of liturgy for the first Sunday, it is very easy to use that same structure and some repeated words to create both continuity and specificity in the following weeks. Like a screenwriter, you are creating a particular "voice" and distinctive rhythm for the series that carries the "ethos" or "feel" throughout. My experience bears out that utilizing this technique is easier, less time-consuming, and much more satisfying than constantly searching outside resources for different prayers for each Sunday. As verbal artists, you get to tailor-make something extremely well-suited to the message and can reap the rewards of creativity *and* repetition.

There are many more prayer forms with structures that can be easily followed and taught, including intercessory prayer, pastoral prayers, writing your own psalms, litanies, confession,

To further your liturgical
writing skills, see
thinklikeafilmmaker.com.

and assurance.[57] You can find examples and exercises for these at thinklikeafilmmaker.com as well as my suggestions for "must have" books to further your liturgical writing skills. I want to encourage you to seek out the wordsmiths in your congregation and create a writing group. Write for fun and spiritual nurture[58] as well as tackling writing assignments for worship. Also play with collecting short verbal statements from anyone in the congregation such as "I believe …" or "We gather to …" and then divide them up and fashion them into affirmations of faith or calls to worship for each week in a series. Anytime people hear their own words helping the congregation to express themselves, the ownership, interest, and commitment to the work of worship increases dramatically.

WRITING SERMONS

There is no shortage of good books about the form and content of sermons, so it is not my intention to offer one more theory of preaching here.

However, there are some things to be said about making preaching more sensory-rich and therefore, more memorable. Humorist Garrison Keillor, when asked what the sermon should sound like said, "When a minister stands in front of people, [she/he] is interrupting what the people have come to church for. [They] had better have a good reason for doing that … we go to look at the mysteries, and all the substitutes for communion with God

See thinklikeafilmmaker.com for a bibliography of my favorites.

are not worth anyone's time."[59] Preaching must, along with every other ritual art form, point toward an experience of communion with God.

There are two things that will put congregations to sleep, and they are something I've already mentioned in this chapter—the need for the verbal to be both visual and visceral. The failure to engage listeners visually happens with overly didactic, heavily concept-based,

I-did-my-exegetical-homework-and-now-I'm-going-to-impress-you wordiness. I see this with new preachers enamored with the research part of the creative process. They think everyone will find all of it as interesting as they did rather than gleaning and communicating just that kernel of wisdom that turns assumption on its head or reveals a twist in the story we've never considered. Directors, actors, and screenwriters know much more about the backstory and context of the setting, the time period, and the characters than they ever are able to convey to the audience. The research helps to drive decisions in the writing and production process, but isn't ultimately the main focus—the message is. I also see what I call the "TMI syndrome" (too much information) with preachers whose creative timeline never allows them time to actually edit what they have prepared. Too often I hear a preacher come in for a landing on what I think is going to be a well-crafted sermon, and then they turn the corner for "one more illustration" or "one more bit of information" or one more, often unnecessary, way to make the point. Usually they haven't actually rehearsed it out loud, or they probably would have felt the places where the story gets sidetracked.

The second way to lose the congregation is the failure to engage them viscerally and kinesthetically. Repetitive, monotonous, and predictable rhythms of speech have lulled many a congregation into a stupor—no matter how compelling the content might actually be. The sermon can lack shifts in energy and "voice," resulting in stagnant prose rather than dynamic movement. Michael Hauge, an author and consultant to screenwriters, says that no matter what kind of story you are telling in what mode or for what audience, knowing the "turning points" of the journey "will strengthen your ability to enthrall your reader or audience."[60] Stories must move in order to take us along for the ride, and we must always be aware that we are going somewhere. Too many stops along the way, and people disembark prematurely and start making their grocery lists in their heads.

"People just don't absorb much of what they hear," says communications expert and Harvard Management Communication Letter editor Nick Morgan.[61] But spoken presentations persist because their primary impact is an emotional one. Trust, motivation for action, sparking insight and change are some of the reasons why the spoken word is vitally important for groups, especially those whose purpose is to work together to bring something about. Unfortunately, most speakers, he says, don't understand and utilize the most important aspect of effective communication—kinesthetics. Inspiring trust and action requires that an audience have a "kinesthetic connection" with the speaker and that the message be communicated on a visceral, personal, and emotional level. There is a "primal hunger" to experience the message on a physical level, and this is created by kinesthetic speakers who create potent non-verbal messages. Speakers can vary their aural inflections such as *volume, speed,* and *pause* to keep the audience interested. Visual stimuli, like the speaker's own gestures and movements in space, objects, projections, or video clips can keep congregants' kinesthetic attention. All of these choices convey energy patterns that "match" the kinesthetic experience of the audience, infusing the presentation "with a legitimate sense of authenticity."[62] Does our energy, movement, and inflection convey that we, too, are inspired by this Word proclaimed? Are we modeling the kind of engagement that we hope to get from those who are listening?

Even if you have been preaching for years, it is important to regularly evaluate the effectiveness of your communication style. Good actors keep working with coaches long after they are established in the business. Writers get feedback from people they trust before it goes out for public consumption. Screenwriter Allen Palmer says, "It is heart first, head second. So after you've written your screenplay, don't read it with a view to how comprehensively you've satisfied the theory; read it for how it makes you feel. And encourage others to whom you entrust your drafts to do the same. Does it move you?" If we believe that worship and preaching are to offer inspiration for transformation, the question of whether the story moves us is a valid one. And anyone who aspires to bring unforgettable messages week in and week out must hone and revise their craft on an ongoing basis.

One of the most difficult things to get used to when I embarked on my performing career was watching myself on video. It is difficult to see yourself from the "outside." Even though we were an internationally renowned performing company, rehearsals involved constant evaluation to be sure that we were continuing to bring our best to the audience. Inevitably, we would find some nuance that could be heightened, or something that was not quite right, or a way to more effectively communicate a line or phrase of movement. When I am working with preachers one on one, we watch videos together. It is an incredibly vulnerable thing to do, especially to watch yourself while someone else is watching, too. We begin to "see" through their eyes, wonder what they think. But this is exactly the point. Unless we practice seeing ourselves through the eyes of our congregations, we can stay in denial of the improvements we may need to make. I remember my first acting class. I had no awareness of my midwest accent, rhythms of speech, and regional inflections of certain words. There was nothing wrong with having these, but I had to become aware of them in order to then try on a variety of ways of speaking, depending on the roles I was to play. Likewise, we may not be aware of speech patterns and vocal intonation that decreases our effectiveness or limits our variety or range of energy.

Giving the text a particular "voice" is of eminent importance in preaching professor Jana Childers' analysis of communication in preaching.[63] Childers notes that speech-communication research shows that "55 percent of all meaning communicated in a face-to-face setting is communicated by the body, 38 percent by the tone of voice, and only 7 percent by the actual words spoken."[64]

> Preaching's nonverbal aspects require a body that is ready to express the widest possible range of ideas and feelings, from the most subtly nuanced theological thought to the largest of human emotions. Preachers deal on a cosmic scale; their bodies must be up to the scope of the task.[65]

We will revisit this in our chapter on Dramatic Arts when we discuss training readers. But I wanted to introduce this important aspect of communication—too often overlooked—at this point because I believe that *how* we write and prepare a sermon ought to be influenced at the git-go by the way we will offer it orally. Turning a written-for-the-page sermon into an effective oral event is more difficult than writing with the live end-product in mind. Whether you will preach with a manuscript, notes, or nothing at all as a prompt, writing the sermon should involve getting up from the computer every once in a while and talking to the cat … or the dog or plant or whatever happens to be there to discover the rhythm and tone and feel of the story. It can involve closing your eyes and putting yourself in the scene, seeing details that can weave themselves into the narrative. It can involve gathering inspirational images and considering utilizing them as media projections or hearing a song that eventually weaves its way throughout the sermon. The act of creating the sermon can be a sensory-rich experience just as the sermon itself can be.

As you write, consider utilizing a poetic format right away rather than writing in paragraph form first. Let there be lots of blank space and write it out in the phrasing you would speak it. Let the words move on the page rather than boxing them into justified margins and nice, neat sentences and paragraphs. Here is one example of an Advent sermon I wrote some time ago:

"This is my body, this is my blood …" *[pause]* … SHE SAID.
"This is my body, this is my blood …" SHE ALSO SAID.

"This is my body, this is my blood," the two woman-voices rang as
  their wombs wove wonders for the world.

*In those days Mary set out and went with haste to a Judean
town in the hill country, where she entered the house of Zechariah
and greeted Elizabeth. When Elizabeth heard Mary's greeting, the
child leaped in her womb.*

The woman-child had barely begun to know the power of her body …
    … the ebbs and flows of mysterious yet knowing surges of
        womanhood
    … the advent of a new rhythm that left childhood behind.
The joy of expected "expecting." But she had not expected this:

*The Holy Spirit will come upon you, and the power of the Most
High will overshadow you; therefore the child to be born will be
holy; he will be called the Son of God.*

The woman-elder knew all too well the rhythms, those telling surges
    describing her pain … the flow again and again revealing her
    barrenness, unrelenting in its regularity.
She prayed for it to change.
She expected it to stop, actually, for her time of harvesting was surely
    drawing to a close. But she had not expected this:

*… Elizabeth will bear a son, and you shall name him John.
You will have joy and gladness and many will rejoice at his birth
for he will be great in the sight of the Lord.*

Adolescent and menopausal — at the very edges of the time to bear.
Together, poignantly, powerfully, they worshiped God, bearing rites
    of adoration and praise.

At this point, the sermon "voice" changed, turning to a bit of con-textualizing about the precarious situation for both of these women (Mary's "betrothed" status and Elizabeth's barrenness) based on what scholars tell us about women's rights at that point in history. The rhythm of poetry and word play woven with scripture passages in this first section was ready for a "turning point"— a change in dynamics that would be a set-up for the next "turning point" of the sermon, which focused on Mary's *magnificat* and talked about the dangerous and prophetic nature of raising "Halleluiah's"—the language of emancipation, bolstered by two modern-day stories of courage in the face of oppression.

Read the whole sermon at thinklikeafilmmaker.com.

As I wrote this using a more poetic format on the page, I could see where the change in voice occurred. It even propelled me to think about actually using different voices to read the scripture pieces woven into it—voices only heard, not seen. If not, then I knew I would need to change postures or my position in the space for those parts to indicate the change in voice. I spoke it aloud as I wrote it and reformatted it to reflect the pauses I would need to effectively let the poetry sink in.

Steven Spielberg has said that he knows when he is editing a movie, he must change the energy dynamics at least every six minutes or he will lose the audience.[66] It doesn't matter how compelling the content is—a tender love scene or an adrenaline-hyped car chase. Too much of a good thing is still too much. Words must move, in order to move us. As verbal artists for worship, we pray that the words we employ will make a difference in someone's life, in the life of the community, and in the world that so desperately needs life-giving and hopeful stories that will speak loud and clear among the bad-news clamor of our times.

CHAPTER 5

THINK LIKE A COMPOSER:
MUSICAL ARTS IN WORSHIP

Music is powerful. A swell in the music can swell our hearts. A single instrument playing a plaintive melody can set the stage for an intensely poignant moment. Music underscoring words can help us hear the words in a new way. And going from music into silence can usher in a breath-held moment of suspense. Simply put, the power of music is in its ability to evoke emotion, an integral part of what worship helps us do—acknowledge the magnitude and intersection of life and faith. Our life stories are filled with the drama of moments of waiting, listening, fearing, rejoicing, longing, hoping, dying, and so much more. Our faith story is filled with the intensity of human failings, God's promise of presence, the stories of Jesus' radical ministry of hospitality, healing, teaching, and passion. Worship crystallizes this intersection when we engage our cognition and our emotion.

Music was one of the first ways that humans helped to establish rapport within communities. In his fascinating book *Music, the Brain and Ecstasy,* Robert Jourdain describes French archeologists who explored prehistoric caves by singing in them. What they discovered is that the chambers that had the most resonance for singing were also the places where the most prehistoric paintings were found on the walls of the cave.

Storytelling and music-making and ritual seem to have always walked hand-in-hand for our species.

> In the view of many anthropologists, music first evolved to strengthen community bonds and resolve conflicts. This idea is anything but far-fetched. Many animals employ their vocal apparatus to convey fine gradations of emotions and intention ... As humans evolved language, with intonation inherent in every word, it seems inevitable that formal expression of emotion would gradually coalesce into something like melody.[67]

MUSIC AND EMOTION

Music owes much of its development to its connection to our need for emotional expression. The rhythm, melody, pitch, tone, and movement of music create physiological responses that literally trigger feelings. Janalea Hoffman, a music therapist, was inspired by a study which showed that rhythms we encounter in our lives have power over our own heartbeats. She began to explore using music at very slow and steady rhythms to relax her clients. "The listener's heart responds to the external stimulus of the slow, steady beat of the music and her/his heart rate begins to synchronize."[68] "Power instruments" such as brass or organ can facilitate feelings of inner power. Flutes and strings may help free the imagination.

"Every sound is a bundle of different qualities," says music theorist Theo Van Leeuwen.[69] For instance, music which emulates a "caress" may be realized by *melodic* means (a slightly descending and undulating melody) combined with a *rhythm* choice (a medium tempo), in a particular tone that evokes a *distance* (soft and close), and a vocal *timbre* depending on the location of the sound in the nasal passages. Change even one of these attributes, and you end up communicating something else—a caressing tone can become a whiny one. The dynamic range associated with musical components such as pitch, timbre, rhythm, and melody has a "semiotic force" based on a range of "holding more energy in" or "letting more energy out," which Van Leeuwen calls the emotive confinement or expansion.[70]

Film composers are expertly attuned to the mix of sound and content in human expression. It is their business to know how musical qualities affect us because their very role is to intensify our emotional experience of any given moment in a movie. Poignant moments in film create physiological responses in us as we see images, hear words, and—sometimes only subconsciously recognized by us—hear music that underscores the story's emotional impact. There are several ways that music contributes to a film, says Roy A. Prendergast in "The Aesthetics of Film Music." He says that music helps "realize the meaning of a film" and makes potent "the film's dramatic and emotional value."[71]

The energy dynamics produced by film sound are perhaps the most important components in this discipline, rather than melody. The term "color" describes film music that creates an atmosphere and a mood, much like the way visual artists' use of color affects our emotions. A particular instrumentation can evoke a place, or a "feel." The effect, says Prendergast, is immediate, visceral, and therefore psychological and emotional. The ability of music to underscore or refine "the unseen implications of a situation" is subtle, making it one of the most valuable contributions to the film story. Music conveys feelings and thoughts "better than any other element of a film … It has a catalytic ability to change the audience's perception of images and words."[72]

Thinking like a film composer has dramatically affected the way I think about the role of music in worship. By the end of this chapter, you will see your role as a musical ritual artist expanding much beyond simply "filling in the slots" of songs, hymns, and "special music." I want to invite you to see your role as creating a "soundscape" for our experience of the Holy that engages us on a visceral and emotional level.

UNDERSCORING

Jon Boorstin reminds us "the chances are that all the emotional high points of your favorite Hollywood films were underscored with music." But we may not remember exactly what that music was because "music can be so precisely placed that properly used it is invisible, a magic pixie dust that intensifies the emotions and evaporates."[73] The film composer knows that the music is there to serve the story. In the same way, musical underscoring in worship can create an emotional landscape for hearing words—it deepens our immersion in the story, not only holding our attention more profoundly but searing its place in our memories. *Under the Tuscan Sun* features a brief yet important monologue by one of the minor characters (the flamboyant former actress) played by Lindsay Duncan. She is pulled from the fountain in the town piazza and ushered by Frances into her apartment toward the end of the film. There's dialogue between the two, and the only sound is night crickets and an occasional passing car. These sound effects are simply there to establish time and place. But then the camera moves in for a close-up in a pause just before the monologue begins, and this moment is the composer's opportunity to enter and create a musical container for this moment of the story. Strings create a bit of anticipation for us, and delicate, simple notes high on the piano invite us to lean in and listen intently. The monologue is the beginning of a sequence of events that show the breaking loose of Frances' grief to make way for a renewed faith in love. The music has helped us notice this moment as important to the transforming storyline.

Oliver Sacks was a neurologist and the author of *Awakenings*, a book made into an Academy Award-nominated film. He studied the effects of music on Parkinson's patients. The movement of the music they listened to helped override their brain's faulty motor symptoms for a time, allowing for smoother movement. "Music overcomes Parkinson's symptoms by transporting the brain to a higher than normal level of integration. Music establishes flow in the brain, at once enlivening and coordinating the brain's activities." Music works on us all in the same way. "It lifts us from our frozen mental habits and makes our minds move in ways they ordinarily cannot."[74] By its movement and careful design, music helps to clear away the ordinary meanderings of our thoughts and focus them on the moment. Simply put, we listen better to words when music is supporting them.

One of my closest collaborators and Worship Design Studio guest expert, Chuck Bell, has a long career of being a church musician, but his college degree is in commercial music—including scoring films. His underscoring abilities are amazing. When we lead worship together, Chuck is listening intently to the words that I say and offering what he calls a "sound bed" underneath. And because he is playing, I know that I can pause to let the music respond. It becomes a duet rather than simply two things going on at the same time. This is when underscoring becomes a slightly more "foreground" activity than a "background" one.

> Generally, such [film] music is treated musically in a recitative style reminiscent of the opera: blank spots in the dialogue are filled with fragments of music, which come to the foreground momentarily to comment on the dialogue and then drop back into the background when the next line is said.[75]

The Psalms are a wonderful body of work to start experimenting with this kind of "dialogue" between reader and musician. Psalm 139, one of my favorites, begins, "O Lord, you have searched me and you know me." A pause at the end of that line to let a musical voice enter evokes the presence of something other than the reader—in a sense becoming the presence of God. "You know when I sit and when I stand, you understand my thoughts from afar." Again, the musical voice comments, adding movement and placement to that presence. "If I go to the highest heights (the music ascends and suspends) … if I descend to the depths (we hear a chord in the lower register, still suspenseful) … you are there (the chord's resolution brings a period to the aural sentence)." Together, words and music are combining to further the message of the presence of God in our every waking moment.

See a video of Chuck and I preparing and doing this Psalm at thinklikeafilmmaker.com.

While Chuck is a very accomplished improviser and composer-in-the-moment, an accompanist who only reads music right off the page can learn to do this as well. I've seen Chuck coach someone to simply play the notes of the downbeat of the measure and hold it while the speaking continues and then move to the next chord at the beginning of the next measure. I've seen him suggest taking the written music up an octave and slowing it way down to create a tender, gentle feel or move the bass note of a chord down one step to create suspense and anticipation. With just a few techniques and time to play around with it outside of worship, pastors and musicians can begin to experience the joy of collaboration in creating emotive, meaningful, and memorable moments.

Film composer Jim Ellis says that you really don't need a whole lot of musical material to do the kind of underscoring that is more in the genre of "background" music. He calls it "going nowhere in a hurry." This kind of underscoring happens under speaking that doesn't have as many opportunities for pause—such as a verbal synopsis at the beginning of worship or under instructions about coming to prayer or communion stations. Jim warns not to use melody at these times because as soon as we hear melody, our brains will latch onto it (especially if it is familiar), and it begins to compete with the words being spoken. If melody does come in, it must be slowed way down or so much in the background that the listeners don't notice it.[76] The music is more "sound effect" at this moment than "constructed music."

Aaron Copland describes this kind of musical contribution this way, "This is really the kind of music one isn't supposed to hear … It's the movie composer's most ungrateful task. But at times, though no one else may notice, he [she] will get private satisfaction."[77] Even though it may not be "heard," it is carrying out a very important task—to create a particular mood and to keep the energy moving forward. When I go through a worship script in the final stages, I always consider having music under some of the most pedantic, or "instruction-y" moments. This keeps the congregation in a worshipful state and helps prevent having the energy drop and then needing to pick it back up.

Just as important as *when* to underscore is when *not* to underscore. As I've mentioned before, "boring" is about monotony. Underscoring everything can become monotonous. It is important to look at the entire worship design and determine how much is just enough. For example, if we've woven verses of a hymn and underscoring throughout a reading from the Hebrew Bible, we might decide not to include music under the reading of the Gospel text. If we've been having a verbal/musical dialogue throughout the beginning of a Great Thanksgiving (communion prayer), we might take out the underscoring during the Words of Institution ("On the night he was betrayed, he took bread …"). One of the wonderful effects of this is that when the music does go away, the "soundscape" of silence underneath makes the words "pop" with intensity. The juxtaposition of music and silence creates interest and focus in yet another powerful way.

Making decisions in the worship script about when we need musical support is akin to what film composers call "spotting." A film director and composer will work together to identify where to use music and for what purpose. Of course, this analogy also works for collaboration of pastor and music director in discerning the placement of songs, hymns, and anthems. But thinking like a film composer will push you to consider taking the time to "spot" for those places where music can provide emotive power, set the mood or "feel," or keep the energy flowing.

THEME SONGS AND THRESHOLD MOMENTS

"Music can create a more convincing atmosphere of time and place."[78] Film scores help build the drama by creating a "sonic landscape" that immerses us in the context of the message. Nowhere in the art of film composing is this more important than in establishing a musical "theme." We hear this in the opening minutes of the film, and its rhythm, tone, intensity, and melody create a "feel" or a "flavor" for the movie. It sets us up for the way we will experience the story. Filmmakers spend more time and attention, proportionally, on the first two minutes of a film than on the rest of it. They know this is the moment that audiences will either "buy in" to the story or not. If the beginning is not strong, the rest of the film is an uphill trek.

As I have developed my art of designing worship in series over the years, I have progressively leaned toward creating a moment at the beginning of worship (well, after the announcements) that takes us beyond the ordinary and into a spiritual journey. When I began to study what filmmakers could teach me about sensory-rich storytelling, the idea of a "threshold moment" solidified in my mind. Creating that kind of moment involves finding the right "soundscape" or theme song that will launch us into the message. And like a theme that shows up repeatedly throughout a movie, the theme song for a worship series will repeat each week and even find spots during worship to be revisited.

As you watched *Under the Tuscan Sun,* you probably noticed the theme melodies. We hear the melody played slowly in a plaintive manner by one solo instrument at the moment Frances enters the house and feels some "buyer's remorse." When work on the house is flourishing, we hear that same melody with more instrumentation in an upbeat way, creating a joyful energy and movement. We hear the same melody in a sweeping, romantic quality during an overhead shot of the convertible heading to Positano at the blossoming of Frances' infatuation with a suitor. Each time, the musical theme simultaneously acts as a continuing thread and interprets the mood of the moment in a unique way. In 2012, I worked together with another one of my musical collaborators, Mark Miller, along with Chuck Bell on a theme song for a series of worship experiences for the United Methodist Church's General Conference in 2012. The worship theme was "Discipleship by the Sea," and each day featured a different story of Jesus at the shoreline of the Sea of Galilee. I wanted to set the scene for the people at the conference in our opening worship. At the time for worship to begin, the lights went down and we heard the roaring thunder of a storm brewing and saw lightning around the space from projected media. For those of you who know about the dynamics of a denominational conference, where policies are debated and voted upon, you know that this was an apt metaphor for our context. But it was also beginning to place us at the shoreline (we'll talk much more about visual and sound effects in Chapter Six). We heard the rain subside and then the sound effects of waves lapping on a shoreline as the first sparse strains of the piano began. A solo voice began to sing the theme, "Shall we gather? At the water? At the water of God's grace?" Dancers began to assemble as I poured water from a vessel into a baptismal bowl in a couple of measures of instrumental interlude. The singer continued, "At the shoreline … at the water … can you hear the voice of God?" I then wove the spoken synopsis as the dancers began to move up the aisle toward the front. The musical underscoring continued under the narration along with the gentle wave sounds as I spoke:

The water of Jesus' baptism, of our own,
becomes the point at which we embark on a journey
together in these days.

River flows to sea,
baptism flows to discipleship,
the Jordan flows to the Sea of Galilee ...

At the shoreline we stand in the midst of all possibility.
We gaze out to the horizon,
we wait to receive what comes in with the tide.
We leave our boats and we climb into boats,
we rock in the gentle give and take of the Breath of Life
and we strain against the storms together.

At the shoreline we stand in the midst of all possibility.
And we hear the voice of the Teacher calling once again ...

And then the theme song went on, "... calling 'Follow me, follow me, follow me to the heart of eternity, where the reign of God is unend-

See a video of this threshold moment at thinklikeafilmmaker.com.

ing.'" In this opening service, the music went on to other hymns. But in subsequent worship, the congregation repeatedly sang the simple theme refrain together in the opening moments of worship, always drawing them back to the shoreline before hearing the particular story for that day. Over ten days, I wanted them to return again and again to the place where Jesus first called the disciples so we could remember our own call to be disciples in the world. The repetition of the music and sound effect was a powerful device for centering us—especially in the midst of the intensity and distraction of the business of the church. And it provided continuity over ten days of worshiping together.

Jim Ellis says that learning to listen "is the single most important thing any film composer can do." By truly listening, we can analyze a moment in worship to discern how music might create the right feel to accompany its message. But how can musical artists learn to do this? Ellis explains, "Start with the simplest thing. How and why does the story move you?"[79] As a worship designer, once I can "hear" the mood of the music we will use in the threshold moment, I can begin to imagine where we will go from there. Just as the visual palette and symbolic objects jumpstart the design process, so does this crucial piece of mood-setting music. "Finding just the right sound can be as exacting a task as finding just the right image."[80]

Chuck and I wrote a theme song together for the Worship Design Studio worship series, "Gifts of the Dark Wood," based on a book by the same name[81] by another frequent collaborator of mine, Eric Elnes. The overarching message of the book is that even in the "dark woods" moments of our lives—lost in the midst of uncertainty and emptiness— there are gifts that can open us to living more wholeheartedly. I knew the tone of the series would be reflective, and I wanted to create a threshold moment for each week that would place people on the journey through the dark woods. I wrote some poetry and had a melody line in mind when Chuck and I met together. I described to him that we needed to feel like we were walking together. What transpired was an underlying piano accompaniment in the right hand that evokes slow and steady steps. Every two measures, the left hand offers a rolling bass line that propels us forward deeper into the woods. The timbre is a bit dissonant but not ominous. There is a resoluteness that we are where we are, but we are not stuck. The poetry solidly states both the trepidation we feel for the journey *and* the assurance that God is inviting us to awake and discover something we may not have expected for our lives. The whole threshold sequence looks like this:

Threshold to the Dark Woods

[lights dim … soloist sings as they move from
back of the sanctuary to front]

There's a path … though it winds its way through darkness
We would choose … to avoid it if we could
We awake … to an unexpected calling
God says, "come … there are gifts in the Dark Wood"

[pastor meets the soloist at the front and offers this synopsis to the people
as the music continues to underscore]

Week One Synopsis: Today we begin a journey in this season of Lent. Our worship series, "Gifts of the Dark Wood" is about "seeing life through new eyes." When we allow ourselves to accept the journey within the Dark Woods, the Holy Spirit Guide tends to nudge us, awaken us, to a fuller life. But life is messy. Life is uncertain. Rather than a problem to be solved, what if we saw uncertainty, failure, emptiness, and loss as gifts? What if we saw how these uncomfortable times can actually help us let go of all we cannot know so that we can live more wholeheartedly? Let us begin the journey …

[soloist sings refrain again from the front
and the choir processes in slowly, singing the echo]

*There's a path (echo: **there's a path**) … though it winds*
its way through darkness
*We would choose (**we would choose**) … to avoid it if we could*
*We awake (**we awake**) … to an unexpected calling*
*God says, "come (**God says, "come**) … there are gifts in the Dark Wood"*

Prayer

[music continues to underscore]

Unexpected Love, enter our lives
and open us to the gifts residing deep within the Holy Darkness of
our lives.
Walk with us,
speak to us,
call to us.
In your many names, we pray. Amen.

*[underscoring comes to a conclusion and segues
into the introduction to the Opening Hymn/Song]*

I wanted the congregation to be able to participate without difficulty—without music or words in front of them—so the first part of each line in the musical composition has room for the choir (the first Sunday) and the people (on subsequent weeks) to echo. Hearing the community's voices singing together provides a sense of togetherness on the road. The repetitive nature, both of the melody itself and the use of the song every week, allows us to go deeper and deeper into the experience. It also becomes a "hook" that we carry with us even outside of worship throughout the series.

Hear this threshold
moment at
thinklikeafilmmaker.com.

Of course, you may not have the skill set in your team to compose a theme song for every series. You may just be looking for a refrain that will work wonderfully for your theme. But taking that time to carefully consider what sounds will immerse your congregation in the message—and doing this in a collaboration between verbal and musical artists—will fast-track the whole design process. As soon as I had a sense of the opening moments for the "Gifts of the Dark Wood" series, I began to imagine with ease the flow of the rest of the worship experience. In fact, the theme song came back as a Benediction Song at the end of each week, with different words:

> *There's a path* (**there's a path**) … *and it leads us out together*
> *To the wood* (**to the wood**) … *where the darkness hovers still*
> *We are sent* (**we are sent**) … *and the Spirit goes before us*
> *God says, "go* (**God says, go**) … *be my presence in the world."*

With these strong bookends in place, plus another musical "thread" throughout in the form of a song we composed called "Come and Rest" for the Prayers of the People each week, the form of the series began to take solid shape, and we were well on our way to a complete design that offered the "a-ha!" and "oh yeah" of creativity and familiarity—a winning combination.

MUSICAL TRANSITIONS

Imagine this moment: The bulletin says it is time for the anthem. The choir director stands and moves the music stand into place in front of the choir. Then comes the motion for the choir to stand. Then everyone gets their music open to the right place while the choir director waits. When it seems all are settled, the choir director looks to the accompanist, and the accompanist nods to indicate readiness. The choir director looks back to the choir to make sure all eyes are focused, that all members will be ready for the downbeat. Finally, the anthem's introduction begins. Certainly a "moment" has been created, but for what purpose? As all of these machinations have been occurring, the congregation has sat watching it, pulled out of the story and into an approximation of what they might experience at a concert hall.

Imagine another moment: A sermon in the midst of a worship series called "Moving Out of Scare City" that focuses on the Gospel good news in the midst of a culture of fear has just finished, with the preacher almost whispering an invitation, "Be still, quiet your heart, and know that God is near." The worship guide indicates a time of silence. The lights are dimmed in the sanctuary. Out of the hushed silence, an unaccompanied voice eventually sings from among the still-seated choir. *"I will come to you in the silence …"* The voice pauses to breathe and then stands slowly with the next line. *"I will lift you from all your fear …"* A few more voices from the choir join as they slowly stand … *"You will hear my voice, I claim you as my choice, be still and know I am here."* The piano sneaks in softly. The choir director moves slowly into place as the rest of the choir slowly stands. The lights in the choir loft have slowly come up, mimicking the timing of the choir slowly standing. The choir begins to sing the refrain, *"Do not be afraid, I am with you …"* and the good news of the sermon begins to be embodied in the music, having flowed seamlessly without breaking the mood of the moment for preparations.[82]

At a concert, we present a piece of music for the sake of maximum appreciation of that piece of music. In that setting, the audience expects to sit quietly and wait while the musicians ready themselves for the first strains of the composition. In worship, however, as in film and musical theater, the music is there to develop the message of the story. Anything that pulls us out of the story has little place in the progression of events. "Hollywood technique, no matter how flamboyant, at its best prides itself on being invisible, on serving the story. 'If you're admiring the work,' the saying goes, 'it's not working.' You have been pulled out of the picture."[83] While not every anthem has to be as dramatically staged as the example above, planning the flow into any element of worship must be approached with intention.

I've been called "the flow queen" (hopefully lovingly!) by many ritual artists who have worked under my direction. This is because I am adamant about rehearsing transitions. I had a dance mentor once tell me, "dancers who can do a triple pirouette are a dime-a-dozen. What distinguishes a technician from an artist is knowing how to get out of that triple pirouette and into the next step with ease and beauty." I know that worship in which transitions have been intentionally attended to is worship that flows. And worship that flows is worship that keeps us "in the story." Music is one of the key components in smoothing transitions from one element in the order of worship to another. We will speak more about this in Chapter Eight when we talk about cue-to-cue rehearsals in the final steps of preparing the worship series. For now, let's hear what filmmakers know about the role of the music in the editing process:

> Music can tie together a visual medium that is, by its very nature, continually in danger of falling apart. A film editor is probably most conscious of this particular attribute of music in films. In a montage, particularly, music can serve an almost indispensable function: it can hold the montage together with some sort of unifying musical idea. Without music the montage can, in some instances, become merely chaotic. Music can also develop this sense of continuity on the level of the film as a whole.[84]

Worship can often feel like a "montage" of disjointed pieces. A rousing hymn finishes, and you can feel the energy crackling in the room. Because the reader who is leading the Call to Worship forgot when to move into place, we all stand in the silence, watching them walk up the chancel stairs to the lectern. The energy we've just created plummets as we suffer through the awkward pause. Or the children are invited forward for a segment with the pastor, and the extended time it takes because a couple of them are "wandering" on their way forward creates a vacuum of energy that has to ramp up again when all are settled. In both of these examples, some impromptu "traveling music" from an instrumentalist could have alleviated the pregnant and unintentional pause in the energetic movement of worship. Empowering musicians to be alert to the possibility (the probability) that this will happen on occasion can keep them at-the-ready to provide important support in the moment. Actually planning for musical transitions when you know you will need one (as in the case of children moving up and back) is also a good idea. Musical transitions can also be planned for in rehearsal when you see the need to move the energy from one dynamic to another.

All of these scenarios require a sensibility about *what* to play in the transitions. This requires musicians to develop a keen awareness of the flow of the overall narrative. What energy is happening at the moment? Do we need to continue that energy, or does it need to move toward a "resolve?" Do we need a sense of anticipation and suspense? Will we bring in an echo of the theme song, or will we stick with a softer version of what we just did musically? What musical component is coming up, and can we use an extended introduction to fill the transition?

These questions and choices are akin to how film composers discern the sonic texture of a moment.[85] Many musical components combine in countless ways to create various dramatic and energetic effects: *pitch* (determined by frequency of vibration); *harmonics* (the complex motion frequency wave forms creates as an object vibrates that determines the pleasantness of the resultant sound); *timbre* (the combination of frequency, harmonics, and overtones that gives each sound its unique coloring and character); *loudness* (determined by the intensity of the sound stimulus); and *rhythm* (a recurring sound that alternates between strong and weak elements). "Sound envelope" (or phrasing) components include: *attack* (when the sound begins and reaches its peak later, whether quickly or slowly); *sustain* (when the sound remains steady and avoids sudden bursts of level changes); and *decay* (when the sound decays to silence with a decrease in amplitude of the vibrating force).[86]

An example of music's ability to mold and transform the dynamics of a moment is the "toilet bowl scene" in *Under the Tuscan Sun*. We are introduced to the idea that work on the house is in full swing with a shot of the workers constructing a wall outside, accompanied by the theme music in a rhythmically bouncy, energetic, and light mood. The scene cuts to Frances in her library, working at her computer, suggesting that her writer's block has passed and the creativity is beginning to flow once again. She stops to reflect, and then her attention is pulled to a point off-camera. The music transitions in that reflective moment, changing from the rhythmic quality that evoked movement to a completely a-rhythmic and sustained note as our anticipation is raised about what has caught her attention. We don't yet see it. The elongated musical treatment is empathizing with Frances' curiosity and our own, stretching and slowing time as she gets up and moves slowly toward the sound. What we

See Chuck Bell and I discuss these choices at thinklikeafilmmaker.com.

finally see is the iconic spigot that is a symbol throughout the movie. This time it is dripping slowly into the bucket beneath it. The suspense is broken by a character's voice calling out to Frances to come check out the toilet bowl, but the moment and symbol associated has already made its impact—things are beginning to flow again in Frances' life. In a very short amount of time, the music created various emotional encounters with the story through the use of the musical components making up the "sonic texture."

If, at this point, you are dizzy with new ways to think about the role of a musician in worship, I would encourage you to start with simply paying attention to the music during transitions, aiding smooth transitions and keeping us "in the story" with the use of music. The change from what I call "herky-jerky" worship to an entire experience that moves us along the highs and lows of a spiritual journey can make one of the most profound, immediate, and well-received differences for your congregation.

CONGREGATIONAL MUSIC-MAKING

There is no formula for picking hymns and songs every Sunday. Vibrant and sensory-rich worship comes in many forms and utilizes various kinds of music and musicians within it. One "style" or repertoire of music is not better or "more worshipful" than another. One size does not fit all churches or all Sundays or all liturgical seasons of the year. There's merit in balancing what feels "indigenous" (familiar and rooted) to the community with that which will stretch them in ways that expand their worldview and spiritual formation.

Some people choose congregational song mostly for the content and how it fits the message. While this ensures cognitive cohesion, sometimes it can lack sensitivity to the mood of the moment, or the melody itself might be difficult to sing. I've seen pastors insist on choosing hymns and songs because they want control of content, yet their lack of musical training can derail a good experience of that very content when the congregation stumbles through unfamiliar or difficult melody lines. Sometimes choices will be made based on familiarity or what is most popular at the time. This focus might ensure good participation in singing but may derail the focus of the message. This can happen easily when music directors are making choices without enough collaboration with pastors. I've seen this many times in my consulting career, but for various reasons. It may be that music directors prefer to do what they like or feel competent in, and sometimes it is because pastors aren't working far enough ahead to communicate the proposed message in time for musicians to adequately rehearse. In either case, the "siloed" effect works against the best interests of the community.

In actuality, choosing congregational song is a matrix of several factors. Cognitive content (articulated theology and story) is important. A balance of familiar and new repertoire is important. Considering the liturgical purpose of the moment is important. But I believe it is also important to understand the actual effect that *hearing music and singing* has on the congregation in order to be able to make choices that immerse us in the story, thereby creating unforgettable messages that are resonating deeply within our very bodies.

Song "charges" the body, so says liturgical theologian Bruce T. Morrill.[87] It heightens awareness and receptivity as well as helps the assembly orient itself. Self-awareness, awareness of others, as well as a sense of the holy are heightened through the vibrations of sound. A congregation singing together produces "some degree of synchrony among their bodies as their heartbeats and breath process the entraining rhythm, pulse, and pace of the music."[88] The quality of the community's sharing the word of God and its sense of the living God in their midst depend in large part on the kinds of "vibrations" present in ritual music.[89] For instance, "rising pitch can energize, rally listeners together for the sake of some joint activity or cause. Falling pitch can relax and soothe listeners, make them turn inward and focus on their thoughts and feelings … our experience of what we physically have to do to produce a particular sound creates a meaning potential for that sound."[90] We create tense sounds by tensing our musculature. When we get excited, our vocal tones tend to ascend, and we increase our vocal effort. As we descend in pitch, we relax the effort, and the effect is calming. The rate and use of our breath can denote intimacy or excitement. When we need to be heard—gain more power—we often get louder and higher in intensity.[91]

In other words, the "sense of the living God" and the meanings we attach to that sense have a kinesthetic quality derived from our experience of the rhythm, pulse, and pace of a piece of music—whether heard or sung. Energy dynamics involve diverse frequencies of vibrations which, in turn, "charge" the body in a diversity of ways. The pattern and quality of those vibrations impacts mood, forms dispositions, and fosters habits and memories "that shape the outlook and ethical action of persons."[92] In other words, both *what* we sing (the content) and *how* we sing it (the dynamics, vibrations, mood, and tone) make a difference for how the story enters our consciousness and shapes us.

Anyone who has been to my workshops knows that I travel everywhere with a West African drum called a *djembe*. It is a drum that has been with me since I graduated from seminary 20 years ago. Experiencing rhythm together in worship can connect a group faster than anything I know. In my PhD research, I began to be fascinated with this idea that our very bodies respond to the stimuli of different rhythms. Because we now have significant studies that substantiate the holistic connection between our bodies, minds, and spirits, I had an inkling that the rhythms

For more on drumming in worship, see thinklikeafilmmaker.com.

of our bodies have something to do with how much we resonate with certain kinds of music and styles of worship. And I surmised that paying attention to how encountering various rhythms actually form us spiritually could help us understand the effects of our worship design choices. And so in my dissertation, I wrote about what I call "Primal Patterns," based on a theory in the field of kinesiology and the neuromuscular research of Josephine Rathbone, Valerie Hunt, and Sally Fitt, and the movement analysis of Betsy Wetzig. In a nutshell, those scientists who study human movement have declared that we don't all march to the beat of the same drummer! We move through the world with a set of rhythms that feel more "indigenous" or familiar and comfortable to us. These "home patterns" are determined by

To read a more academic article on this subject, go to thinklikeafilmmaker.com.

the force and timing with which the nerve cells of our muscular system are firing off. My mother moves through the world with an explosive and highly active pace that has slowed little even as she approaches her mid-seventies. This kind of energy is "home" for her, meaning that she has the most energy at this pace as well as the most relaxation—this energy is "effortless"—to her. Others would be exhausted by her rhythms of life. Indeed, her home pattern is not mine. I can certainly engage that kind of energy (we all have the ability to do so), but it will zap my energetic resources much more quickly.

My mother's rhythmic home pattern is one of four "primal patterns" that the researchers identified. We can look at the music we make in these four categories as well because we *are* bodies at worship—these same rhythms come through in the music we make and sing. And we can see how each is important to consider when choosing congregational song. If you move through the world with "things to get done," making lists and moving with purpose and goal like my mother, you have the *Thrust* energy dynamic. The gifts of this dynamic are decisive movement toward a goal, passion for change, and rallying toward action. Theologically, this dynamic shows up in stories of a transformational God—a God "on the move" who makes a way out of no way. This is music that inspires us to action. These songs often have a driving beat meant to be sung strongly and with conviction. They are most successfully used after a stirring invitation to acts of justice in a sermon or at the close of a service. Some examples of the *Thrust* dynamic in congregational song are "We Are Marching in the Light of God," "What Does the Lord Require of You?" "Thrive," "For Everyone Born,"—all of which have themes of justice in their content, driving beats, and soaring melodies. Any hymn or song that ends with an exclamation point musically, especially with an ascending melody in the last phrase (essentially anything that feels like it needs a fireworks show at the end), is most likely in this energetic category. In singing these songs together, we feel the "thrust" of energy needed to accomplish our work in making this world a better place. These would not be good choices if an introspective mood is what you are after. And equally important as choosing the right moment in the worship for these kinds of songs is leading them strongly, in ways that encourage people to join in with confidence and vigor that matches the intent.

If you move with reserve, are perhaps careful or exacting in your movement, like for things to be organized and in order, and are very satisfied to find a way to do something and repeat it, you are moving through the world in the *Shape* pattern. This dynamic focuses less on getting to a goal and more on proper structure and form. The gift of *Shape* in worship is that it communicates a theological image of a God that is eternal, steadfast, and enduring. This is very different from the theology described above that thrives on change. This is a firm foundation—God who is "rock"—the same yesterday, today, and tomorrow. Indeed, music that has a melody whose phrasing lands squarely and resolved in a descending pattern evokes this solid dynamic. The hymns "The Church's One Foundation" and "Holy, Holy, Holy" fit this bill as well as many musical doxologies. Hymns with strong four-part harmonies communicate a sense of *Shape* as we sense that each part contributes to the whole. This is music that connects us to the timeless, ageless foundations of faith. Song leadership in this pattern will more likely utilize schooled gestures of conducting that facilitate the congregation joining their voices in a solid rhythm together.

The next pattern involves music that creates celebration, community, and relationship—the *Swing* pattern of energy. Indeed, for those whose home pattern is *Swing,* it is difficult not to sway, rocking from one foot to another, especially in the presence of music. Because of the back-and-forth nature of this energy pattern, if you like to have your hands in many projects and love to make connections with others, this is likely your home. Music in this style can be an upbeat Caribbean tune like

"Halle, Halle," the jazz, gospel, or blues-influenced feel of "Stand by Me" or the slow rocking of a ballad like "Sanctuary." This musical style offers fluidity in what are too often immobile and stiff worship postures. This dynamic is often the most difficult to achieve in congregations where worship habits have not permitted hand-clapping exuberance. Like the image of a relational God that this energy dynamic models, song leading in this style will need to lean towards the informal, being relational and encouraging, giving permission for the heights and depths of our spiritual journey to be present.

The last of the four patterns embodies a "go with the flow" attitude. Persons whose home pattern lies here will be more indirect in focus, preferring the "big picture" to the details and will be more apt to meandering than any of the other patterns. The *Hang* pattern of energy in music draws us close to the "still small voice" of God and the deep wells of our souls. It is content with prolonged silence and meditative singing such as the repetitive and cyclical nature of songs from Taizé (a community in France that produces chant-like compositions for worship). This dynamic is one that most North-American congregations can use more of. Too often we pack our worship with so much that we don't incorporate a contemplative dynamic that can give us time to "dwell" with the Holy. Worship feels as rushed as our everyday lives rather than unhurried, like a place to "practice" the calming presence of the Spirit that we so desperately need in order to be spiritually renewed. This musical dynamic facilitates a feeling of "hang" time, where there is nowhere else to be except resting in the presence of God. Cyclical songs (repetitive refrains such as those from the Taizé community or contemporary music genre) draw us deeper, slow our breathing, and even offer us moments of visionary insight. This energy is one that can lead us into or out of times of silence. Song leadership in this pattern will be subtle—perhaps a simple gesture to get us going or to indicate a *decrescendo* or *ritard* to the end.

As our bodies encounter these various dynamics through all the worship arts (we can draw examples of color and movement and even the timing of the progression of projected media as well as music), we are spiritually formed in various ways. We are formed as people who come to their feet, who are ready for action, inspired for action *(Thrust* energy). We are formed as people who name and claim God's reality, who embody the vision of the reign of God, who share with others the sure foundation that is God (*Shape* energy). We are formed as people who love deeply, relate personally and intimately, who feel the ebbs and flows of life and emotion, and respond to a hurting world (*Swing* energy). And we are formed as those who can listen for the still, small voice leading and guiding us—able to simply "be" present, steeped in awe-filled moments, guiding others to the presence of the ever-mysterious God (*Hang* energy).

As we "synch up" with the energies of worship, of each other, and, ultimately, of God, patterns of action are formed. In a word, we are "moved." And so, as we consider the criteria for the choice of congregational song—indeed any musical offering that is heard, played, or sung—the energy that is produced by that music is an important consideration. When the energy patterns and their effects on us coincide with the intent of the message, the "feel" of the series and the attribute of the holy that we are focusing on for this moment (the theology), we experience that message more fully, more meaningfully, more memorably. Choosing music becomes more about spiritual formation than simply filling in a slot. And evaluating our selections over time can help us see where we may be too narrow theologically. No one genre of music is "shallow" in and of itself. But too much of a good thing is still too much. Any one of these patterns can go into "override" to the exclusion of others, creating monotony in our musical repertoire and blandness in our theological diet. The pounding energy of the *Thrust* dynamic can become relentless if used too much. Many of our churches have certainly *Shaped* themselves to death with a steady diet of four-stanza hymns. Singing too many songs about my "personal relationship with Jesus" is the *Swing* dynamic gone toxic. And too much "meandering" in a *Hang* energy can

See a video of Marcia teaching about the Primal Patterns at thinklikeafilmmaker.com.

begin to feel indecisive and lost. The point is not to have a little of everything every Sunday, as if worship were a smorgasbord. Rather, the "feel" of the message of a series or of the liturgical year will drive various dynamics to become more or less prominent at various times over the course of a year. The Primal Patterns construct can help us make sure we are well-rounded in telling the whole of the narrative over time.

As you have seen in our examples of the patterns, *how we lead* the congregation in their performance of the music is equally as important. The number-one purpose of a song leader is to model the energy we want back from the congregation. Because we have amazing "mirror neurons" that enable us to soak up and entrain with the energy around us, congregations led by a sensitive leader (one who is modeling the preferred dynamic that matches the intent of the song) will sing more fully. When choral directors want their singers to crescendo in volume and dynamic, their bodies take on that energy in order to spark and encourage a similar response in the choir. Good song leaders will treat the congregation like a choir, and congregations will generally respond in kind. When people can hear each other sing, they also will sing out more fully. There are various reasons why congregations may be anemic in their singing. The space itself may not be resonant, and people may not be able to hear each other. No one will sing out if it feels like they are singing alone. In spaces like this, it is even more important to have a song leader amplified. Or it could be that the accompanying instruments are too overbearing, making it difficult for us to hear one another. This applies to organists as much as it does to bands. One of the most energizing moments in rock concerts is when the solo artist points the microphone at the audience and stops singing, and the crowd hears itself singing out the well-loved lyrics. The crowd goes wild as their sense of each other and the common experience heightens, bonds, and excites them.

Singing *a cappella* often can be a way to build up the sense of "the whole" in worship, whether a whole song, refrain, or simply one verse. I had some training in Bobby McFerrin's "circle singing" process and have begun to use this with congregations. One part of the congregation is given a musical phrase to sing and keep repeating, and then the leader moves on to another portion of the group to overlay another musical phrase on top of that. The process continues with another couple of segments of the group until all are singing parts that overlap, creating a delightful experience of collaboration. Chants in parts, rounds, canons, verses sung only by women and then only by men, sprinkling a hymn with a verse sung by the children's choir—all these techniques develop an active, singing congregation whose experience of making music together can ignite other active, collaborative, supportive attitudes outside of their worship.

When all the musical artists—whether related to vocal or instrumental music—have a bigger picture of the powerful role of music in the storytelling endeavor, they begin to "think like a composer" of film scores. Sensitivity to dynamics, a sense of flow and mood-setting, and collaboration with the other ritual artists can make for musical nuance that has a powerful impact on our praise, prayer, and proclamation.

Chapter 6

Think Like a Cinematographer:
Media Arts in Worship

In the late 1960s, the term "multi-media" was coined to convey specifically the combination of sound, light and projection. My own introduction to multi-media performance was in my first career as a professional dancer in the Nikolais Dance Theater. Alwin Nikolais ("Nik") was a pioneer of combining music, dance, lighting, and projection in the 1950s and beyond. He had the first MOOG synthesizer, on which he created all his own music, and he put colored paper on glass slides in order to project textures, not only on walls and the backdrop of the stage but on the dancers themselves. We traveled with dozens of slide projectors that were hung and stationed on the floor to create timed effects much before the advent of LCD projectors timed by computer programs. Nik played with shape, motion, and color in order to create environments of wonder, awe, and delight. As an international sensation throughout his career, he was the "grandfather" of companies like Pilobolus, Momix, Blue Man Group, and many of the effects used by Cirque de Soleil. I remember seeing his company perform when I was a college dance student. I was absolutely mesmerized and hooked. Within two years, I had the great privilege of landing a role in that company and traveling and teaching with Nik for several years. I never lost my

See photos of Nikolais' work at thinklikeafilmmaker.com.

awe for his multi-media work. Unlike other cho-reographers, he was paying attention to not only communicating through the dancers themselves, he also knew that the magical environment he cre-ated for them to dance in would have a profound effect on the audience.

Cinematographers (directors of photography) "paint with light." As we saw in the visual arts chapter, art directors choose colors and textures and objects in order to create a "dominant mood, to give a sense of completeness to the whole film; cameramen choose a particular color of light for the same reasons."[93] They choose camera angles, speed of motion, lighting for the purpose of capturing the "ethos" (feel), move-ment, and rhythm of the story. Much like Nik's attention to the whole environment, they capture "the world" of the story, helping us to feel part of it in a visceral way.

THE ART OF CREATING A "WORLD"

My own love of creating sensory-rich environments in worship— from the basic to the very complex— is deeply influenced by my time with Nik. Simply using media projection for words alone never crossed my mind. To my thinking, if all we do is project static images and words on a screen, we are just creating a really big bulletin. Yes, it may be informational, but is it artistic and, therefore, inspirational? Further, when those who choose images for projection simply pick stock images unrelated to the palette being utilized by the rest of the ritual artists, we can end up with competing art forms that distract from, rather than enhance, the main thing … the message.

When Nik created a piece, he paid close attention to how all the media worked together as one palette. Granted, as an avant-garde artist in the late 20th century, he was not big on telling stories or conveying emotion, but he was adamant about creating a "world" into which the audience would be immersed. His example taught me to ask myself this question at the beginning of the design process for a worship series: "Based on the main message, what is the world into which we will enter for this spiritual journey?" This question leads me to the discerning process about what the sanctuary will look, sound, and feel like—which is a collaborative conversation with the whole team, especially the visual artists, who will work with the tangible, visual elements of the space, and music artists, who are creating a "sonic landscape" that sets an overall "tone" for the series. How do media artists contribute?

Under the Tuscan Sun is a story about transformation. It is a "character piece" and, seemingly, the main character is Frances—or *is* she the only "main character?" The house itself becomes a metaphor—a symbol—of Frances' own transformation. Having arrived in Italy after an awful divorce and in the midst of writer's block, she initially encounters the house that she has impulsively purchased in dimly lit and dusty-colored camera shots. Through this lens we see holes in the ceiling, empty wine bottles, and dried-up grapevines. Her first days in the house are characterized by rain and a ferocious storm. All of these design choices create a world that point toward the tempestuous and depressed state of her soul. There is nothing here of the gorgeous, vivid color and bright intensity that comes later as the transformation is underway, or the brightest, most colorful scene of all—the wedding reception in the voluptuous gardens of the house at its completion. The story is communicated through rich symbolism—some of which is dependent upon the lighting and color ratio and particular lenses—the art of cinematographer Geoffrey Simpson (for which he garnered praise).

The job of media artists is attending to the "palette" of image and color, movement and rhythm, sound quality and sound effect that will best support and convey the message. "Overall, the 'look' of a picture can create emotional expectations … the look creates an emotional space that allows for a certain range of emotional response."[94] The range of emotional response in Lent will not want to hit the kind of emotional "highs" that we will feel in the Easter season. As the story moves from introspection and wilderness wandering to resurrected hope and joy, like a cinematographer who chooses the lens through which we experience the story, media artists will choose color for series' slide templates and lighting choices that create a sense of transformation in the "emotional space" of the congregation.

For a long time, most of our attention has focused on the front of the worship space as the "canvas." However, like our discussion in the visual arts chapter, more immersive communication strategies invite us to consider the whole of the worship space in our planning. Tangible, visual elements may be repeated alongside walls or flown overhead. The entry to the worship space may introduce us to symbols we want people to engage with up-close. Media artists will want to work with the visual artists to highlight these with special lighting to create shadows and contrast or by taking photos of the tangible visuals to use on screens or environmental projection.

Besides creating a "world" for the series itself, each moment of the worship experience will be filled with considerations for media artists. Would this segment of prayer-time be aided by dimming the lights as we move to a more intra-personal and meditative experience? With what timing should the slides progress for this song, depending on its tempo and feel? Where is the focus of the congregation at this moment, and do we need to keep the image on the screen static so we don't draw attention? Is this an opportunity for the moving imagery on the screen to be the focal point, taking us deeper into the message visually?

These are all questions that require an artist's craft, intuition, and intention. For too long, audio/visual personnel and volunteers have not been understood to be an integral part of the worship team. Projections and word slides and sound board volunteers did their work without the benefit of more participation in the process of design and rehearsal. Their jobs have been considered "technical" and treated differently than the artistry of the choir, band, or preacher. This is changing along with the advances in the aesthetics of the media art form. When multi-media began to hit churches in the contemporary worship movement of the late 20th century, graphic art aesthetics were enamored with cartoon-like clip art, and projections served more like enlarged bulletins. Images were static and sparse, especially with overhead projectors being the first step for many of us. And then when video players hit the scene, projecting movie clips for sermon illustrations was all the rage, even if we had to roll a TV into the sanctuary to do it and cue it up to the right place. Then computers and LCD projectors became more accessible and affordable, and we transferred clip art and movie clips to this technology. But we've come a long way, and so much more is possible now. The aesthetics of graphic art have become much more sophisticated with the ease of transferring photography to presentation software in mere minutes or less. And moving images, synthesized or filmed, have become truly artful and used as backdrops for lyrics, as moving "texture" on screens or directly on walls. Likewise, ritual artists who create video pieces based on scripture and liturgy are transforming the way media functions—not solely as "background" or support for other art forms but as proclamation of the Word.

New terminology for media artists has emerged as media-theologians have begun to influence worship forms. "Visual worship leader," "curator" of visual experiences and "worship VJ" (visual jockey) are some prominent descriptors of the shift from "techies" to artists. Stephen Proctor, a pioneer in this movement, says,

> A visual worship leader takes on a new responsibility: recognizing the powerful impact visual imagery can have on

a worshiping congregation, stewarding that awareness well, and being intentional about every visual aspect of your worship gathering.[95]

Stephen's message is that just as a musical leader guides the musical experience of the congregation toward the message, so, too, does the "visual jockey" create an atmosphere and tell a story, especially as worship becomes more sensory-rich, multi-layered, and non-linear (for instance, those times when we invite a congregation to prayer stations and extended times of engaging in ritual action). "More and more, those who are designing, planning, and leading worship are identifying with the title 'worship curator' and seeing themselves as 'makers of context' rather than simply 'presenters of content.'"[96] The media arts can help place us in the context of the story through a still or moving image, for

See a video clip at thinklikeafilmmaker.com.

example, of the shoreline of the Sea of Galilee and sound effect of a brewing storm (read about this example in the music chapter which involved the close collaboration of media, music, visual, and dramatic artists). In larger, more contemporary-genre churches, a worshipVJ's responsibilities may be more extensive than that of a smaller church that is just beginning to use projected images. But the identity of those who choose and execute the visual experience is the same no matter how simple or complex—"displaying imagery with a discerning spirit."[97]

VISUAL SUPPORT FOR HOLY SPACE

The first forays in the development of projection technology for worship was "for the sake of better communications, evangelism, or increased congregational participation, not for the creation of liturgical art."[98] Still, many churches' first attempt at utilizing this technology is focused more on its role in providing information—announcements, words to songs, and liturgy. But if a production designer for film operated in this way, the lighting, sound, and lens choices would be driven primarily by the need to make sure the audience can see and hear. When we think like a filmmaker, we begin from a place of understanding support to mean further immersion in the story. Projection of the information can be infused with inspiration, making the slides we create more artful. I have fallen in love with the media art form and love to produce media art for worship, but I won't pretend to be the expert on its many technical facets. There are many good resources to train media artists in the particulars of working with the technology. Let me simply share what I have learned that can jumpstart your practice or offer another perspective for what you already do.

Projections don't have to feel "foreign" to the space. If you have the gift of blank walls on which to project, there is no reason to have screens installed. The images are there when you need them and not there when you don't. Projection surfaces have also become more diverse and creative. I've projected on stretched lycra in various shapes, white "scrim" fabric hanging from the ceiling, and screens that are lightweight fabric stretched over frames like a pillowcase that easily go up and come down off of walls when needed. The application of highly-reflective paint produced specifically for this purpose can make any surface an economical possibility for projection, although simple neutral colors on walls, especially in smaller spaces, usually provides a fine-looking projected image.[99]

Another strategy that I have taken great pleasure in doing in order to make screens more compatible with existing worship space is to take high-quality photographs of the architecture, windows, and artwork present in the space already and incorporate it into the projected images. Close-ups of stained glass details that the naked eye could never comprehend because of the distance are brought into sharp relief, offering the congregation an enhanced way of experiencing the art already in the room. A church I consulted with a few years ago had a screen that electronically raised and lowered during the worship with an awful loud noise, while everyone sat and watched it do so. They were desperate to figure out how to eliminate this distraction from their worship. They wanted it to go up when the screen wasn't in use because they liked seeing the cross that hung on the wall behind it. They were engaged in an "either/or" debate—to keep the screen or not. When I arrived, I experimented with inserting a photo of the actual cross perfectly proportioned in the slide to match its position behind the screen. When we used it that Sunday, the congregation gasped (in a good way) when we projected the image, realizing that the symbol could be experienced without multiple interruptions to the flow of worship.

I can't emphasize enough the collaboration of media artists with visual artists, who are caring for the tangible, visual symbolism. Too often I see great care going into the "feel" of the room through fabric colors, textures, and objects that bring an aesthetic that supports the message, but then slide backgrounds for projected media are chosen from the limited stock that came with the presentation software and may not complement the setting—or may downright clash with it. Digital photography has created the ability to almost instantaneously create backgrounds out of the customized palette you already have. What this means is that when I am preparing for a series, I will go ahead and insert all the words needed for songs and liturgy as soon as the scripts for the whole series are done. I use white letters on a black background because this is likely the color the text will be. White letters on a darker background are easier on the eye. The opposite is fine to use for when background images are light in color, but I tend to make that the exception. I go ahead and give all the words a drop shadow effect because when I add the background image, the drop shadow helps lift the words off the image, allowing better articulation for the eye. I don't worry about placement in the frame yet since I'm not sure what the background will be, and I don't worry about font style just yet until I know more about the feel of space (although font style should ultimately be about readability, not simply design).[100]

When the visual artists begin to work on their installation of fabrics and objects, I begin to take photos. Some photos will be shot very close-up so that I'm getting mostly a visual "negative space" (a solid or slightly textured space to put words on) with some visual interest on the edges as a kind of border. I'm always shooting the photos with an eye for "where would the words go on this shot?" I take photos of candles (especially if their surroundings fade into black) in the visual installation so that when they are on the screen, we are seeing the pattern of the physical candles in the space repeated on the screens. I also take photos of the visual installation that don't have as much "negative space" and use a cropped portion of it as a bottom or side border on a black slide. I also look for a good full-screen image of the visuals that I can use with a section title such as "Prayers of the People." Sometimes the photos will need enhancement such as slight blurs on the edges or another special effect, but generally these can be done right in the photo application installed on your phone or computer.

Basically, I'm creating a template of background images based on the actual visuals in the room that can be used throughout the series, providing continuity for the series and continuity with the rest of the room. This does not mean that I *only* use those template slides, but it gives us a base—a recognizable "brand," so to speak, for the series. It is also true that I have been inspired for the tangible, visual design by templates from one of the many stock companies producing projection backgrounds (still and motion). The point is to be sure that the two art forms are communicating and supporting one another and that what is on the screen feels "indigenous" to the room.

See examples and resources for creating backgrounds from your own photos at thinklikeafilmmaker.com.

On the other hand, media arts may transform the room into a completely "other" environment. One of the most exciting things I see happening in the media arts now is something that Nikolais did decades ago—essentially coloring outside the lines of the screen surface and onto the surfaces of the walls and ceilings. In other words, some churches are now utilizing multiple-projector systems on much bigger surfaces than just the two side screens or one middle screen we installed 20 years ago. If you have one of these plain-walled worship facilities that became popular with the emergence of the contemporary worship movement, you are in luck, because "triple-wide media" can help you create any environment and immerse the congregation in a "world" just like Nik was doing in his theatrical productions. Multiple projectors are hung and networked together so that a very large image can be spread out over a large surface—called "environmental projection."

I had the pleasure of using this technology at one of the General Conferences of the United Methodist Church for which I designed worship. Rather than use only the stock images of the company we were contracting with, I also wanted to integrate the images related to our theme (the "shoreline" anchor image I previously mentioned) and the actual tangible, visual art objects that we would be using in the space. I wanted to blur the boundaries between screen graphics, our immediate space (a generic expo hall), the water and shoreline just outside the conference space at our location in Florida, and the narrative of Jesus at the shoreline of the Sea of Galilee. So about a month before the conference, we took the "holy hardware" (objects and fabric for the tangible, visual installation) that my collaborator, Todd Pick, had collected, and we went out to the shoreline to do a photo and video shoot of these things on the beach and in the water. The effect was amazing, creating a seamless palette of imagery that located us both in our immediate environment and in the faith story. Every worship experience of the conference featured still photos and video footage across a ninety-foot expanse of projection surface that echoed the beautiful altar/table settings physically on the platform. While we were filming that day at the beach, large sea birds (egrets or cranes) had landed next to the vases and stood very still for quite a while. Then they began to walk slowly around them and eventually flew off in a dramatic display of their large wings lifting them in flight. We decided to use that footage, slowed way down, on the large digital backdrop during morning prayer the day those same large vases would be on the platform in the visual installation. Seeing the vases echoed in the video footage and physically before us in worship was sensory-rich. But then add the moment when, in the midst of a spoken

See images from this conference at thinklikeafilmmaker.com.

meditation inviting the Spirit to lift us, the great birds took off in slow-motion flight across 90 feet of digital backdrop, and ... well, you can imagine how the message became verbal, visual, *and* visceral.

Camron Ware is one of the foremost experts on environmental projection.[101] In our interview with him for the Worship Design Studio resource library, Camron describes the roots of this art form. Rather than being inspired by the IMAX film phenomenon, environmental projection for churches came from a desire to reach back to the sensory-rich experience of ancient cathedrals, when the message was proclaimed not just through words but tapestries and frescoes and stained glass. Indeed, when I ask people about some of their most profound worship experiences, they describe worship at camp, or a retreat or maybe on vacation in one of those massive cathedrals in Europe, or at a worship experience outside. And when I ask them what about that experience was meaningful, they describe the environment as being really significant; the environment drew them closer to God because they were immersed in the awe and wonder of creation, of a forest, of sun coming in a stained-glass window and streaming to a cathedral floor, of a starlit night or a candlelit chapel.

As we talked about the origins of "story" in Chapter One, we remember how our human ancestors found the most opportune times and places for their stories and rituals to be experienced—in a cave with light and sound amplified because of the natural chamber or around a campfire at night, where the flickering light created a sphere of attention. Environmental projection in worship creates the same wonder and delight of being surrounded—immersed—in the glory and mystery of the Holy. What filmmakers know about audiences' desire to be "in the story" applies to the ways media artists, like cinematographers, can carry on the tradition of creating the best possible environment for encountering the Word.

If you are a church with the resources and space to consider environmental projection, I would not hesitate to investigate the possibilities. But if you are one of the majority of churches that don't have a large expanse to project upon—or perhaps even any blank walls at all—and if your worship space has a lot of natural light spilling into it, this doesn't mean that you can't utilize environmental projection. Play with some portable projectors in your space. See what it looks like to project a forest or even a Hubble space photograph over your existing architecture at night. Imagine how utilizing a star-lit night slide from a projector pointed at your ceiling could create an immersive environment on Christmas Eve. Think about putting extra effort into creating Holy Week services that utilize projected images in various places around the sanctuary. Play with this idea in a basement or smaller room setting, where you can control the light, perhaps for a special series of services or youth events. You may even be inspired to begin an alternative worship time at night for a season to take advantage of these techniques.

VISUAL LITURGY, VISUAL WORD

Supporting the verbal artists by projecting liturgy and scripture is another common usage of projected media. Again, too often I see these functions taking on a didactic rather than artistic quality. There is nothing wrong with putting entire scripture passages on the screen in paragraph form for people to follow along with the reader, especially if the preacher will be doing some unpacking of that text in an interesting way. But a consistent diet of this isn't adding anything special to the visual and aural quality of encountering the story. Just as adding music underneath a reading can help focus our attention on the underlying emotion of the story rather than just the comprehension of the words, the right images on the screen accompanying only *some* of the main phrases of the passage will be more engaging and communicate the text more powerfully.

No one does this better at this time than Travis Reed at The Work of the People (TWOTP), an independent ecumenical platform that produces and publishes multimedia "to stir imagination, spark discussion, and move people toward discovery and transformation." Travis is creating "content that doesn't decorate but *declares*."[102] Their visual liturgy spans from scripture to prayers, blessings, and poetry (they also have an impressive collection of video reflections by prominent theologians). I've used and recommended their work for years because it truly embodies how media arts for worship and the techniques of filmmaking converge for powerful, prophetic proclamation of the Word. Besides their fully curated visual liturgy, complete with text, voiceovers, musical underscoring, and moving imagery, they also provide a library of loops without sound that are wonderful to use as a base for making your own visual liturgy. One of our Worship Design Studio series is called "A Future with Hope." The anchor image (the grounding metaphors for the series) is a tree, but, more specifically, seedlings whose growth symbolizes future hope. I've used Travis' video footage of gardens and someone digging in the earth, planting a seedling, and washing their hands with the Jeremiah "future with hope" scripture read as bits and fragments of the words ("plans for you ..." "plans for peace ..." "I will listen to you ..."

"you will find me …") fade in and out over the images on-screen in time with the reading. The footage then continues to play as a soloist sings Mark Miller's "Sower Song." When I designed the series "Gifts of the Dark Wood," I was thrilled to find several loops at TWOTP of a person walking and sitting contemplatively in the midst of a wooded area in winter. The bare branches and black-and-white effect in the video were perfectly suited to the visual installation of bare branches in the worship space, and the overall tone of the message and became a perfect visual complement to a time of prayer (it is important to invite people to pray with their eyes open, engaging the visual imagery on the screen as a meditative practice).

There are more free sources of photography at our disposal than ever before. Photographers are making their work available through creative commons licenses that require attribution but not a monetary fee or

For a list of favorite websites for free photos, go to thinklikeafilmmaker.com.

through websites that offer photos that have gone to the "morgue"—the term photo houses use to describe stock that they no longer want, many of which require no attribution at all. As soon as you have an anchor image and synopses for the frames of a worship series, invite people who love to hang out on the computer to search for images that evoke and inspire—all they need are some keywords from you.

The use of modern-day images alongside ancient faith narratives is a powerful storytelling tool. I developed a Holy Week experience based on a journal written by the 4th-century pilgrim Egeria. She dramatically describes the rituals of the church in Jerusalem at that time. I knew I wanted the experience to be media-rich and immersive because the Holy Week story is one that continues to repeat itself throughout history. I juxtaposed Egeria's description of the Palm Sunday parade with images of marches for justice in the 20th and 21st centuries around the world. After reading her description of hundreds of candles in the 4th-century Good Friday vigil, I designed a time to sit in somber silence watching images of modern-day candlelight vigils for victims of violence as dramatists slowly came to sit with candles at the base of the screen.

Sometimes we're not so blessed to find just the right thing in pre-packaged form—which actually can be a blessing in disguise. If we are really committed to a "plan together and plan ahead" strategy for worship design, we probably have time to produce something we just can't find already prepared. This is a wonderful way to get people involved in the media arts ministry who are not as keen on compiling slides or hitting buttons in the A/V booth. Consider developing a photography group that can take on commissioned projects for upcoming series. Imagine this scenario: after the Visionary (pastor) comes back from their retreat, they share the idea of a series on "Pilgrimage" coming up for the Lent season. The anchor images are paths and walking sticks. The church hiking group is going out to walk a trail through a wooded area that ends up at a high point in the surrounding hills. They are asked to take walking sticks along on this hike. The photography group (which may also have a video camera or two as well) goes along and snaps beautiful photos and takes video footage of the trek through the woods and of people sitting, looking out over the horizon at their destination. The media team works with the still and moving images—cropping, playing with color filters, applying special video effects like slow motion—to create a stock of imagery for the upcoming series. Now we've extended the artful enterprise to many persons—hikers, walking-stick makers, photographers, and media artists—whose connections to the images on the screen will be deeply embedded in their experience, which now symbolically expresses the spiritual journey of the theme.

I relish the opportunity, as a preacher, to combine the sermonic art form and the use of media arts. I don't think this has to be the rule or the exception. In fact, I think the message itself will dictate when adding components of the media arts will truly benefit the communication rather than act as an "add-on." When I do decide to use projected media within a sermon (actually, I always use it in my teaching and presenting), I want it to feel seamless and indigenous, and to add something energetic to what is said. Nancy Duarte leads a company that creates presentations and offers training based on something they call the VisualStory™ methodology, which "applies storytelling and visual thinking to craft persuasive communications designed to shift audience beliefs and behaviors."[103] Nancy believes that if you communicate an idea in a way that resonates, change will happen.[104] Powerful stories come to life with a combination of graphics, animation, and live-action footage. This is not to say that simply communicating verbally is not an option, but if that's what you do, you still have to provide concrete imagery and movement (see the verbal and dramatic arts chapters for more on this) that literally "moves" the hearers. For now, let's assume we are going to add visual media to the sermonic form. The process of creating flow and shape to any presentation is akin to the "storyboarding" technique many filmmakers use.

> Storyboarding helps you plan your visuals. Even though it sounds like a tool from the motion picture industry, don't let storyboarding intimidate you. Many of the concepts work in other forms of storytelling, like presentations. A filmmaker likes to visualize the entire movie before going into production. They'll usually tape the storyboard on a wall and begin by looking at the sequence, transitions, and framing—making sure it hangs together structurally, conceptually, and visually.[105]

When I am preparing to teach, preach, or give a presentation utilizing media arts, I begin by laying out the structure, highlighting the most salient points and imagining the visual symbols that will bring out the best in each section (storyboarding). In essence, I apply all the things I know about sensory-rich communication in worship to the subset of this 15–20 minute piece of communication (in the case of a sermon). When there is movement or a shift in the sermon, I'm going to mirror that with a shift in the visual. When I want people to focus intently on the story I am telling and on me telling it, I am *not* going to insert any transition in visuals on the screen—which *always* pulls attention away from the speaker and to the screen. And when I think an image or series of images can tell the story better and more economically than I can in verbal form, I let the images do their thing, and my verbal contribution is merely summative rather than descriptively detailed. I pay attention to the timing and dynamics of the transitions between slides, and I prefer to use my own remote to change them because I know my rhythms of speech. For instance, a slide that contains a quote can't appear before I have begun to speak it, or else the congregation is reading it while I'm finishing the introduction to it. A slide that serves as "punctuation" on a salient point or something that will be humorous has to be perfectly timed for maximum effect—just as timed as the rhythm of the speech itself. If you aren't controlling the progression of the slides yourself as the speaker, rehearsal with the media team will be imperative.

The possibilities are exciting, I believe. I have used still photography, video loops, brief excerpts of others speaking, snippets of music, movie scenes, you name it. When preachers begin to incorporate media arts, it can be electrifying as they collaborate with media artists to see messages come alive and congregations engaged in compelling ways. The point, as I hope you continue to get, is not to use "bells and whistles" for the sake of being "cutting edge," but to utilize all the communication tools at our disposal in the 21st century when they will authentically amplify the message.

So just as important as *when* to use media is when to refrain. "The idea of being intentional about our use of media is nothing new, but what about being intentional about *not* using our media?"[106] In the verbal arts chapter, I described a "layered sequence" using the 23rd Psalm and a song called "Shepherd Me, O God." At the beginning of the sequence, the piano begins to play softly as I invite people to imagine their favorite body of water—water being a strong image both in the Psalm and in the song. When I do this, I do not show a nice photo of a body of water on the screen, although I certainly could. Why? Because I want them to imagine *their* favorite body of water. Sometimes the best visual is the one living in our memories and imaginations. If we continually feed the congregation imagery chosen by us, we do not allow for their own interpretation. I also made this decision because the whole experience of the song and Psalm is a very *intra-personal* one. I want them to remain more inwardly focused. Changing images on the screen will draw us out of our inner story. Stephen Proctor says we can do "visual violence" when media creates too much noise and clutter. "It's also good to think about the idea of 'visual stillness,' where your atmosphere is simple and quiet for the eyes. You might use more still imagery instead of motions, and keep visual changes to a minimum so that you create an environment of rest and 'selah.' Less is always more."[107]

This is an important consideration when your media arts also include IMAG, an acronym that means "image magnification" through live camera work projected onto screens. When I am designing worship for a conference in which I know the still and moving imagery generated by media artists will also be flowing in concert with live cameras, I produce a tech script that includes highlighting important moments to capture on live camera (the movement of a procession that starts in the back or a person dipping their hand in water as they say, "Remember your baptism and be thankful"). My tech scripts also include moments when I *do not* want live camera to intrude on our experience. During a prayer I might suggest a static close-up on a candle, Bible, or other symbol until the prayer finishes. If people have been invited to engage with each other in conversation or in a ritual action that warrants privacy, this is not the time to be getting close-up shots of the congregation.

Through the camera lens

When directors and cinematographers work together to plan out shots for a movie, they take various degrees of distance into consideration. There are several fractions of these categories, but in general, filmmakers use a *long shot* (or *wide shot*) to allow us to see the actor in relationship to the environment—generally serving the purpose of "placing" us—helping us to know where action is taking place. *Medium shots* will show more of the actor, thus letting them communicate through gesture and bodily communication more effectively, and the audience will feel more of a sense of being in realistic proportion to them. *Close-up shots* are reserved for intimate moments when facial expressions are subtle and filmmakers want to invite audiences to the inner world of the character.[108] These same principles will apply to IMAG in the worship setting. There are times, as I mentioned above, that I want everyone to get a sense of the whole space and a procession moving through the entire body of worshipers. This requires a wide-enough shot for us to get the visceral feel of the community around us. When a presider is at the communion table and I want the congregation to feel like they are "at the table," a medium-shot can help us feel closer while still engaged with the gestures and postures of the presiders. Close-ups on speakers and singers will be most effective when the pulse of the moment is slow and intimate.

Camera crews can do their best when they are informed by an annotated script of the worship that empowers them to "dance" with the flow, action, and emotional landscape of the worship. This is true of all media artists. When a contemplative song is accompanied by word slides whose transition is a jarring cut rather than a carefully timed dissolve from one slide to another, the energy change distracts from our spiritual journey. It is essential that slides be checked by musicians for accurate spelling, line phrasing, and the timing of dissolve between song slides. When sound personnel are operating without a script to tell them which reader with what microphone is coming up next, congregants and reader/singer are likely to be distracted from the content and flow of the moment by the dreaded lag in amplification. Collaboration depends on timely and clear communication for all the pieces to complement one another.

PAINTING WITH LIGHT

Color and lighting contribute to the energy of the moment—whether that is a cool and calming energy or a bright, vibrant, and celebratory effect. Have you ever wondered why it is difficult to get the congregation to participate energetically in a dimly lit room or why you can't create intimacy and warmth under fluorescent lights? Ask a filmmaker why. The wrong lens on a camera or botched lighting on a set can call for an extra day of shooting just to correct it. It really is that important to the experience of the story.

Analyzing the light in your worship space is important to understanding what you have to work with and how it is affecting—good or bad—the feel of the room (see the description of analyzing your space in the visual arts chapter). "Light defines mood."[109] Does your lighting offer options? If you have a fully sunlit space, turn the lights on and off. Can you tell a difference? If you can, even this little bit of difference can offer the opportunity to differentiate between moments of outwardly-focused, bigger energy and inwardly-focused, meditative energy. Dimming the lights as we go into a contemplative time can frame the experience and encourage deepened participation as our pupils change and breathing slows. As lights come back up, so, too, does our bodily reaction move in an "upward" and outward direction. "The way a scene is lit influences both how we understand the scene—what we can see in it—and how we experience the scene emotionally."[110] If all you can do is install dimmer switches for overhead lighting, even that would make a difference.

If your space allows lots of control, are you utilizing it fully? The number of lighting instruments will determine how flexible your use of light is. Here are some basic things that I want to know as a worship designer when considering the light design for a worship experience in a new space. Do we have the ability to create "warm" or "cool" washes of light—which completely change mood—or are we dealing with one "feel" in the lighting? Is the lighting all *soft* and *diffused* in order to cover maximum territory (*overhead, front,* and *back lighting*), or do we also have the ability to utilize *hard light* for more dramatic effect in spots and for creating shadows and contrast? If so, where are those lights focused? What are my "playing areas"—in other words, are all the lights focused on the chancel/platform, or am I still lit if I want to lead or preach from the floor level, getting closer to the people? Do we have some "floating" instruments and LEDs to help highlight visual installations or give architectural interest to flat walls in the form of *up lights*? Do we have control of the *house lights* in the congregation so that we can raise them and see one another (and the preacher can see us) when we need to increase the interaction and energy in the room or lower to cloak us in darkness when the focus is elsewhere?

If you are a smaller church with some chandeliers overhead and a couple of spots—one on the pulpit and one on the table—and are almost belly-laughing by now, hold on. There are things that you can do to actively engage lighting as media art. A set of utilitarian floodlights and a set of under-cabinet pin-lights from the hardware store, along with a few battery-operated headlamps from the sporting goods store can go a long way. Light creates focus. The pin- and head-lamps will come in handy when you are asked to help the visual artists highlight their installations, shining light up through bowls of water, creating highlight and shadow on various objects and fabric. The floodlights are especially

Go to thinklikeafilmmaker.com for links and resources about lighting for worship.

wonderful for creating architectural interest in a bland space if you create simple boxes to hold them upright and place a few against the walls (or pipe-and-drape surface), creating columns of light from the floor. Lighting "gel" (colored transparent material) placed on top of the boxes gives you the flexibility to choose and change colors.

SOUND EFFECTS, SOUND SYSTEMS

Good amplification is the first thing that churches should invest in to enhance their worship, no matter the size of your space. Nothing is more distracting to congregations and to leaders than difficulty with sound systems. The irony of amplified sound is that when it works, we are not aware of it. "Sound [in film] has a subliminal role. Sound is working on its audience unconsciously."[111] Cinematographers, lighting designers, and sound engineers for film spend the largest percentage of their work in preparation for the actual moments of being on-set. They immerse themselves in the script and make their own lists of objects, actions, environments, emotions, and transitions. They draw visual maps of the flow of the story and its "sonic structure." They meet with the director to confirm choices and get feedback, and they create a "sound map" so they will be sure to have the right equipment for all aspects of the shoot and for sound effects needed in post-production.[112] Preparation for an excellent experience of sound is also necessary for the worship media artist. All of the preparation makes possible the invisibility of sound, ensuring we amplify in the best way possible without drawing attention to amplification.

Before we get to the use of sound systems, let's spend a moment on how media artists can contribute to the sonic landscape of worship. While media artists for worship might not be using this very much, the use of sound effect is also something we can learn from filmmakers. David Sonnenschein is an award-winning sound designer for films. His training for new sound designers includes not just the technical aspects of the role but also the need for creativity. Much the same as the way music affects us, sound effect can place us in the story and contribute to the emotional ethos or "feel."

> As the narrative in a film represents a state of being for the director, sound designer, character, and audience, it can be explicit (conscious) or implicit (unconscious). The poetic function of sound relates to the meaning of this state of being through allusion, i.e., its indirect significance. Like dreamscapes, the language of sound imagery has parallels to the figures of speech in our verbal tradition [simile, metaphor, allegory, etc.].[113]

The dripping spigot protruding out of a wall that appears several times during *Under the Tuscan Sun* has a very important symbolic role in the movie as it parallels the state of the main character's soul. The first time Frances tries to turn the faucet on, it squeaks. Whether that faucet on-set actually squeaked or not, the intentional inclusion of this sound effect helps us perceive, on a more visceral level, the absence of water. Later, the spigot begins to drip. The subtle sound effect of that drip helps us to notice and "get" this important beginning of transformation. The end of the movie features a deluge of water coming from the spigot with an appropriate gushing sound as well as the sound of the water hitting the floor. Sound effect has deepened our experience of the metaphor.

I am always on the lookout for opportunities to use sound effect … umm, "effectively." In the music chapter, I described the opening scene of a conference that used "shoreline" as our anchor image. As I was designing this worship, I wanted people to place themselves at the Sea of

Galilee. In my research, I found out that there is a reason why so many of the biblical stories describe storms "suddenly appearing" at this location. The geography of the lake and the hills around it frequently creates unexpected storms. Then I found out that the location of the conference (Tampa, Florida) actually has the largest number of lightning strikes per year of anywhere in the United States—and especially around the time the conference was to be held. So I determined that both the faith and life narrative would warrant the use of a storm in light, video, and sound effect. It was not simply a gratuitous use of drama to get a reaction. It had a profound effect in furthering the story emotionally and viscerally.

I have used a ticking clock in a "series trailer" (see more about trailers in Chapter Eight) for a Worship Design Studio series called "Busy: Reconnecting with an Unhurried God." The clock set up the visceral sensation related to the stress of a busy life, deadlines, and the passage of time—more of an *explicit* or "conscious" use of sound effect. It faded out and into more soothing music as the synopsis called us to reconnect to God. I have used the sound effect of footsteps (walking on crunchy gravel) underneath a reading about Jesus' walking with us and the walking alongside one another we are called to do. The sound effect I found on iTunes (a great place to search for sound effects) was too fast, creating a more harried feel, so we had to slow it down to match the pace of the poetry, making it a compatible choice. And of course, we had to try it with the reader for timing and sound level so it was more of a background accompaniment—more *implicit* or "subconscious" rather than something that would distract from the content of the poem.

Listen to examples of this at thinklikeafilmmaker.com.

I also enjoy creating ways that sound effects can "set the stage," so to speak, as people arrive. The same principles apply to sound effect that apply to musical "preludes"—What is the feel of the room when people enter, and how can this immediately help them enter the narrative? If we are doing a worship series that features our relationship with creation and nature in a prominent way, I might think about what nature sounds we can have playing as people arrive. Sound effect can also be produced and highlighted from live sounds such as water poured into the baptismal font, handbells ringing out in an unexpected but dramatically appropriate moment. You'll want to play with amplifying those sounds adequately if needed. Whatever the sounds that you choose, Sonnenschein reminds us that "noises can energize, release pain, and dissipate tension … but a sound can also bring about negative changes." Headaches, disequilibrium, stress, and internal effects that cause an unbalancing effect can occur if we aren't carefully choosing and testing out the volume and duration of the sound effects we use.[114] As in the case of the thunderous beginning I used at the conference, we had to let the thunder begin at a lower level and build so worship wasn't interrupted by paramedics! But keeping an "ear" out for when sound effects can enhance the message is a wonderfully creative endeavor that can help messages be unforgettable.

Sound, along with all the other media arts we have covered in this chapter, involves a lot more detailed technical knowledge than I can include here. So my goal is to simply express some of the things I've learned over the years related to an awareness of how sound affects worship and worship leaders. Firstly, is your sound system "good?" What I mean by this is, do you have quality *and* flexibility in your system? The quality of your system and microphones will depend on your size of room and needs (consults from reputable A/V companies are a must), but

For resource suggestions see thinklikeafilmmaker.com.

essentially we want speaking and singing voices and instrumentation to be amplified using microphones that bring out the best for those various purposes. Not all microphones do the same job. Directionality is important—being able to stand several people around a microphone and hear them without each person moving in front of it (*omnidirectional*) is helpful for dramatic readings with multiple people, for multiple vocalists on one microphone, instrumentals, and choirs. Microphones that respond to sound coming from directly in front of them (*unidirectional or cardioid*) are better quality for soloists, one reader at a time, or a single instrument—especially because microphones need various placement in relationship to musical instruments for the best sound (of course, there are a host of attachments for amplification of instruments as well).

A *flexible* sound system will allow you ultimate placement in the room. As we get more sensory-rich in our worship expressions, we may have need for readers, preachers, and singers to be placed in the congregation, on a balcony, to the side, etc. Cordless microphones, both handheld and hands-free, are essential for sensory-rich worship. Because I am a leader who likes to be able to be in many places in the room *and* play a drum or other instrument at the same time, it is discouraging and even disabling to my leadership when I encounter a sound system that is not equipped for either *lavaliere* (lapel) or *headset* microphones—both of which are hands-free options (headsets will offer the best quality since the microphone moves with your head). The latest and best in headsets at this moment are over-the-ear microphones that speakers can inconspicuously and comfortably wear. A tip: I always use face tape or the end of a bandaid to hold it fast to my head, eliminating any unwanted movements of the microphone and keeping my hair from catching and flipping it off of my ear. Make the switch, and I'm sure you'll agree: having full use of your hands and the ability to move around will be such a gift to preachers, presiders at communion, and any worship and music leader who is engaging actively with the congregation.

Many churches I have consulted with have sound systems that are quite functional—or they used to be. As years go by and A/V volunteers change, persons who once had knowledge about how to set and run the system may be hard to find. If this is the case, I always suggest that the company who installed the system come for a "tune-up" and re-training (preferably at a time when you have your musicians and preachers available). It does no good to have the equipment but no information about getting the most out of it. And having multiple volunteers "tweak" it can make a good system sound terrible. Training days are important, whether you are getting expert outside help or simply an in-house brush-up. In the dramatic arts chapter, I suggest a training day for readers. A great idea would be to coordinate their training to include A/V volunteers so that you can work on best practices from both sides of the equation. Have instrumentalists/bands/singers come for part of the day as well. Spend part of the day on audio, and use the other part of the day to develop skills in other media—lighting, slides, and video production.

For a sample training day schedule, see thinklikeafilmmaker.com.

Once you have a good, working sound system, test it also for whether you can leave some microphones "live"—such as the pulpit or lectern throughout worship—rather than turn them on and off. The best way to simplify the work of audio during worship is to have the least amount of "fiddling" with buttons as possible. My mantra is "set it up, let it run, when you can!" Along these lines, the more improvisational a leader is, the more they need control of the mute button while their microphone remains "live" at the board. Sound technicians won't always share such a leader's desire for control over the audio system. I have to promise them I know what I'm doing and will take full responsibility if I leave it on when I run to the restroom! My own style of leadership—and this will become more common the more sensory-rich your worship becomes—involves verbal or musical transitions that may or may not be planned or completely scripted. I don't want to have to wave down a soundboard operator to turn on my microphone every time I decide to use it. That may have worked with the plug-n-play, predictable, and disjointed worship of the past. But our techniques have to change as our worship does.

No matter who has control throughout the service, it is vitally important to provide A/V personnel with full worship scripts that include descriptions of what is happening when, where, and by whom. I'll discuss this in Chapter Eight, when I talk about writing scripts, but just let me say here that when we hand a worship guide (bulletin) to someone who is in charge of making sure microphones are live at the appropriate place, we are not doing them any favors. This means that they must guess at who is about to speak and from where. You will inevitably get the typical situation where a leader starts talking and sometime later the microphone comes live, confusing and distracting the reader, preacher, or singer and distracting the congregation from the content of the moment. Like any movie set, the more information the technicians have before the scene begins, the more their role supports the action rather than distracting or delaying it. Those whose art form may be more "technical" or behind-the-scenes are still as important as those "up front" and ought to be considered equal members of the worship team with access to all the information. And when they begin to understand themselves as such, they will begin to see how important it is to be present at rehearsals rather than simply stepping in last-minute on a Sunday morning.

Finally, sound checks are important in the ½ hour before worship begins. Whether or not you set levels at rehearsals sometime during the week, there are "gremlins" (either human or machine-related) that can confound us with their unpredictable ways. Making sure all settings are ready to go, batteries are fresh, placement of microphones is correct, and people using them are aware of how to use them is just good practice. Making sure recorded sound from a computer or elsewhere is coming through and is at the appropriate level can prevent some mighty embarrassing moments for the media team. This is true of all technical systems, audio or visual. Just as preachers are making sure their notes are in the right place and readers are making sure they know when to make their move and musicians are going over all their music, media teams must be fastidious in their preparation so the Spirit can soar in the moment!

Chapter 7

Think Like a Director:
Dramatic Arts in Worship

The saying goes, "You don't think your way into a new kind of acting, you act your way into a new kind of thinking." We spend a lot of time focusing on the content of our worship in words, tunes, visuals, media—as we should—but the way we *do* those things might be even more important. We may sing a good song about being community, but do we actually *look like* community? Or do we sit in rows, never interacting with one another? We may talk about the call to serve others, but if only the clergy serve communion every time, we may be communicating the idea that only the professionals are called to serve in ministry to the world. Indeed, actions often speak louder than words.

Most discussions of action in worship would focus on the obvious art forms of drama and dance. But I want to ask you to open your perspective beyond this, just as I have invited other ritual artists in the previous chapters to expand their understanding of their roles. Language is visual and visceral, music and its dynamics play a part in our spiritual formation, and visuals produce an ethos or a "feel" that communicates a message. So, too, even the most basic and simple actions of our worship (or lack thereof) are powerful. They shape our understanding of ourselves either as active disciples or passive church-attenders. I want us to imagine drama and movement in a much broader sense than a skit or sketch or even a passion-type play. I'm not excluding those, of course, but when we consider the drama of worship, we are standing in a long tradition of the mission of worship. Worship seeks to take a concept and give it tangible expression through a set of symbols—and some of the most powerful symbols are the embodied kind. So in this chapter, we will talk about the impact that actions and words-in-action have on creating unforgettable messages through sensory-rich worship.

THE IMPORTANCE OF EMBODIMENT

One of the most important questions I ask of myself as I'm designing worship is "How can we *embody* that which we proclaim?" We don't just *have* bodies, we *are* bodies. When we come to worship, we experience the story in and through our bodies because it is the only way we connect with the world. Cognitive concepts are embodied because they are shaped by our bodily perceptions and sensations. What we do with our bodies in worship makes a difference for how we understand and connect with God. The church has not always been convinced of this, however. The Enlightenment era (1700–1800) brought rational thinking into view as a sacred edict, bringing with it a decline in a variety of the visual and dramatic arts. The physical and visual were dissociated from the inward and spiritual. For René Descartes, the preeminent philosopher of this time period, what it is to be "human"—in other words the essence of being human—is the capacity to think, to reason. This is the first principle of Cartesian philosophy, "I think, therefore I am." And so, in the Western philosophical tradition since then, there has been a tendency to insist upon a gap which is thought to exist between our cognitive, rational side in contrast with our bodily, emotional side. This crept into Christian doctrine, emphasizing a dichotomy of body and mind for the post-Enlightenment church.

Although sacred dance had flourished during the Renaissance … in the post-Renaissance period, the door was firmly closed on its creative expression … As the Roman Catholic church became more centrally authoritative in Rome and published conforming edicts, there was little chance for creative and fresh exploration in the sacred dance. In general Protestant Christians felt that the portals of the spirit were to be entered with great seriousness through the mind and not through the senses.[115]

For Roman Catholics, "the liturgy [became] something that is watched by the people from afar."[116] For Protestants, participation meant understanding (intellectually) what they were experiencing—mostly an experience of verbal discourse.[117] This also led to attitudes about what kind of bodily behavior was acceptable or holy. Christian theology itself was to become associated with liturgical "uprightness," and the vocabulary of action in worship narrowed, holding more active and ecstatic expression at bay along with the emotions that accompanied them. For example the "enthusiasm" of early Methodists was held suspect because "rationalism simply could not tolerate such enthusiasm."[118] Diverse forms of expression have always found allies in the bodies of those not under the thumb of dominant Western ideology or by those who were, by virtue of class, race, gender, or any other marginalizing factors, excluded from "upright" society in the first place.[119]

This history of the depreciation of bodies has had a lasting effect on some denominations' worship practice. Many of our congregants still hold attitudes about embodied expression that can be difficult for them to overcome. Because my first career was in dance and drama, I encountered firsthand the resistance to embodied art forms. I realized that I had to learn about this history and to talk about it in a way that would invite people to a new appreciation for a fuller incorporation of our bodies in worship. In my studies I found much from both religion and science to back me up. The biblical texts are full of descriptions of communities praising God through dramatic movement—whether of celebration (drumming and dancing) or lament (wailing and tearing of clothes). Bodily expression in the midst of life's emotional circumstances have historically found a home in ritual through such actions as exuberant processions or subdued kneeling. The body has given Christians throughout history the ability to encounter God and to act as "the Body." Scholarly thought is now catching up with that reality as new philosophies and theologies "in the flesh" embrace our embodied nature as the source of knowledge itself.[120] Neurobiological science is helping us understand that rational thought is not possible

To see how theology and ethics are derived from bodily practices, go to thinklikeafilmmaker.com.

without the gut reactions called "somatic markers" that come from our intuitive bodies. Somatic markers increase the accuracy and efficiency of our reasoning processes. This is a partnership of cognition and emotion that makes rational thought possible.[121] Our brains are interpreting our bodily experience. How our bodies experience the stimuli in worship practices (music, words, actions) influences the interpretations of the sensory information the brain faces in that moment. That information is part of what gets assigned to our mental concept of who God is and how God feels to us.

We might not think about watching movies as a particularly "embodied" experience, but Clive Marsh reminds us that it is often a *visceral* experience. Our emotions, cognition, and reactions combine for a "visceral attentiveness" that facilitates concentration on and absorption of the story. For Marsh, this is akin to Christian worship as "visuality, emotion, and embodiedness" combine and the story is "made real" to us in an incarnational way.[122] When we are a witness to someone singing, speaking, or moving with emotion, we are wired to test out that emotion ourselves.

> Long before we can talk, we are attuned to the shifting sands of [facial and bodily] expression ... the eye instinctually searches for emotion in the human face. And we are not passive observers of those emotions. The emotions of others create a matching urge on our part.[123]

Directors of film know that the story comes alive when audiences engage emotionally with it. When movie-goers are having a visceral experience, they are more likely to respond empathetically to the characters, and therefore become involved at the level of *caring about them.* "What a film reveals ... is the director's sense of emotional truth. The director is the one who decides, 'Yes, that will do, that feels right to me.'"[124] While emotion is not the only outcome we are searching for in worship (if it is, then we have crossed over into the treacherous waters of manipulation), if we want congregations to be motivated to action, we must present the narrative of faith in such a way that we begin to care about how we will respond as disciples in our own contexts. We must strive toward an engagement with story that invites empathy, and therefore, action.

Under the Tuscan Sun's director, Audrey Wells, says that the scenes in the "divorce hotel"—where Frances resides after leaving the home she shared with her husband and before going to Italy—were meant to feel like "purgatory" to the audience. The room is small enough to be claustrophobic. It is bland in color, and the furniture is decades old. The walls were thin enough to hear the wailing cries of the man in the next apartment. The superintendent of the building is slumped and indifferent. This is a low point for our main character, and her hair and clothes demonstrate that she is in a holding pattern—a space of not caring what's next. She lies on the floor in despair. While there are comedic aspects of these scenes, the director is ultimately taking us to a place that many of us recognize—especially those of us who have known rejection in relationship. But we have all perhaps felt despair, loneliness, and perceived helplessness. It is this empathetic journey into Frances' state of mind that is the genesis of our caring about what happens next for her and our ability to stick with her during the transformation toward wholeness, and finally, to viscerally revel in her joy.

One of the most dramatic moments in our liturgical year is Holy Week. We recount the agony of the crucifixion, hopefully with enough power to draw us uncomfortably close to the agony that continues in our world. It is this experience of despair that makes the story of resurrection so powerful. It is our own experience of despair that makes those times when we are able to turn our lives around—to experience our own resurrection of life and hope—all the more meaningful. And it is what motivates us to bring renewed life and resurrection into reality for others. Active discipleship begins when we begin to *want* life and liberation for all people. Bringing the drama of the faith story to life in actions such as lighting candles, washing feet, anointing foreheads or kneeling at a cross is an art form with great importance as it forms us for discipleship.

MOVEMENT IN COMMUNITY

When film directors plot out the action of a movie, many of them storyboard the whole movie so that they can see the patterns of energy, making sure that there are ebbs and flows. "[V]isceral space is defined by movement, visceral time is defined by rhythms. Action by itself, no matter how frenetic or skillfully portrayed, palls; to keep the freshness of surprise, movement needs to ebb and flow."[125] Monotony, as I have said, comes in many forms, and monotony is the enemy of the kind of engagement that makes for unforgettable messages. A creed or affirmation of faith recited every week has the power to form us, but if we stop actively engaging with it, the practice can become rote. Just a slight change to the congregation's bodily posture, such as reciting the creed while standing and facing the center of the room, where the Christ candle is held aloft during a worship series called "Gathered as One," can wake us up again to the power of speaking a set of beliefs together in unison. Facing one another as we face the candle adds an "embodied theology" to the moment. We are those who gather as one around the Light of the World, and when we turn to see that light at the center of our community, we see one another. "Now that will preach," as they say! Add a theme song refrain bookending the creed as the candle is brought to and from the center, and you have done what I call "blocking layered sequences."

Blocking is a theater term also used in rehearsals for film scenes. A director blocks the movement of the actors to add emphasis and interest to the dialogue. This task in films also has the purpose of letting the camera crew know where the actors will be and where they will move. The movement and camera angles combine to give the audience a particular perspective that feels more *live* and *alive*. Of all the ritual art forms, the direction of the action of worship as a whole is really where I am most at home. Like the director of a film, I hold the big picture of the worship—where it needs to go in the ebb and flow of dynamics, energy, and participation and how all the pieces fit together smoothly as a congruent whole. "Setting the blocking (physical movement) and creating pace and tempo-rhythm" are two crucial duties for film directors besides the analysis of the script, says directorial coach Judith Weston. "A film script is an idea for a movie ... not the movie itself."[126] Directors must adapt the written document in order to bring the story alive for the audience, translating it into a facsimile of lived experience with which we can empathize. As worship designers, we too are called to translate the rituals of the church into a communally lived experience.

I want to return to the scene I began to describe in the verbal arts chapter from *Under the Tuscan Sun*. It is the scene right after the baby is born when Frances picks up the baby, repeats her name, and carries her to the window. As you may remember, the narration tells us that the word for "giving birth" in Italian is *dare a la luce*—to give to the light. The blocking for this sequence is for Frances to open the window, where we see the sunrise and hear the church bells pealing. Really, how many ways can the director say to us "this is a moment!?" The director has deepened our experience of this tender moment by layering words, visuals, sound effect, and motion.

Now let's imagine a baptism in our worship—a "once in a lifetime" ritual. Most of our traditions will have words prescribed for this ritual that we say every time. And there are also prescribed actions, such as pouring water into the font as we pray God's blessing over the water; and then there are the actual baptismal gestures, such as pouring, sprinkling, immersing—depending on your tradition. Let's imagine taking a cue from the film scene just described above. What if immediately after the words of baptism are pronounced, we hear handbells gently pealing from the balcony or corners of the worship space? Perhaps the bells are octaves of G's and D's on the musical scale so that a slow and simple melody ("I Was There to Hear Your Borning Cry") sneaks in under the bells as the baby (in the case of an infant baptism) is walked up and down the aisle, as many pastors are doing these days. The movement of the pastor holding and showing the baby to the congregation is now underscored with music that acts as an emotional nudge, connecting us more viscerally to the moment and to the child. Then what if the family comes to join the pastor in the aisle in the center of the worship space? The congregation is invited to stand and turn to face the family, in effect "surrounding" them. The people sing,

I was there to hear your borning cry
I'll be there when you are old
I rejoiced the day you were baptized
To see your life unfold[127]

With piano still underscoring, the pastor then invites the family to look around at the congregation. "Remember this moment and the faces of these people surrounding you because they are about to promise that you will never be alone in raising this child. We are your community, we are your family." And then the pastor invites the congregation to the prescribed words that are the promises made at every baptism. The promises to "love and surround" this child and this family are not just lip-service. They are made more palpable because at the moment of say-ing them, the congregation is literally surrounding them bodily and energetically. The family feels it. The congregation feels it. There is nothing rote about this moment. I have used this example in my workshops for a few years now. More often than not, someone will respond by saying, "there isn't even a real baby, and I'm crying!" Some of us can more easily let emotions flow than others, but the point is that involving the congregation in the action and bringing them literally closer to it helps them to feel more emotionally connected to the story (and the family) as well.

See a video of this experience at thinklikeafilmmaker.com.

What actions or postures can the congregation engage in that will solidify the message in their very bodies (and therefore, their minds)? This is the question for dramatic artists. Communion is a powerful ritual action that can be made more meaningful and wake us up to its many theological facets by inciting intentional thought about how we embody the ritual. Feminist liturgical theologian Marjorie Procter-Smith has writ-ten that all of our worship languages must be "emancipatory," to draw us into a "depth of dialogue" which is the heart of worship and the key to transformation.[128] Seminary students who studied with her recount that she made all of her students memorize the Great Thanksgiving (communion) prayer. While most students were mortified about memorization, they all report that the effects are astounding. When presiders at the table are able to use their full bodies freely, making gestures and eye contact intentional and engaging, the congregation's response is also more engaged—the "depth of dialogue" (rapport) between presider and people is more fully realized. While it is unlikely that specially written communion prayers will be memorized on a regular basis, my advice to those who preside at the table is that we *must* rehearse in order to give our bodies the chance to have lived the liturgy, determining what parts can be done without looking down and what rhythms, tempos, pauses, and gestures will bring the text to life. This, too, is a kind of "blocking" for the presider.

The communion prayer is meant to be a prayer of the whole assembly, not just the presider. How can we facilitate this more fully? I will often design the congregation's responses as an echo so that they do not need to have any paper in front of them or any words on the screens. This keeps them engaged visually and aurally with what is happening at the table. For instance, here is an excerpt from a communion prayer I wrote specifically for intergenerational participation (no reading required):

Presider: Friends, God is ever present with you!
Liturgist: And the people say, "And also with you!"
People: "And also with you!"

Presider: Turn to the people around you and tell them this news: "The peace of Christ is always with you!"
People: "The peace of Christ is always with you!"

Liturgist: Listen! *(pause)* The body breathes in together… and out. As close as breath, the Holy is present with us. *(pause)* So we lift up our hearts. And the family says, "We lift them up to God." **People: "We lift them up to God!"**

Presider: Let us give thanks to the Holy Living One because it is the right thing to do, not only now, but always, for "always" is when God is with us.

Liturgist: I invite you to open both palms upward in the sign language for "give."
Presider: *(as the motion is done)* … We thank you, Creator God, that you formed us, giving us your image.

Liturgist: Now place your hands together in the sign meaning "to be with."
Presider: *(as the motion is done)*…We thank you, Sustainer God, that you are here with us.

Liturgist: Bring your hands close to your face, in the sign for "prayer." Become aware of your breath on your hands… *(pause)*

Presider: *(as the motion is done)*… We thank you God for breathing into us the breath of life. Even when we have turned away, you have remained with us, close as breath. When we have been frightened, hesitant, still you are patient. You have time and again reached out your hand to free us, for your promise is steadfast.

See the whole prayer at thinklikeafilmmaker.com.

And so, we open our eyes, our hands, and our hearts to your will for us as told to us through your prophets. We join our voices together praising you with all the saints, repeating after me:

Holy, Holy, Holy God! (the people repeat)
Everywhere we see your Glory! (repeat)
Hosanna in the highest! (repeat)
… and the widest… (repeat)
… and the deepest… (repeat)
… place in our hearts. (repeat, pause)

The exercise of making this prayer intergenerational, and therefore interactive, was a wonderful way of pushing myself to a more embodied expression of the liturgy by the congregation. I knew that I would have children of various ages who would need to keep connected through movement. But I also wanted to keep the traditional pattern and language of the prayer, following my belief that you don't have to throw the baby out with the bathwater in order to be "creative." When you watch the video at the website, you will see that, later in the prayer, when we get

See the video of this communion prayer at thinklikeafilmmaker.com.

to the *epiclesis* (the name for the moment we petition the Holy Spirit to transform us), I invite the whole congregation to raise their hands upward "in the ancient Christian posture for prayer." This is called the *orans* position and was the posture of prayer in the early church for all the people, not just the presider. It is an open stance that has the effect of putting us in a posture that connotes a sense of "receiving." And then at the end of the prayer, just before we ask God to "make us one in ministry to all the world," I invite the congregation to "find a point of connection, a hand on a shoulder, holding hands—whatever is comfortable to you." These gestures by the congregation serve to strengthen our connection to the words being said. We are opening ourselves to the transforming Spirit, and we are seeing and feeling our connection as "the Body," unifying on behalf of the transformation of the world around us.

I wrote out my exact words in both of these invitations above because they were purposefully composed. Adding movements might feel "weird" to your congregation at first, especially if gestures are not common in your worship. In the first instruction, I made sure to connect raising hands to the ancient Christian practice. Anytime we can connect a new experience historically or theologically, it goes a long way in people opening up to that which feels new. And by giving people options for connecting with each other (hand on a shoulder, etc), I've given them an idea of how they can connect if hand-holding feels difficult for them for whatever reason. The use of sign language is a wonderful beginning step because it is a way for us to make the connection between gestures and language. When incorporating bodily gestures, it is always important to be invitational in our language, introducing this in incremental steps (not too much at one time) and offering options, including the choice to participate by watching only. You will build trust, and a "stiff" congregation is more likely to eventually appreciate the benefits of being more physically engaged.

There are many ways to engage a congregation in more embodied worship practices, limited only by your imagination. Simply keep asking yourself, "How could we symbolize this message or concept through our actions?" I have done prayers of confession that used a simple movement from clenched fists to open palms, asking the congregation to identify those things they are holding onto that they need to give up to God. All I did was introduce the gesture and the meaning behind it and then let the congregation take their time to do this, either in silence or with music playing. I have taught sign language to "Spirit of the Living God" during a time with children and then invited the congregation to join us (this is a good tactic for introducing the use of gesture—start with the children). As I discussed in the visual arts chapter, inviting people to go to stations around the room—interactive visual installations such as a table for lighting candles, a bowl of water to place dissolving paper, a place to plant seeds, or a "wailing wall" for placing rolled-up prayers (all depending on the subject of your series)—is a practice that infuses worship with movement other than "stand up and sit down." The way we take communion can vary depending on the message. For an emphasis on repentance during Lent, you might want a kneeling posture for receiving communion. But an emphasis on celebration and resurrection during the Easter season would be better embodied by being upright to receive, perhaps by intinction (dipping the bread into the cup). A series focus on community could be symbolized beautifully by serving one another in pairs or creating a large circle around all the pews and having servers move around the circle. The message proclaimed then drives our response in ways that further solidify the Word into the Body.

MOVEMENT AS PROCLAMATION

I have had the great honor of dancing in churches all over the world. When I was dancing with the professional secular companies of Alwin Nikolais and Murray Louis and for several years in a collaboration with the Dave Brubeck Jazz Quartet, the international acclaim of these artists created invitations that took us far and wide. As soon as I found out our itinerary for the next tour, I would begin contacting churches in the places we would be on Sundays and ask them if they would welcome an experience of dance in their worship. They all said yes! I danced in churches in East Germany before the wall came down and the Soviet Union during Gorbachev's *perestroika*. I danced in churches in Paris, Rome, and Tokyo and many other cities. The fortunate thing about dance is that it is something of a "universal language," which enabled communication and connection with congregations whose first language was not my own. Actually, we might claim that movement *is* everyone's first language and one of the things that helps to break down barriers. We first learned to interact with the world through gestures and reading faces. We fall back on hand gestures and facial expressions when trying to communicate with someone whose language we cannot speak. But dance is more than gestures trying to compensate for words, as Tex Sample observes:

> In dance as worship and witness the relation of God's story to dance is clear. Its display of God's powers, its capacity to present human action and will, and to display human bondage and spontaneity bespeak its narrative power. Even more, dance does presentationally what story in word can never fully achieve. It embodies and enacts what cannot be adequately said but must be shown and done.[129]

My professional dance career was in the field of modern dance. One of the things I love most about modern dance is that the exploration of movement goes much beyond the storytelling genre of classical ballet. Rather than a set of steps showing off a bravura of talent imposed onto a storyline, modern dance allows the storyline to drive the movement choices—to evoke a message through the components of movement itself. Dance may communicate a moment in a story such as the wrestling of Jacob and the angel or Jesus carrying the cross (yes, I played a cross one time, arms outstretched and body stiff, hoisted on the shoulder of a man making his way slowly up the aisle). Dancers may simply bring the energy of a moment in the story more alive, such as by adding big, sweeping, grand gestures with palms at the beginning of a Palm Sunday procession. And dance may simply evoke a human emotion or experience. For instance, lament may be characterized through heavily weighted movements or a tension evoked by manipulating a piece of stretch fabric, as with Martha Graham's famous "Lamentation." Ms. Graham describes the tube of fabric she chose as a costume/prop as a "skin"—a way to express the emotion of grief inside one's own body. She relates a story about a woman who had not been able to cry since she witnessed her young child killed by a truck. But the dance broke something loose in her, and she realized that grief is "honorable and that it was universal and that she need not be ashamed of crying for her son." Martha Graham reminds us, "Realize that there is always one person to whom you speak in the audience."[130] It is vitally important for trained dancers to understand the narrative power of dance in choosing movements. The point is to communicate the message in a way words cannot. If we gesture upward every time we mean to evoke "God," then we are limiting the theological range of who or where we believe God's action to be. If we always put our hands together when we mean "pray," we are doing no more than sign language can do. This merely mimicks the words rather than getting inside the message to draw out the intensity of lived experience.

Download my guide to creating a dance for worship at thinklikeafilmmaker.com.

Watching someone move can be as viscerally powerful as doing it yourself. Our *mirror neurons*, which I touched upon briefly in the visual arts chapter, allow sympathetic brain responses that mirror the action and energy we are watching. This happens to entire movie audiences, especially with suspenseful scenes or action sequences. We sense everyone around us "jumping out of their skin" at the same time. This is what makes any movement so powerful whether or not the congregation is physically involved. And I am convinced that it is also why some people have a harder time accepting dance in worship—it has a sneaky way of making us more present to our emotions. If we are uncomfortable with emotions in worship, preferring our religion resemble Descartes' intellectual "knowing," anything outside of those bounds may take a while to be appreciated. What I can say to dancers is "cultivate relationships" and let the Spirit do its work. While I was dancing in New York City, I attended Christ United Methodist Church and danced quite a few times there. One of the elderly members worked for a milliner in the 1930–40s, and at that time I loved wearing hats to church. She ended up giving me her hat collection, and we became very close. But there was always one thing that stood between us—she just had a hard time accepting dance as "holy enough" for the sanctuary. But one day after a worship service in which I had danced, she said, "I tried my hardest to be mad. But then I realized that I was moved. You moved, and I was moved."

Incorporating movement in worship as proclamation doesn't have to wait until you have trained dancers in your midst. The simplest movement can be the most profound. I remember an Advent series based on the words that appear more than 100 times in the Bible—"Do not be afraid." Usually this is a messenger of God delivering some news that will change people's lives. It particularly abounds in the Christmas story. Each week we had people processing lanterns into the worship space in the place of typical taper candles for an Advent wreath. On Christmas Eve, I brought in a final lantern, larger than the others, that would reside in the middle of the four other lanterns. The sanctuary was dimly lit. We entered into a time of silent reflection, and after a while I came in, walking backwards and shining the lantern toward one side and then the other. I moved slowly and looked into people's eyes and said, "Do not be afraid." I barely held my own emotions at bay as people's eyes welled with the assurance that they are not alone in this life—no matter the changes and difficulties they are facing or will in the future. You don't have to be a trained dancer to walk backwards and move a lantern around or walk the space with a group of people with glass pillar candles, process symbolic objects up the aisle with grace and focus, or learn to sprinkle the congregation with water to remember their baptism. This is the kind of simple movement that can dramatize a moment powerfully, searing it more indelibly in our memories.

Like writing liturgy, I believe anyone can participate in symbolic movement as long as you have a good structure to help with the task. There are two methods I want to mention here that you can use for non-dancers that don't require a lot of choreography and rehearsal. One of them is what I call "sculpting." I have used this with intercessory prayer statements such as "We pray for the earth and commit to protect its resources and creatures." Two people work together to come up with a still pose that can represent the statement. Perhaps one person is circling their arms as if encircling the globe and the other is hovering over it as if protecting it. Other pairs of people work on sculptured poses for other intercessory statements. The various pairs of people are placed around the worship space where they can be seen well by the congregation. They stand in a neutral position until their line is read, and then they move slowly into the pose and hold it during a brief period of silence to let people enter the prayer with their eyes and their ears. This progresses

See a video of "sculpting" at thinklikeafilmmaker.com.

until all have finished. The whole movement group comes together for a final pose, which could be as simple as making a circle, holding hands, and raising those hands high for people to see the connection as the reader ends with, "Hear our prayer, Holy One, and call us to be your people, with and for the world. Amen." If you have control of the lighting in your worship space, dimming the lights and shining a floodlight on the group can cast shadows on the walls behind them, making their silhouettes very large and adding to the dramatic impact. This can also help new dramatists to feel more comfortable if they know people are looking more at the shadows than at them!

The second form for non-dancers is improvisational and is made up of stillness and slow-motion movement. A scenario is set such as a group of people keeping vigil at the cross on Good Friday. As meditative music is played, the group changes position slowly and stops at a new set of emotive gestures. One person is reaching up with outstretched arms, and another one is slumped over, hiding their face. Another one is gazing off as if looking for someone (where did Peter go?) and another is staring in disbelief. This is held for a bit, and then the group moves again, slow-motion, and settles into another set of poses. This can be as powerful for those who move as it is for those who watch. Putting our bodies into the story can bring elements of the narrative into symbiotic relationship with body memories of our own postures with which we react in real life. Filmmakers use slow-motion to stretch time when they want an audience to sit with the power of a moment.

See photos of this at thinklikeafilmmaker.com.

This same technique in drama and movement can allow a congregation to reflect contemplatively and to steep us further in the story. One of my favorite uses of this was when I directed people at a long table in the series "We Are Family." The dramatists started out with gestures of loving relationship, but then, a couple of poses into it, two of them started showing signs of animosity that spread to the rest of the group and eventually settled once again. Extending these actions into slow-motion allowed the congregation to get a visceral experience of family just before the sermon, which explored difficult relationships in the human (and church) family.

EMBODIED SPEAKING

Paying attention to movement is vitally important to speakers and readers as well. Nowhere is this more important in worship than for the preacher—and it is rarely attended to. We began to talk about this in our chapter on verbal arts. The *how* of communication should be thought about even as we are thinking about the *what* of the verbal content. Indeed, whether or how we respond to the content of speech is highly dependent upon the performance modes of that speech. Ray Birdwhistell introduced the term "kinesics" in 1952 to describe "the science of body behavioral communication."[131] Research in this field (now more commonly called "kinesthetics") began to uncover the ways that messages are amplified and distinguished, moods are generated, and relationships conveyed through the dynamic use of energy and the speaker's use of space.

I introduced you to the work of Nick Morgan in the verbal arts chapter as we began to explore the connection between what we write and how we present it. Morgan cites the advent of film and television as a turning point in the kinesthetic expectations of audiences. Previously, the energetic power of a speaker came from "grand gesture, voice projection, and other methods for addressing huge crowds."[132] However, the advent of speakers on-screen created an expectation of the kind of intimacy from a speaker that is created cinematically, using a small frame with a close-up head shot. This is the way we began to understand "connection" with a speaker. And while public presentations have become more conversational and speech more informal in an attempt to recreate that kind of intimacy, the *kinesthetic* connection receives less thought for settings like worship and is not covered nearly enough in seminary education.

Crowds "tune out" without any kinesthetic stimulation. "The effect is to disconnect the speaker from the message, the message from the audience, and the audience from the presenter's desired action—the main reason for the communication in the first place."[133] Kinesthetic stimulation occurs when the speaker's actions are aligned with their words, creating the appropriate energy and accent to communicate particular content and modes of speech.

Choreographed movements throughout a presentation, like changes in the volume of a speaker's voice or the variation in a series of slides, provide the stimulation that helps keep an audience engaged. They also punctuate the presentation by signaling changes in content and by highlighting the most important points, giving the audience the helpful signposts so often lacking when words are spoken rather than written.[134]

When rehearsing sermons, one of the most important things to pay attention to are the *shifts* between sections or trains of thought. These are moments to consider shifting your placement in the space, your posture or direction of the gaze. Blocking a sermon may include deciding when distance between speaker and hearer should be changed, moving closer to the people for a more intimate, conversational, or personal story. A shift in distance—even just a step forward with a lean, can say, "I really want you to hear what I'm about to say right now." A move back to a more open and wide stance, perhaps with arms outstretched can say, "Look at the vast implications of what we are talking about." Film directing coach Judith Weston says that she is able to decide on blocking by getting to it kinesthetically—she needs to physically try it out rather than simply visualize it.[135] Everyone works differently, but I would tend to agree with her. Some things we just can't imagine until we try it on for size in the space. Rehearsing a sermon in the worship space in which you will speak it as opposed to your living room allows your body an experience of the content in context, and the blocking choices you make are more likely to feel second-nature in the real worship event—allowing your brain, your heart, and your spirit to focus on your convictions about the message and your connection to the people.

Those of you who use a manuscript or notes while preaching may be thinking that I'm insisting you give up these prompts. I'm not, and I don't think it is an either/or situation. You might play with using a music stand that can be easily moved to the center of a chancel area or taken down to the level where people are seated and allow your body and movements more visibility for the congregation. Sometimes when I block my sermon, I will decide to start at the pulpit and move to a stand at a crucial point when I want to be closer to the people. Because I know I'm going to move, I don't have to drag my notes with me. I simply place the notes I need for that segment down on the stand before worship begins (I also keep a backup in my worship notebook in case someone decides to move the stand or picks up my notes after having used the stand before the sermon). I also encourage manuscript preachers to choose at least one segment of their sermon to commit to memory so they can have an extended time of engaging the congregation without looking at their notes, allowing the possibility for movement away from them.

If moving away from notes gives you heart palpitations, kinesthetic engagement with listeners can be achieved through gestures and vocal intonation, but this requires just as much time and attention as blocking movement. Tones of voice and "tone of body" must ebb and flow within the sermon, just as we are aware of these variations in the whole of the worship experience if we are to be offering memorable proclamation of the Word. Bar none, the most common work I do when coaching preachers is to focus on patterns of speech. Many of us have no idea about the singsong-y habits we get into. I call it the "preachy voice" when we begin to speak in a habituated and highly predictable pattern. Usually within minutes of watching a video with a preacher/client, they themselves can point out repeated vocal patterns that literally numb the listener. Vocal patterns have kinesthetic implications. No matter how good the content is, when there is little rhythmic or energetic variety in our voices and bodies, it will be difficult for listeners to "stay tuned"—much less take away a memorable and transforming message.

TRAINING AND PLACEMENT OF READERS

All of these factors are true for those who read scripture as well, and yet most churches I work with have never held any training for readers at all. Usually we figure that if someone can read without stumbling too much over words, we are good to go. But the difference between simply reading a text and actually communicating the story is significant. "A commitment to energy" is one of the attitudes of actors, says homiletics professor Jana Childers, and it's one worth exploring for those who perform the spoken word in worship.[136] This "energy" can also be called "presence," "projection," or, simply, life.[137] "When it is present, the people in the pews … may not think about it at all; but they are guaranteed to notice its absence."[138] Because words originate from the body, vital energy is demonstrated through bodily processes, from particular vocal intonation to the ways performers hold themselves, direct their eye contact, and move in the space. All of these aspects have to do with the performance of text—indeed the text becomes "known" in worship through its performance.

> "Expression deepens impression" as Leland Roloff has said. And it is peculiarly true of Scripture texts, so many of which began life in oral form, that the preacher or interpreter/performer can not be said to know the text until he or she has given it his or her voice and body.[139]

Reading written text is an *oral interpretation of literature,* which makes it more than just reading words from a page. Our task is to help make the words alive to the people, and being alive means both intellect and emotion. We interpret with our voices so that people can comprehend the words but also enter *an experience* of the words. For this to happen, we must have had an experience of the words *ourselves* as readers.

A process that I take readers through in learning how to prepare a text involves incremental steps that help get the reader do three things: get inside the narrative they will present, get a feel for how the reading will be embodied (gestures, eye contact, blocking if any), and prepare their written page to support them in communicating well.

I start with a *body warm-up* with the purpose of getting in touch with our bodies. Loosening up through simple movements and extending our energy into the space will cue the body that we are about to use our energy in a larger way than usual. A *vocal warm-up* comprised of deep breathing from the diaphragm, sighing out loud from a very high pitch to a low one, and articulating "silly syllables" in phrases not unlike a choir's vocal warmup (without the singing) open up our vocal range so we have access to the whole instrument. The next step involves reading through the text to be presented once, simply for diction. At this point we are not worried about understanding the passage, but we simply ask, "Do I know how to pronounce all the words, and are there any whose definition I need to learn?" This is the first time you hear your voice read it aloud, and it's all about just seeing what the words feel like in our mouths. Unfortunately, this is about as far as most people go in preparing to read aloud in worship.

The next step involves reading the passage silently for deeper comprehension. Is it a narrative story? What is it about? Who is involved? Do I need to know more about the context in order to understand what is going on? Is the passage more like a poem? What are the main metaphors and messages? What meaning does it have for me? People who read scripture on a regular basis can benefit from accessing commentaries and learning exegetical processes just as preachers do—of course, not as extensively. Such preparation can help them get into the heart of the message and think about the "backstory," just as actors do in order to enter the mindset of a character more fully. Doing this doesn't change their actual lines, but it helps them be more connected to the lines and communicate those authentically.

Once this process is done, the next step is to tell the story or describe the passage to someone else *in your own words.* This feels really awkward and difficult at first to most people. Especially when dealing with scripture, we are often afraid to leave anything out or change the words. The benefit of doing this part of the exercise is that we really find out if we've comprehended what we are reading. This process is repeated, now for a different reason. This time tell it in your own words again, but notice your voice inflections as you do. What things do you emphasize? Our voices naturally change *volume, intensity, pace, pause,* and *pitch* when we are in conversation, depending on what we really want people to notice about what we are saying. Notice where you slow down, what words you emphasize, the words that seems to matter the most or need some inflection to help people who are listening to grasp the meaning.

Make some notes on the page related to what you just learned about emphasis as you spoke the story in your own words. Now read the actual words of the passage again, making choices to bring out the nuances in your vocal intonation. There may be only a couple of places in the text where you have significant changes in vocal intonation. That is good. When we begin to "doctor it up" just to be dramatic, we can come across as melodramatic and draw focus away from the story instead of supporting it. At this point, reformat it on the page if you need a larger font or would be helped by having it in a poetic format rather than a paragraph format (see the section on formatting sermons in the verbal arts chapter for more about this).

It is time to practice the reading in the space. This step involves knowing about the microphone you will use, practicing moving your hand down the page if needed, being sure the placement of the paper is the right height, looking up on the important phrases (too much bobbing up and down can be distracting), and feeling what gestures might be appropriate (if it feels awkward or "put on," it probably is). If the reading involves several voices, notice the rhythm created from one voice to another. The reason I like to have reader training days (usually a couple of hours is fine) on a regular basis is so that people who have committed to being part of this kind of worship leadership have a chance to "play" in the worship space. What I mean by this is that they get to feel the size of the space and try out what it feels like to speak into the microphones without the added pressure and anxiety of preparing something they are about to actually do next Sunday. We get to try different kinds of readings on for size, experimenting alongside others and encouraging one another. Then when we are asked to read, we have a bodily memory and experience to lean on.

For a training day format, see thinklikeafilmmaker.com.

Readings by one person are only one form of presenting dramatic texts. During the brainstorming stage, dramatic arts team members will look for ways to embody the spoken word by looking at the verbal material for the whole series and imagining how some readings could be given vitality through the participation of multiple voices. If scripture is read by one voice at a lectern all the time, it is much more difficult for the congregation to stay tuned in. Giving the congregation a "part" in a narrative scripture reading can help them begin to see from that particular perspective. In this one, the congregation takes the words of Jesus.

Reader: Then Jesus went with them to a place called Gethsemane; and he said to the disciples …

> ***Congregation:* "Sit here while I go over there and pray."**
> *Reader:* He took with him Peter and the two sons of Zebedee,
> and began to be grieved and agitated.
> Then he said to them …
> ***Congregation:* "I am deeply grieved, even to death;
> remain here, and stay awake with me."**

Some narrative readings will give you the opportunity for several different leader voices. Sometimes the text itself is suggesting the types of readers that would bring a deepened sense of the meaning, as in this reading from the book of Joel that prophetically declares the Spirit's movement among all people—young and old, all genders, all stations in life:

> *Reader 1: (woman)* I will pour out my spirit on all flesh;
> *Reader 2: (young boy)* your sons and your daughters shall prophesy,
> *Reader 3: (older man)* your old ones shall dream dreams,
> *Reader 4: (young girl)* and your young ones shall see visions.
> *Reader 1:* On all, male and female, bound and free,
> in those days, I will pour out my spirit.

Litanies, affirmations, and creeds can involve several people for the leader parts. Our ears perk up when we hear different voices in a typical leader/people call and response format. Choral readings by multiple voices are fun to write and to prepare. This is a great way for people who don't feel skilled enough to be in a musical choir to have an ensemble experience. Whenever I am rehearsing multiple readers, I have all of them read through it the first time in a circle so they can feel each other's rhythms, pace, and intonation in close proximity. After giving some direction, I have them read it again there. It is only then that I have them go to their places in the space where I have

Try multi-voice readings at thinklikeafilmmaker.com.

imagined them being—especially if they will be some distance apart, such as surrounding the congregation.

The placement of readers can be symbolic. Hearing voices coming from the midst of the congregation or surrounding them creates an embodied experience of worship as the work of all the people and the priesthood of all believers. A reading that involves water imagery might invite a placement of the reader near the baptismal font. A Psalm that refers to God's "high mountain" might be read from a balcony, and someone reading from the book of Isaiah, "comfort, comfort my people …" might stand close to the people, like a comforting friend would do, as opposed to standing at a lectern in a position that feels more separated. All of these examples show how "dramatizing" a reading need not require many rehearsals or even specially written scripts. The simple choices of readers and placement can bring deeper comprehension and relationship to the words spoken, making verbal expression sensory-rich.

For a sneak peek at my Holy Week drama, go to thinklikeafilmmaker.com.

Of course, specially written dramas can be an incredible gift. I was fortunate to grow up in a little rural church that had musically and dramatically gifted pastors. The most memorable moments, ones I can still see in my mind today, were the first-person monologues that one pastor prepared. We even went out to the city lake for a picnic complete with fishes and loaves on the shore while he did Jesus' Sermon on the Mount and other narratives. Sensory-rich indeed. I have written a drama for Holy Week that includes monologues by six biblical characters who were with Jesus that fateful week. Each one tells their powerful story from their perspective, and then the congregation engages in a ritual action like washing hands, anointing with oil, lighting candles and receiving communion. Monologues such as these can be done as memorized presentations if you have experienced dramatists in your midst or simply as reader's theater, requiring less preparation and no memorization.

CHILDREN IN WORSHIP

There are so many ways to draw on the heightened storytelling that drama provides. This book's website will point you to some of our favorite resources, including dance, drama, and storytelling associations to help you deepen your skills for this area. In the Worship Design Studio, we also include "The Gifts of and for the Younger Church" (what I call the "children's message" or "time for children") as part of the dramatic arts. While I believe wholeheartedly that it is important for children to be welcomed in worship, if the only time we make worship more "engaging" for children is when we gather them up in the front, we have missed important opportunities for the whole of worship to be more engaging. When worship becomes more sensory-rich, I have found that children and youth have little problem staying engaged. Parents will frequently approach me after I lead worship at their church saying, "I didn't even have to send my child out or tell my adolescent to pay attention." Besides the attention of children and youth, their leadership is important as well. If

For links to dramatic arts resources, go to thinklikeafilmmaker.com.

we utilize youth leadership only on "Youth Sunday," we've missed a very important point. Children and youth are not the "church of tomorrow," they are part of the church right now. They can regularly help lead age-appropriate lengths of readings, help put together a visual installation, be part of creating a photo compilation for projections, or be part of the music and dramatic arts teams.

But there are times when we want our full attention on children in worship. Worship Design Studio guest expert Mark Burrows has opened my eyes in new ways about this art form—both small segments within a worship experience and entire worship services geared to children and their families.[140] One of the most mind-blowing things Mark has taught me is that the age at which children's brains begin to comprehend analogies or metaphors is much later than we think. The most common structure I've witnessed with "children's sermons" is relegated to "object lessons"—comparing that nature of God to this or that object. Bringing children to the front to just make them sit and listen is no more engaging than the rest of the service for them (even with props). *Action*—getting children actively involved—is the name of the game, says Mark. What can we *do with* the children that will invite them to *experience* the message?

See examples and Mark's resources at thinklikeafilmmaker.com.

My paternal grandmother lived into her 90s even though in her 70s she began to lose her memory. Even though she did not know who any of her family were anymore, she played the piano almost until her last days. "Procedural memory"—the memory of our actions, is the most indelible in our brains. And so we come back around to the "main thing" for the dramatic arts—embodiment. Whether or not you have dramatists and dancers in your midst, the movement of leaders and congregations is vitally important to making worship "M-M-Good"—meaningful and memorable. When we think like a director, whose job it is to bring scripts to life and encourage actors as they embody their roles, we add a visceral dimension to the experience of the whole Body as they bring their lives before God.

THINK LIKE AN EDITOR:
PRODUCTION CONTINUES

I t's time for the rubber to hit the road. The whole team has engaged creatively and faithfully in the brainstorming and resource-gathering process, and now it is time for all of that work to become a cohesive whole. As I outlined in Chapter Two, "production week" is scheduled about four weeks before the worship series begins. During this week, a core group of people work diligently to move from lists of great ideas from the whole team to detailed worship scripts for the whole series. Once that is accomplished, the entire team is on board again to carry out the tasks needed to get everything prepared—readers and drama-tists scheduled, music rehearsed, items found and purchased for visual installations, projected media elements compiled and publicity launched. Only after this process is complete do we turn our attention to the items that will be completed week-to-week once the series begins—cue-to-cue rehearsals, sermon preparation, and worship guide production. Our "plan together and plan ahead" strategy has paid off by moving the whole of the creative process—from visioning to completion—out of the stress of a one-week time frame and into a more liberating process that invites participation of the people. If we are to offer artful, sensory-rich, memo-rable experiences of the story steeped in both tradition and innovation so that people are inspired in their faith journey, we will embrace that this takes time and attention. You can throw together an agenda for a meeting the night before, but you cannot create the opportunity for unforgettable messages that way.

THE CUTTING-ROOM FLOOR

The editing part of the process can be daunting. Editors are one of the most crucial members of a filmmaking team, and editing is an essential skill to develop for worship designers and leaders as we discern the movement and flow of the series as a whole, and of each worship experience within it. In filmmaking, "the editor is confronted with a block of marble, the footage, and has to take away everything that isn't the film ... Filmmakers usually walk out of dailies buoyed up; they leave first cuts weighted down." The first round of editing on a film usually still comes in too long. "If a movie is a series of scenes where all the actors have nothing but moments too good to lose, it can end up a wonderfully acted, almost unwatchable film."[141] After the resource-gathering process, we will *always* have too many good ideas to use. We will have to weed some out in order to find the ones that further the story most effectively as well as pay attention to balancing several factors.

The balance of *repetition and innovation* is vitally important as we seek to ensure both the "oh yeah" and "a-ha!" experiences of the congregation we talked about in Chapter One. We will want some deeply familiar acts of worship as well as some that become familiar through their repetition. We will also want those unique expressions that act as surprising wake-up moments for the congregation. Films thrive on plot twists that keep us on the edge of our seats, open and engaged with the story. In worship, this can be as simple as a reader whose voice comes from an unexpected place or a video that sets up the sermon in a humorous way.

Strive to balance *theme-based material* with resources that are *not so obvious*. If the central symbol is "life-giving water" for the series, you can't have *every* song be about water—this gets ridiculous and predictable. While footage of the renovation of the house in *Under the Tuscan Sun* was rife with metaphors for the renovation of the main character's inner life, the movie couldn't become a movie about renovating a house, says director Audrey Wells.[142] It had to be about restoring faith in love and relationship at its core, and so finding a balance between focus on the house and focus on the other ways the theme was carried out was key in keeping the movie on track.

Finally, evaluating the *balance of dynamics* is another consideration for what ideas "make it" in the final cut. There must be a balance of activity and contemplation. In my professional dance career, I danced with a company that toured the world for five years in a live show with the Dave Brubeck Quartet. Along the way we would teach master classes on improvisation at universities. One of my favorite things that Dave would say was "You have to have the 'do' and the 'be' for the 'do-be-do-be-do.'" In other words, you need the notes and the silences between the notes for a satisfying rhythm. In worship we have to have the "doing" and the "being" in order to embody the ebbs and flows of life and liturgy. In those master classes, I liked to follow up Dave's joke by saying "if all you have is the 'doing' without the 'being,' all you are left with is the 'do-do.'" The joke was effective then, and the memory now always reminds me to make sure I don't fill worship up so much that we don't have time to just "be."

First drafts are where you begin to see—literally—the concrete result of your brainstorming and resource-gathering. For me, this is a turning point in the whole process that comes not without labor. I liken the creative process to having a baby. In the visioning process, when I'm working with the possibility of a theme, I am thrilled and excited. I can do this freely because I am not faced with a to-do list about it yet;

I am living only in the "land of possibilities." The horizon is beautiful because it is "out there." Brainstorming and resource-gathering are like decorating the nursery, imagining all the wonderful, deeply heart-warming moments that this new creation will bring. The excitement in the worship design process during brainstorming and resource-gathering, when we are dreaming without having to make too many decisions about what will ultimately be left on the cutting-room floor, is fun and intoxicating. I've had worship teams stall out during the script-writing process because they just love coming up with ideas so much but have a hard time whittling it down. But in order for anything to actually be born, actual labor has to ensue, and all is not so pretty. At the beginning of my process of creating first drafts, I see the due date approaching, and anxiety sets in. A mantra, "What was I thinking?!" sets in, quickly followed by the knowledge that there is no turning back. I can't imagine how I will be able to know what to do with all I am faced with. I also wrestle with including everyone's ideas, which, of course, is impossible—like new parents trying to incorporate the copious advice of well-meaning grandparents.

Where is the turning point? When I sit down at the computer. For me, after I look over all the possibilities gathered during the resource-gathering process, I sit in silence and begin to imagine the moment of people gathering for worship—expectant, yearning, hurting, rejoicing—a gathering of all that life brings. I hold the metaphorical "baby" in my arms for the first time, and I simply begin to do what my God-given intuition urges me to do. I start to write what I see, what I hear, what I feel. And when it is time to imagine the first word, the first song choice, the first sound, something of what I've been steeping in from the resource-gathering lists comes to the fore, and things begin to unfold. I know—it is a bit mysterious.

Intuition is an essential component to a film editor's job. While careful attention to detail is another, perhaps-more-technical, asset, editing is a lot about intuition, says Brad Schwartz, Emmy-winning editor. "You have to learn how to tell a story from a specific point of view."[143]

> Editing isn't just about pushing buttons or using the latest software; it's about the psychology behind the edit. Editing comes down to one very simple moment—when to cut. This may sound easy, but knowing when to cut requires an extensive understanding of the psychology of storytelling, emotional intensity, pacing, visual flow, continuity, and editorial aesthetics.[144]

Yes, a lot of things go into the "mystery" of how things come together in the script-writing process. And honestly, sometimes it isn't so spiritual. Sometimes I just have to get something—anything—going, and the inspiration will come when it comes. More often than not, it is the material itself, such as an idea for a theme song, that will help me get into the flow of getting it all on paper. I also believe wholeheartedly in the ability of the structure of worship to guide the decisions.

THE ORDER OF WORSHIP—NARRATIVE FLOW

Screenwriters, directors, and editors all have to be keenly aware of the structure of the story. This creates a common journey that shapes the decisions needed to put it all together. The ancient storytelling device called the "hero's journey" is one of the common building blocks for storytelling in film that mirrors our own stories of growth, challenge, and discovery as humans. One description of the stages of story in film is: 1) the set-up; 2) the new situation; 3) progress; 4) complications; 5) the final push. Not all screenwriters use the same verbiage to describe this structure, but all teachers of screenwriting sound the same clarion call—you have to have a structure within which to create a flow of narrative that makes sense. Christian ritual has a structure, and no matter what style of worship or denominational tradition, this ancient four-fold pattern not only grounds us historically, but it makes a lot of sense. The worship pattern of *gathering, proclaiming, responding,* and *sending forth* mirrors the rhythm of human interaction—our coming together, sharing stories of life, responding to those stories through our actions, and moving apart to continue living our lives, having been moved and formed by our time together.

Gather—The *gathering* part of the pattern is the threshold, the moment of entry into a different mindset, the moment we acknowledge that we are community gathered, and we are introduced to the journey upon which we embark together. Think about all we do to prepare when we host a dinner party at our house. We take special care to be ready at the appointed time, to have the house feel inviting, perhaps with a special decorative theme to celebrate something special, and music playing in the background that sets a mood. As leaders, we want the space, the sounds, and the preparations to be just right as people enter. It is true in most things, including worship and film, that first impressions are long-lasting.

> There is a critical period when a movie begins, the first five or ten minutes, when audiences haven't yet labeled it. They have suspended judgment while they decide what they are dealing with. This is a crucial time for a filmmaker, for here he or she must define the expectations the viewers will carry throughout the film. Here the audience takes its cues for pace, for tone, for what to accept as "real."[145]

The "threshold moment" concept that I teach originated from hearing filmmakers tell me just this—that the first minutes of the film give us cues about the rest of the experience. Setting the tone at the beginning is crucial to how we experience the rest of the story. Too often in worship, we don't introduce the storyline at the beginning, and, therefore, anything that happens before we have any clue about the message will not benefit from having had our minds "set" toward the story. Threshold moments give us a frame of reference and send us powerfully into the story. Threshold moments in my designs usually include a theme song, the synopsis for the week and another spoken piece—opening prayer, call to worship, affirmation of faith or confession (depending on your tradition)—all tied together with the musical thread. Then the typical order of worship such as an opening hymn would begin (if you haven't seen the examples of threshold moments in Chapter Five on the musical arts, go there now).

Generally, I would place other gathering elements before this threshold moment. These would include the music that is playing when people arrive. Contrary to what some musicians believe, my experience bears out that we need not compete with the energy of people gathering together by expecting that they will sit quietly through a "prelude." The function of music as people gather is to set an atmosphere. If there is a piece of music that you want people to listen to with intention that furthers the message, I encourage you to either let it be part of the threshold moment or place it during the next section and let it be part of the Word proclaimed. Welcome and announcements have important functions in hospitality and invitation to the congregation's journey and life. But I prefer

For my two cents on making announcements more meaningful, go to thinklikeafilmmaker.com.

them "outside of the ritual," so to speak, meaning before the threshold moment. In some series, I have included gathering the joys and concerns of the congregation as a way of creating a greater orientation toward the gathered body and of invoking the names of those who can be with us only in spirit but not physically present. These then are summarized in the pastoral prayer in the *responding* section of the four-fold pattern. The point of the *gathering* section is to do everything you can to instill a sense of the community on a spiritual journey together.

Proclaim—Having gathered together, we move to the purpose of being immersed in the story, in the message. The question for this moment of editing is "How will we offer the story in this particular moment in a way that weaves together what we hear, what we see, and what we do?" Elements in this section can include many forms of proclamation. This is where I place a time with the children. Rather than always being a "children's message" that functions more like an age-appropriate mini-sermon, I consider whether one of the scriptures or readings might be presented in a creative way utilizing the children as participants.

This section is where readings will be presented—hopefully in a diversity of ways determined by the ideas generated by verbal and dramatic artists. I will often include a congregational song that weaves itself among the readings and the content, the dynamic of which will help us to hear the verbal components more fully. Anthems or music presented by ensembles and bands may be included in this section. If they are, my preference is to title these "The Word in Song" rather than "anthem" or "special music" in order to help the congregation see these as one more way that the Word will come alive. The placement of this music in relationship to the sermon will be determined by whether its content and energy prepares us for the sermon or works better as an exclamation mark after the sermon. As a preacher with musical abilities, I will often find ways to weave such musical offerings within the sermon itself. All forms of proclamation of the story, whether they be music, dance, drama, video, or a typical sermonic form reside in this section (unless the art form is actually functioning more in the vein of one of the other sections of the four-fold pattern—such as a choral piece whose content is more a response to the sermon).

Response—Here is our opportunity to offer ourselves in many ways having been moved by the message we've just experienced. Determining what kind of form the prayers of the people will be offered in during the series—such as intercessory or pastoral—or whether the Lord's Prayer will be spoken or sung is part of the editing process. Repeating the same form within a series is a way to have continuity and familiarity as well as set the "feel" for a series. You may have found a song in the resource-gathering process that can bookend or weave during the midst of the prayers. We offer our gifts (offering) during this section of the four-fold pattern. Ritual actions such as baptism, communion or other interactive opportunities, such as going to stations, are made rich by their relationship in response to the Word proclaimed.

Many churches use an order of worship that places the sermon at the end and these responsive elements before it. That order of worship really is a hold-over from the revival pattern of worship that swept early America. But in revivals, altar calls served as a significant response to the Word proclaimed. When the popularity of revivals affected the order of worship on Sunday mornings, the altar call was eventually lopped off and replaced by an invitation to membership. If your order of worship has the sermon at the end of the order of worship, with only a closing hymn (and perhaps an invitation to membership) between the preaching and the rush for the door, I invite you to seriously consider this more ancient order of prayers and offering *after* the sermon, in this *response* section. I think you will find that the sermon gets time to settle in us, the prayers can be inspired by the Word we've heard, and we can get creative about the ritual actions we use to solidify the message. I'm also not a purist on this issue, and there may be times when the content of your series theme will warrant an order more like the revival pattern. For me, however, this is an exception rather than the rule. This is especially true in traditions that have a historic connection to this four-fold pattern but engage in both classical and contemporary worship forms.

Contemporary repertoire can live comfortably and powerfully within the classic four-fold structure. Churches with historical roots in the four-fold pattern need not adopt an order of worship from traditions outside their own simply because they are utilizing music that originated in a different tradition. There are many ways to be creative within this basic structure that gives a common shape throughout the year but can also invite flexibility from series to series. Change happens in incremental steps, and you may not want to change too much all at once. Try a different order for a series and see how it feels; then go back to what feels familiar for the next series. This sets up a pattern of experimentation without people getting anxious that this is how it will be forever (more on this in our final chapter).

Sending forth—The fourth movement comes when we have been inspired by the message and are *sent into the world* to live the message. Who are we as a result of what we've experienced? The closing songs, blessings, and words of dismissal underscore the message we've heard and send us out as transformed people ready to "go and do likewise" in the world. The Light of Christ heads out of the doors, and we are compelled to follow, taking our own renewed passion to make the world a better place for all people. These closing elements help define our identity, remind us of the overarching message, and instill in us the courage we need to go into the world as disciples. A congregational sung refrain after the benediction is a terrific way to add emphasis and focus to a series' message.

LAYERED SEQUENCES

Montage theory of film was developed by Russians during the silent film era. "The Soviets, for the most part, looked at the shots themselves as meaningless atoms or building blocks and claimed that meaning first emerges from the images though the juxtaposition of the shots."[146] One of the final scenes of *Under the Tuscan Sun* is the wedding of two young lovers, one of the Polish workers Frances hired and the neighbor's daughter. Everything about the scene is beautiful—the church, the couple, the music. Our main character cries tears of joy through the whole scene. But on its own, this scene could have been any wedding scene. The tears we as the audience shed (or at least those of us, like me, that cry at the drop of a hat in movies) are prompted because of this scene's juxtaposition with the subplots of heartbreak throughout the movie—especially the one that might have kept these two young people apart forever. Frances' tears touch us because we know of her loss and struggle to find her own internal resurrection from brokenness. And at this point in the movie, joy is not just in the wings, but making an appearance fully on stage because love has come to Frances in the form of her "adopted" family surrounding her in this new home, now a cradle of love instead of the harbinger of neglect and despair depicted in early scenes in the movie.

The meaning of the word *montage* is "to mount" or "to put together" and "edit." As we begin to put together the pieces of liturgy that will comprise the whole, the pieces themselves take on more meaning in the way they begin to relate to each other. A dramatic reading of Jesus' asking the disciples to "stay with me" in the Garden of Gethsemane takes on additional power from the chant "Stay With Me" being woven into the reading and then in the sermon after vignettes of despair from current events. After a message acknowledging divisions in the human family that lead to violence, the song "Make Us One" as a benediction will take on more significance. As we sing it and turn to face the Light of Christ in the

See a transcript of my related presentation at thinklikeafilmmaker.com.

center of the gathered community and then hear a dismissal encouraging us to use this unity for the good of the world, all the pieces come together powerfully. Then, when the next "scenes" of violence or division cross our paths in our everyday lives, the *montage* grows, relating the scenes from our worship to the scenes of our lives.

You've heard this technique of mixing art forms—putting them together—described as sensory-rich "layering" throughout this book. Engaging in the act of editing or *montage* is the act of creating "layered sequences" that will repeat throughout the series. I usually have three or four layered sequences that are structural threads in a series. The first one is the threshold moment—for example, a theme song refrain, synopsis, repeat of theme song refrain, spoken prayer or litany. The second one is a structure for the presentation of readings—for example, song verse and/or refrain, first reading, song second verse/refrain, second reading, etc. The third layered sequence will be a way of structuring prayers and/or ritual action with musical responses, and the fourth may be a sending forth sequence with a benediction song thread. What you see is that I'm making artistic decisions for each part of the four-fold pattern that can act as repeated structures even though some of the content will differ from week to week.

Hear me talk about layered sequences for the "Gifts of the Dark Wood" series at thinklikeafilmmaker.com.

Creating layered sequences throughout the order of worship, rather than treating each piece of the order as its own "bubble," will make worship feel like a journey from beginning to end—this technique aids in better flow. I asked a filmmaker once about why it is that when I go to a good movie, two hours can fly by before I know it; but when I go to a disjointed worship service, sometimes an hour can feel like an eternity. What he shared with me was eye-opening and affirmed everything I'd been teaching about paying attention to flow: when time becomes "segmented" into pieces, we become much more aware of the passing of time—things seem to take longer. This is why the editing process is so important in film—so that the audience is whisked along the story-line without becoming too aware of abrupt scene changes. When the segments of worship are not at all connected and we proceed as if we are checking off a to-do list, time seems to elongate. Creating layered sequences keeps us in the story, and we feel the movement of worship in a much more kinetic way.

SCRIPT WRITING

Once an overall structure and flow are decided, script-writing can begin in full force. This is the point at which you will want to be sure you are aware of all the extra-liturgical components that may not have to do with the series message specifically. Perhaps there is a baptism scheduled for the third week of the series, or a family will be moving out of town on the second week and your church has a tradition of blessing people for life transitions. Maybe Memorial Day falls on the last Sunday of the series or you want to be particularly aware that the first Sunday is right before the general election. Where and how will these things be acknowledged without taking over the movement of the message? When are particular musical groups scheduled to offer their gifts? As you begin to plan further ahead, you will be able to schedule things in ways that support the message more fully, rather than the message being enslaved to the handbell ensemble schedule, for example. You'll be able to ask them to offer something specific to the message for a particular week in the series far enough in advance for members to accommodate the request. While national holidays and happenings are beyond our scheduling control, I believe that there are always ways to incorporate them without interrupting the flow of a series message. For instance, knowing that the July 4th weekend will fall in the midst of a series on communion prompted me to write a communion prayer

To get this communion liturgy, go to thinklikeafilmmaker.com.

that incorporated images of picnic tables we often gather around that weekend as well as verbiage of the real "freedom" that comes with working for justice. At this stage of the creative process, be pro-active rather than reactionary in weaving in all the needed components.

My use of scripts for worship leaders comes from my theater background. A script for theater includes not just the words of the actors but also stage directions and notes about the stage setting, musical cues, object placement, etc. This is similar to what a movie script looks like that includes descriptions of visuals and action. I have found that translating this practice from my theater experience to my worship design and leadership experience has been an asset, and I think you will too, once you get the hang of it. When I have a script with *rubrics* (the liturgical term for stage directions), anyone who has a script can be much more informed about timing and specific actions than someone who is simply working off of the typical "bulletin." Scripts also contain all the words that leaders need so that the congregation's Worship Guide can be more sparse, containing only what the congregation needs for their active participation.

I can tell you from experience that the more sensory-rich and complex worship becomes, the more you will need a script. If you have music underscoring a scripture reading, for example, even if the reader is reading out of an actual Bible, the musician will need the words in the script to help them time out their music. If you want the ushers to help direct people in an unusual traffic pattern, you can describe it in the script, hand it to the "head usher" after you explain it to them, and they will be able to be clear in training the rest of the ushers. If you use multi-media, you will need scripts at the computer, the soundboard, the lighting board, etc. And believe me, there will be times when someone can't get there early enough to go over their part, and if you hand them a script that has their part highlighted in yellow with a rubric that says *"reader moves to lectern during last verse of the hymn,"* their (and your) confidence level goes up, offering both of you the opportunity to really worship rather than worry! Another gift of preparing a script is the ability to have some extras available for folks who might have hearing or long-distance sight limitations. Giving this to them keeps them part of the experience—both verbal and visual. I've even had the pleasure of being able to send the scripts to be translated into Braille for someone. Because of the rubrics, she could "see" what was happening.

You will find your own system of formatting your scripts. The important thing is to decide on a format and stick with it so people get used to the way it looks on the page and what to look out for. I like a center-justified format so that there is space for people to write their own notes and reminders in the margins during the cue-to-cue rehearsal. I'm sure my preference for this formatting also comes from my theater days, as scripts are usually center-justified. I always use italics and a red color for all *rubrics* so that I can clearly differentiate directions from spoken text. I make all words that need to be entered into presentational media software and instructions for A/V the color blue, making it easy for those folks to find it easily and know exactly what needs to be onscreen. I make printed words for readers (especially when there are a lot of words) in 14pt font (at least). When I print out the scripts for readers, I highlight their parts with yellow highlighter for them. And I

To see a script generated in the Worship Design Studio Design App, go to thinklikeafilmmaker.com.

make sure a page never breaks in the middle of a sentence. It is better to have some blank space at the bottom of a page and start on the next.

Once you have the first worship service scripted, you will simply copy and paste to as many documents as you have frames/services for the series (or use our Design App in the Worship Design Studio to automatically generate the other scripts complete with thread items repeated for you). The thread items will remain the same, so there is no need to retype all of that. Simply go through and customize all the material that will change from week to week. And *Voila!* you have all the worship services scripted for the entire series in one fell swoop. I can't emphasize the benefits of this part of the process enough. Some worship teams get so enthralled with the fact they have gathered so many resource-ideas that they put off compiling them into worship scripts, making that a week-to-week task. What they find out is that the details of actually implementing their ideas begin to overwhelm them because they are now trying to accomplish it in a shorter time frame again. Inevitably, things happen out of our control, and our best ideas fall by the wayside as we stop to deal with the wrench that life just threw into the works. By completing all the scripts and having three weeks to deal with details, we are more likely to be able to bring our dreams to fruition.

TASK MANAGEMENT

As I'm creating scripts, I like to be making a "task list" of to-do items that will be necessary to complete in a timely way. Recall our most important rule of successful teamwork: when decisions are being made in the creative process, there are less people involved. Script-writing definitely fits under this part of the rule. But when the scripts are done, we have a very concrete vision of what it will take to pull it all off. This is akin to the lists created when the analysis of the script by the whole film team is complete. Lists must be made of the props and set pieces art direction teams need to produce. Other lists include characters that need to be cast by casting directors, lists of shots by cinematographers and the equipment needed at each location to get those shots, and so on. Production assistants (PAs) on film projects are the worker bees of the process. All the creativity and talent in the world will not be experienced if the thousands of details are not cared for. Just as the brainstorming and resource-gathering parts of the worship design process benefit from the whole team's input, "the more the merrier" is the mantra for task management on the home stretch to the launch of the series.

This is another point at which some worship teams stall. Pastors will try to do it all themselves, especially those who have a hard time asking for help or letting go of the details. But if a director of a film took on making sure there was coffee and bagels available the morning of a shoot, they would not be able to concentrate fully on their job of guiding the actors, camera operators, set designers, etc. If the director is not operating with the focus needed to move the film production forward … it won't. And the people who depend on them will suffer in their tasks as well. A pastor who is rushing around just before worship making sure the candles are lit and everyone has their script is robbing the congregation of their full attention to their most important role in the moment—being the spiritually centered guide of the journey.

If you are a pastor of a small church, I can hear you saying at this moment, "But I'm all there is! We don't have anyone else to take care of things." I've been there, friends. I've been part of small churches almost my entire life. As you've read this book, I hope you've seen the ways that smaller numbers of people gathered can be an asset, rather than a liability, for sensory-rich worship expression. Likewise, in this moment, I hope you will think a bit out of the box about the talents of the people you do have. I'm guessing that you may have someone that loves to talk on the phone and is connected to everybody in the church. This is the person to engage in one task as part of the worship "team"—calling people to be readers. Make a list of how many readers you need for each week, and give them a list of people who have said they will read. You may have someone who frequents the fabric or craft store regularly. Tell them what you need far enough in advance, and they can be looking in the bargain bins for just the right thing. And you may have someone with some land that would be happy to get you a truckload of bare branches for your Lent series. The point is that when we solicit help, we empower people to be part of the process, no matter how small the task. And we begin to draw appropriate boundaries around how much we take on so the sustainability of meaningful and memorable worship is supported.

I mentioned the role of a "series team leader" briefly in Chapter Two. These folks are the equivalent of the film "PA" (production assistant) on the worship team. They can be indispensable in the production part of the process. Their responsibilities can include working with the Visionary to create the design calendar (timeline) for series preparation and execution, working with artist-group leaders (Visual, Media, Music, Verbal, Dramatic) to schedule meetings, assisting in the production of worship scripts for the series, communicating with team members about schedule and tasks, helping with cue-to-cue rehearsals, and overseeing Worship Guide production. They can also be present before and during worship to make sure all participants/leaders are present, rehearsed, and informed about their roles. Of course, you can also decide to have a Series Team Leader and an assistant, or Co-Leaders, to help spread the duties out (this is a wonderful way to mentor youth). Can you imagine how this role will free up the Visionary (primary preacher) to have time to hone sermons

To see more about the Task Manager in the WDS App go to thinklikeafilmmaker.com.

and think about future series amidst all the other duties of ministry? What a valuable contribution to the church!

THE CUE-TO-CUE REHEARSAL

"The art of editing is in large part sensing the difference—feeling that edge where we teeter into boredom," Boorstin tells us.[147] A worship service that *flows* is one where designers and leaders are intensely attuned to the right timing for the parts of the service itself and also the transitions between the parts. "Filmmakers rely on story, what E.M. Forster called the 'and then ... and then.' Things have to keep happening. The child in us that loves a story demands we turn the page."[148] Working through transitions is the single most important key to a worship experience that moves seamlessly from one element to the next, making it feel more like a journey or unfolding story than a business agenda. How do we achieve this?

My theater background instilled in me the benefits of a "cue-to-cue" rehearsal in which we move through the worship script with an eye for artistic and technical details. Likewise, my research into the creative process of directors and actors on a film has revealed that the actual shoot of a scene will be more successful if various team members have "gone through the paces" before the camera actually rolls. In rehearsals, actors get blocking from the director and find their marks (places to be on the set at a precise time) so that when they are performing, they can focus more intently on immersion in the script and character rather than the technical aspects of where to be and what to do. Stand-ins (or "doubles") for the primary actors spend considerable time in technical rehearsals helping the lighting, sound, and camera crews make sure the equipment and their own blocking is correct and ready for the actors when they arrive. Directors have preceded live rehearsals with their own preparation, doing detailed script analysis so they are ready to offer a vision to actors and crew and be prepared to intuit new ideas during the rehearsal as well.[149]

All of these help us imagine the benefits of the cue-to-cue rehearsal. Key leaders (pastor, music director, A/V lead, series team leader) are in attendance at this rehearsal, which I recommend happen early enough in the week to precede any choir or music rehearsals in case any pertinent information comes out of the rehearsal that musicians will need to know. I don't have all the actual participants (readers, ushers, dramatists, musicians, etc.) at the rehearsal—it is more likely that they (particularly readers) will be able to commit only to coming thirty minutes before worship begins to run through their parts. But the cue-to-cue rehearsal allows the key leaders to make clear decisions and come up with clear directions for all those who will need them. After years of directing worship, I can tell you for sure that you do not want to be making decisions in front of the choir, band, readers, or leaders of ritual action. *Everyone* has an opinion, even if they don't have all the facts (this is coming from my experience of wrangling 140 Bishops in a rehearsal for serving communion to 10,000 people). Besides, we want all participants to feel like we know what we are doing! Clear and simple step-by-step instructions that we have thought all the way through will go a long way, for example, to calming a nervous choir ("but we've never done it this way before") about the round they will be singing from the aisles for the threshold moment every week in this series. Making sure leaders feel comfortable and can lead confidently will also make the congregation comfortable and confident even if they are being led in something that is new or different.

For the cue-to-cue rehearsal, we put our bodies *in the worship space.* It is simply not as effective to do a cue-to-cue rehearsal around a table and try to "imagine" what it will be like. We literally "walk through" the worship in order to ensure that we've covered all the details. We will find things that don't work as well as they did in our imaginations and are then able to tweak things to create a better solution. My suggestion is to walk through the worship "from the top" (beginning to end) so you can literally see and feel what needs to happen. The rehearsal requires an eye for detail. For example, how many music stands do we need for the reader's theater interpretation of the scripture, and when do those get into place? Will the dramatists bring them as they move to their places, or will they already be there? If we are going to have people writing prayers on slips of paper, will the paper be in the worship guide or handed to them when they come in? And are there writing utensils in the backs of every pew? Attending to details like these can mean the difference between a deeply meaningful presentation of scripture or act of prayer and an awkward or distracting moment as we scramble for music stands or something to write with.

Rehearsal also requires an attention to "flow." We may become aware that we need time to get the children's choir to their places, and we've got to provide a musical transition to keep the energy from "tanking" after our opening hymn. Figuring out just when to tell the communion servers to come forward may be different this time because we are receiving communion in a special way based on the message of the series. We need to remember to tell them not to rely on their usual timing, or we will mess up that wonderful moment of stillness and silence we are trying to create at the breaking of the bread. If we are paying attention to the overall momentum during the rehearsal, we can see moments that could become too stagnant or make more of moments that need to "stretch," giving us more time to savor them.

"The good editor uses the movements of the shots in an orchestrated way ... so movement leads to movement in a choreographed series of images and the action gains a cumulative momentum. Planning, then is essential."[150] As worship designers, we have three "editing" opportunities:

1) the script-writing process; 2) the rehearsal; and 3) in the moment of the worship experience itself. What little impromptu editing we do during worship will be aided by the editing we do throughout our preparation. After all, some things just can't be changed at the last minute. As the elements of worship become more sensory-rich, making sure they run smoothly so that people can worship without distraction is essential. Inevitably, there will be things that require our adaptation in the midst of worship. But having prepared ourselves diligently means that we can be more open and attentive to the Spirit's movement in the moment, allowing us to improvise with unexpected occurrences and then moving easily back into the "plan." In fact, I *hope* that there will be things that happen in worship—it should make a difference that we are a living body worshiping together. My silent prayer before every service is "O God, let there be something that happens that *isn't* in the bulletin!" I want the carefully planned sequences I've prepared to come off without a hitch—and they will if I've done my work of preparation. But I also want to be open to what the Spirit will do in the midst of the community that is better than anything I could have planned.

For a checklist for cue-to-cue rehearsals, go to thinklikeafilmmaker.com.

The first cue-to-cue rehearsal the week before a new series starts will be the most intense because we are just figuring out a new set of elements, such as the threshold moment. But this and other "thread items" will not have to be rehearsed every week once you have a series underway, so subsequent cue-to-cue rehearsals will not be as lengthy unless you have an especially complex element one week (such as communion or baptism). So allow more time that first week to get a handle on things, and know that other weeks won't take as long. This is true for all the ritual artists—the time preparing before the series begins will be more involved as you prepare elements that then will remain the same (visuals, theme songs, prayer responses) throughout the rest of the series. Besides the benefits of repetition for the congregation, it is also a way to keep from reinventing the wheel every week and burning out staff and volunteers. Years ago, when I really began to explore having threads throughout a series, I was worried that the repetition would become boring to the congregation. To the contrary, I have found that congregations love how repetition deepens the theme each week, and I've certainly found that those who work on worship relish the rhythm of preparation and rest.

WORSHIP GUIDES

I prefer calling what the congregation has in their hands a "Worship Guide" rather than a "Bulletin" because we want to move away from the notion that worship is a list of things to be checked off, and toward an *experience* of God with head, heart, and whole body. The written materials serve as a guide to help the congregation participate, which is the most important thing as we seek to offer unforgettable messages. Therefore, the decisions about what goes into the Worship Guide begin with the question, "At this moment in worship, what do we need written down to enable the fullest participation?" Sometimes the answer to that is "Nothing!" For instance, if I want the congregation to be visually watching the breaking of the bread at the end of the communion prayer, I don't want them to be reading the lines that the leader is saying. And my experience is that if the words are there, people will look at the words on the paper (or the screens) rather than at the action. At every step of the finalizing process, we concern ourselves with the details that invite the participation of the people in clear and concise terms, providing them with what they need yet not giving them too much, so that they can fully enter into a worshipful experience. However, as I mentioned above, I always keep a few copies of the scripts around in case there is someone who has hearing difficulty that will benefit from seeing as many of the words of the leaders as possible.

I believe we should put as much thought into the graphic design for the Worship Guide as we do the visual setting of worship. We are putting a lot of thought and attention into the environment—the feel of the space, how the visuals help set a tone and tell the story. Then, too often, we cram a lot of words onto a little page and slap a picture of the church on the front week in and week out (we just came into the church—we know what it looks like). Or we let the screen do everything, offering nothing in our hands except perhaps a list of titles down the page. This is sometimes not enough. I believe that what we have in our hands is also an opportunity to visually and verbally contribute to the message, theme, and "feel" of the worship.

Consider that the format of the Worship Guide could be different for different series because the "feel" of each series is different. Perhaps a watermark of a stretch of road is lightly in the background of the Worship Guide for a series using an anchor image of "journey." Perhaps a series on "emptying" has no Worship Guide or a very sparse outline on a ½ sheet of paper. Perhaps you center justify everything during a series on "Centered in God." You could copy everything upside-down on the inside of a Worship Guide for a series on "Turn the World Upside-Down." You get the idea. The graphic design software and technology have gotten so accessible and flexible that this is possible for any size congregation. Consider the worship guide as a graphic designer would consider the layout of a beautiful book of poetry—indeed,

See thinklikeafilmmaker.com for examples of Worship Guide formats.

worship is a living book of poetic praise and prayer to the Holy One. My preference with calendar-type announcements or current prayer lists that you want to have on paper each week is to create a separate insert that people can take out and stick to their refrigerator for ease of reference.

Rather than always using weekly guides, consider creating a booklet for one series with all the worship services for the series in it with a beautifully designed and artistic cover and divider pages that reflect the theme. You can even add pages of inspirational quotes, devotions by members, pages of announcements for special projects, a mission focus, meetings, events of the season. If you do a booklet, you could have people leave them in the pews/chairs from Sunday to Sunday. Let people take them at the end of the series. Invite visitors to pick up extra copies on their way out on any Sunday, and/or offer a website address where people can download it in pdf format if they'd like a print version.

If your church is "going green" and not using paper (which is a viable option), or if you are in the practice of putting all the words to songs/hymns on a screen, I want to encourage you to consider printing some number of copies (with your license numbers to do this on it) of the musically annotated versions of the music for music sight-readers in the congregation to pick up on their way in. They will love you for it! And the congregation will sing better with their help. Speaking of licenses, as you create scripts and guides, it is important that you enter "Worship Note" information. This is an essential practice and one not enough churches are doing. It is important to give credit where credit is due—as well as legally required. And I've found some people enjoy knowing

For more information on licenses and worship note formatting, see thinklikeafilmmaker.com.

sources of material. Also, I'd much rather refer to all that information at the bottom of the document rather than in the body of the Worship Guide itself. I'm not sure that listing the arranger of every anthem and song in the body always serves the Guide's purpose: to enhance the participation of the people.

As we talked about in the verbal arts chapter, consider using a format with a more poetic layout rather than a paragraph layout, especially for words spoken in unison. More white space on the page makes us feel *less* like this is a primarily *verbal* event. When the eye can dance on the page rather than focus hard, as if we are reading a book, it has a freeing effect on the eyes. One last comment about Worship Guides—I highly recommend that you have someone on the worship team oversee the creation, layout, and inputing of information rather than an administrative assistant who has no connection to the work of designing worship (or ask them to work on the team). I have found that innocent mistakes will be made when the person arranging the information has no idea how the information relates to the lived liturgy. Assigning this task to office personnel might have worked with "plug-n-play" worship, where we were simply replacing items in an order of worship that never changed. But when we begin to see the Worship Guide as part of the artfulness of ritual, we must bring greater awareness to its creation series by series.

GETTING THE WORD OUT

Call it evangelism, call it publicity. It really doesn't matter because the goal is the same—to make sure that the life-giving message you are offering touches those who need to experience it. Any movie producer will tell you that if you don't get the word out about a movie, you are missing an opportunity to offer the story in the broadest way possible. The art of marketing has changed drastically in recent years, and the advent of social media means that everyone is getting creative about marketing—no matter if you are a large film company or a small church.

Even though I'm including this at the end of this chapter on production, getting the word out will occur much earlier, perhaps as soon as the brainstorming process has begun. Movie posters and trailers are made before filming is complete and certainly before the editing is done. As soon as a worship series synopsis is written and anchor images decided upon, you can make logos, postcards, and series trailers about your upcoming series. All of these things can be done easily and inexpensively and can be quite fun to create.

In the Worship Design Studio, we have several mobile apps and websites that we recommend for creating graphic logos almost instantly (and in most cases, free) for your series. All you need is a title, a photograph that conveys your main metaphor (anchor image), and someone with an eye for design. Logos then can be made into postcards that you can give to your members a few weeks out, making personal invites easy for them. The logo goes on the front of the postcard with a provocative tagline. For instance, our series "Resurrection Stories" has an anchor image of people jumping into the air. We utilized a photo of a person in silhouette jumping in front of a sunrise on a beach and the tagline, "Do you need one for your life?" was placed across the bottom portion of the postcard. On the back you can put the entire 2–3 sentence synopsis you've written for the series, along with the important "when" and "where" information. An electronic postcard with all the information can be made for people to post on their social media accounts as a digital photo.

Learn how to create a logo at thinklikeafilmmaker.com.

Better yet, create a moving postcard in the form of a series trailer video that can be shared on social media and placed on your church's website as a "coming soon" and then "current series" announcement

To see some examples of series trailers, go to thinklikeafilmmaker.com.

after the launch of the series. You'll want multiple photos or video clips that can be edited together to go with your voiced-over synopsis. If you have a theme song that you can legally use (or if you have written your own theme song), use it as a sound score under the spoken synopsis. There are also many free sound clips available to use as background music. Be sure that the music communicates the tone of the series, giving folks a taste of what's to come. All of this can be done with the software that came with your computer or by using fairly inexpensive upgrades.

The work of your worship team can also be a wonderful source of building anticipation. Create a page on your website or on Facebook (even easier!) that is updated regularly with photos of the "behind the scenes" work by the worship team. Show visual installations in progress, do crowd-sourcing for sermons, and invite people in the congregation

See a "Behind the Scenes" Facebook page for a large conference I designed at thinklikeafilmmaker.com.

to upload photos about the theme that could be used in projected media. This is an amazing way to create excitement and even *ad hoc* participation in the design process for people who love engaging with social media.

Friends, the work of production is done, and we are ready for the release. Indeed, "release" is a good word because it is at this point that we release all of our preparations into God's hands. But we do so knowing that God's hand has been in it all along—from the visioning to the smallest detail. God's presence has been working through the actions of each person who has contributed in any way—from the most arduous contributions to the carrying out of one task. We have "planned together and planned ahead," ensuring that we have done our work as co-creators of the Living Word—as the hands and feet of Jesus, the ultimate storyteller.

CHAPTER 9

THE RELEASE AND THE REVIEWS

*They say they built the train tracks over the Alps between Vienna
and Venice before there was a train that could make the trip. They
built it anyway. They knew one day the train would come.*

The final narration at the end of *Under the Tuscan Sun* speaks of
hope. The elements we build and prepare for worship are analogous
to those train tracks ... they are just tracks. They carve an opportunity
for spiritual journey through the vast terrain of possible routes, but it
is not until people inhabit and embody those elements that the journey
truly begins. The train does come, every week. The time for worship
arrives, and we pray that people will trust us—and the Spirit—enough
to get on board. The narration continues:

*Any arbitrary turning along the way and I would be elsewhere.
I would be different. What are four walls, anyway? The house pro-
tects the dreamer. Unthinkably good things can happen. Even late
in the game. It's such a surprise.*

There are so many possible choices we could have made along the
way as we design a series that would have created a different experience.

But like Frances' renovated house, the work we do will be the walls that provide a container—a safe space—for the living, breathing community to dream a better future for all people and then move out to create it. Indeed, unthinkably good things can happen when we release our creative work into the hands of the Creator and the congregation and watch the Spirit take hold, sometimes in surprising ways.

The mission statement for my ministry of more than 20 years has been: *I am committed to building up the church by empowering congregations to celebrate and utilize their inherent creativity and diversity in order to worship God fully, thereby forming disciples to be the body of Christ in the world.* At the heart of this statement is the congregation—the people who gather for worship. Whether they gather in a cafe or a cathedral, whether they number five or five hundred, whether they sing accompanied by band or the bellows of an organ, it is they who *are* the work of worship as they embody the elements of worship we have prepared. Participation of the people is not an "add-on"; it is not optional. "The work of the people" *is* liturgy.

The two attributes I list in my mission statement—creativity and diversity—are human attributes that come into play in the work of worship. We are inherently creative, made in the image of the Creator of all that exists. Creativity merges with the expressive elements at hand—words, music, art, movement—to find ways to express the mystery of divine relationship that then inspires creative action on behalf of justice and love. This creativity, as we have seen throughout this book, can be harnessed as a "work of the people" in the design of worship and in the moment of worshiping. As we are empowered to utilize our creativity, we see and experience our own agency, our own ability to bring about change. The good news is that creativity is our birthright. All we have to do is encourage it, support it, and draw it out.

Diversity is also inherent in the human family. It is God-given and beautiful. It is the reason why we flourish as a society. If we all thought alike, moved through the world alike, had the same perspectives and talents, there is no way our species would have advanced in knowledge and survivability. And diversity is necessary for creativity, which thrives on combining disparate ideas until something new is formed. The more we celebrate creativity and diversity within our communities, the more we are empowered to worship God fully, bringing our whole selves as an offering to God.

I always joke in my workshops, "You know, the Bible says where two or three are gathered, there will be diversity. Actually … it doesn't say that. But I think that is why Jesus said he would be with us whenever two or three are gathered!" No matter what the configuration of people gathered, there will be diversity. This also means that there will be diversity of opinion about what "ought" to constitute the worship of God.

THE POLITICS OF CHANGE

"Everyone's a critic," so the saying goes. As sure as there are movies, there are movie critics. Reactions to anything are based on opinions derived from expectations. For Roger Ebert, perhaps one of the most well-known and respected film critics of our time, the expectations of film have to do with more than simply technique. "For me the movies are like a machine that generates empathy. It lets you understand hopes, aspirations, dreams and fears. It helps us to identify with the people who are sharing this journey with us."[151] Story, and the power of film to bring that story alive for us in ways that make us care about one another, seems to be at the heart of what Ebert was looking for, no matter the genre of the film. But not everyone is reacting out of such lofty expectations. Sometimes people just want what they "like" based on their own proclivities and without regard to what I call "a culture of hospitality."

Some churches I have consulted with are paralyzed by a small but vocal group that threaten (yes, *threaten*) the ministry of the church by withholding their gifts and their presence if they don't get their way—"sing this music, not that; preach from the pulpit, not the middle; add projections and we're out!" Churches often talk a good game about radical hospitality to "those people" outside the walls, and then I see how people treat each other in discussions about diverse worship expressions, and I wonder if we have at all heard the Gospel mandate to love our neighbor. Our "neighbor" may be the person sitting next to us for the last 30 years who resonates with something different in worship than we do. The mission of worship is not actually about pleasing ourselves or any one person. Even if it was, if we managed to please one person, we are guaranteed to have cut ourselves off from reaching someone else. People-pleasing is a game you can't win, and it will suck the life out of your church. You see, the thing about our inherent diversity is that for any one moment in worship, I can guarantee there will be some who "like" what's happening. *And* I can also guarantee that, for someone else, it will just not be their "cup of tea."

Imagine your church is having a potluck. Everyone has brought things they believe will feed the community in a delightful way. You arrive and see a chair at the table open and waiting just for you. The food in front of you is plentiful. You see fried chicken, and you start to salivate. You notice that someone brought mashed potatoes and gravy—prepared *just* the way you like it. Then, out of the corner of your eye, you see the *brussels sprouts*! Oh, no, no, no. You don't like brussels sprouts! What are you going to do? Get up from the table in a huff and leave the gathering because someone dared to bring brussels sprouts to the potluck? Of course not! Instead, you take the brussels sprouts when they are passed to you, and you turn to your neighbor and say, "You know what? Brussels sprouts are not my thing. But I saw how your eyes lit up when you saw them! Here, let me spoon out a nice heaping portion onto your plate *because I want you to be fed, my sister/my brother.*" And then you gratefully accept the mashed potatoes and gravy when they are handed to you, and, instead of over-focusing on the menu, you delight in the gift of being in the good, hospitable, and loving company of friends.

See a video of me presenting this analogy at thinklikeafilmmaker.com.

Do you see the metaphor? I have spent the last couple of decades finding ways to help churches understand, embrace, and be blessed by their diversity as they plan worship rather than being broken down by it. I have seen people and churches transform when they do so. But it takes open discussion about our diversity and instituting good structures within which to "evaluate" our worship. The root of that word is "value." For me, good evaluation happens when we *find out what we value so we can get more of it.* What we value is different than what we "like." In our potluck story, our decision not to get up and leave the table is based on the value of relationship and building community that supersedes our need to please ourselves. If we truly value each other and desire that God's loving presence be experienced by each and every person, there will be times when that value will move us to set aside our personal preferences in a hospitable attitude that embraces a God who comes to, speaks to, and transforms people in diverse ways.

In the first chapter of this book, I mentioned an evaluative exercise I developed early on in my consulting work. I ask people to share briefly with one another a moment in worship that they will never forget—one that was *meaningful* and *memorable* ("M-M-Good"). It is a moment that moved them and pops up in their memory—an "unforgettable message." As people begin to describe these moments, we begin to see just how diverse the descriptions are. Some memories are of quiet, introspective reflection and moments of awe. Other memories are boisterous and full of joyful exuberance. Some have to do with specific art forms, and some focus on a sense of community, surprise, or challenge. The point is, no story is the same. I have sometimes done this exercise with churches in the midst of "the worship wars." By inviting the participants to communicate about a moment when they were moved, they begin to see the reality that people are moved in all expressions of worship. We see how our fellow worshipers, no matter which service they go to or what expression they "like," are filled and growing in their spiritual journey. It is difficult to call "that" kind of worship "bad" when we see how it has truly uplifted our sister or brother. And what is good for one can be good for the whole body, *if* we do not insist on breaking that body apart ourselves with inhospitable words and actions.

But this move toward a more hospitable stance comes only as we begin to *trust* that, because this community honors the diversity of ways the Spirit moves in each of us, there will be times when what we are doing in worship *will* fully resonate with me. I believe that the intensity of anger over worship change is an *unarticulated fear of losing God*. If I have experienced God at this church where we have been doing it "this way" for quite a while, if I have felt God's presence with me in good times and bad here in this worship … and now and *you say you are going to change it*??!! It is possible that what I'm afraid of is that I won't encounter God here anymore. I may feel I am in danger of *losing* my experience of God. But this is a gut reaction most likely anchored in the reptilian "fight or flight" part of the brain, and it is often difficult to articulate reasoning from this place. We simply react. We simply call that which feels threatening "not holy" or "not reverent."

I have discovered many reasons why people react negatively to change in worship. Most often, it touches on something much deeper than reactions to the actual worship expression itself. You would never (hopefully) go to a doctor with symptoms and be treated without that physician first reviewing your health history. Likewise, when dealing with conflict about worship, it is important to dig deeper than the complaint.

Worship is often a safer thing to argue about than the deeper issues at hand. I recently received an e-mail from a member of the Worship Design Studio asking for advice about the fact that she had an uprising on her hands because people didn't like what she was doing in worship. When I asked her what else was going on in the life of the community, she revealed that they are in the midst of deciding if they have the resources to continue to sustain the church. This congregation's pain and grief and sense of failure simply found an outlet in blaming the pastor for the new song they were being "forced" to sing. Perhaps it is their inability to be open to a new "song" (metaphorically speaking) that is killing the church. Conflict over worship can actually help us understand the deeper undercurrents of dys-function. Here are some of the things I've learned about individuals' reactions to worship change:

Download a handout that includes all these points at thinklikeafilmmaker.com.

Reactions to change may be "theological" (our experience of God). But "theological" reasons may not necessarily be in the form of well-thought-out systematic theologies. Theology is a term that describes how we understand the holy. Sometimes our theological reflections are visceral—related to what "feels" holy to us—even down to the habits that make us feel at home. I have a cartoon that shows a disgruntled couple glaring at the visitors who have taken "their" pew seats. This cartoon points to the fact that even where we sit (Sunday after Sunday)—our vantage-point in the sanctuary—becomes part of the memories of our experience of God. Our brains take snapshots of memories that are tied to the neural path-ways of our emotions, and these kinds of neural connections are deeply felt. It is difficult to articulate why we want to sit in the same spot, but we just know we do! If our vantage point changes or something about what we see from that vantage point changes, such as a new placement for the pulpit or the objects on the table in a different configuration, our brains immediately go on alert. We are wired to notice difference as part of our survival skill set. We immediately begin to assess the threat and if disturbed enough, we go into "fight or flight" mode. However, our brains are incredibly elastic, and after we let a few Sundays go by with the new configuration, we discover that our minds relax and are reassured that God is still present. As we get used to things changing with each new series, our brains begin to understand and accept as "normal" the rhythms of change. It is important not to react to complaints too soon and "go back to the way we've always done it" without giving people a chance to adapt. Good questions for evaluation are:

> *If we become upset about a change or a possible change, what experience of God are we afraid of losing? Is our concept of who God is tied only to things that feel familiar to us? Or is it possible that God could show up to us even in new things if we give them a chance? Is it possible that a new thing, given some time, could eventually feel familiar and full of the presence of God?*

Reactions to change may be "historical" (our memories of church). Our concept of "the way we've always done it" is often only a couple of generations long, if that. I have a workshop experience that I call "3000 Years of Worship History—Only the Highlights!" We begin with Miriam and the women drumming and dancing at the Red Sea after the people have escaped slavery in Egypt. Then we go through several time periods, including the first temple, Babylonian exile, the early church, and on through medieval and Reformation movements. We end up in early American worship in three forms: camp meetings, urban, and the "invisible church"—the worship expressions of African slaves. What we find is that the only constant is change—but not simply change for the sake of change. Rather, change happens because context changes, and the forms of worship change with them *in order to keep the story alive.*

The Latin root of the word "tradition" is *traditio,* and it literally means "to hand on or to surrender"—not to "hang on!" Tradition exists only because the story is handed on to the next generation and they continue to tell it in their own way—in a way that will communicate powerfully to their context.

I have a cartoon that shows some folks in ancient clothing and one is saying to the other, "But we've never *used* a ram's horn in worship before!" Yes, in *every* age there have been folks who undoubtedly resisted change. It is in our nature. Memories (or nostalgia) are powerful factors in our opinions of what worship "ought" to be. We seek experiences that relate to our memories—either we are looking for the warm-and-fuzzy things we remember from our past experience of worship, or we are reacting *against* the things we remember that were not so life-affirming.

Getting upset that we are using a different Advent wreath this year could be wrapped up in the fact that this new one doesn't look like what I'm "used to." Our underlying discomfort makes us forget that it is the actual *light,* not the holder, that is the root of the symbol. On the other hand, if we were oppressed by forms or messages of worship in our younger years, anything that "smacks" of that memory will cause conscious or sub-conscious reactions in us. For example, my spouse grew up in a very strict, theologically punitive religion. Now, no matter how liberating the message by a preacher, if there is a "floppy Bible" (soft-sided) in the preacher's hands, the gut reaction of my spouse is negative. Apply this to other reactions to negative past experiences—something that feels "too Catholic" or "too Pentecostal" or "too touchy-feely" or "too stodgy." Here are some questions for evaluation of reactions related to our histories:

> *If we become upset about a change or a possible change, how*
> *is this change related to our expectations of worship based on our*

histories? How could we better educate the congregation about this "new" thing that could expand our knowledge of history—for example anointing with oil—actually an ancient historical practice that might be new to some?

Reactions to change may be "sociological" (messages of what worship is "supposed to be"). We all live with inherited messages about what is acceptable worship behavior. Our religious identity is often wrapped up in various expressions of piety—meaning the quality or character of worship. When I was growing up in my small, rural United Methodist church, we didn't raise our hands in praise. *That* was the Pentecostal church down the road! Even though now I am often in worship environments where raising one's hands would be completely acceptable, I still find it uncomfortable (or non-native) to my body because I still live with childhood messages ingrained in me. Now think about a whole congregation, each one with differing messages about what worship "is" or "is not" internalized down to their very bones. Whew! Even something like whether or not we should clap in church can divide us or whether worship ought to be more formal or informal. Here are some questions for reflection:

> *When we become divided about what worship "ought to be," can we examine the origins of those messages and affirm that all "shoulds" are contextual? Perhaps this would be an opportunity to hear each other's histories and experiences of deeply meaningful worship, even and especially if they are different from our own. Can we figure out a way to include various experiences, knowing that it never has to be an "either/or" but rather a "both, and?"*

Reactions to change may be physiological (what we literally resonate with). Our bodies literally resonate with different rhythms that feel "holy" to us. I talked about this briefly in the music chapter—my research into "Primal Patterns" of energy that form the rhythms with which we move through the world. Our reactions will sometimes depend on whether our very bodies are comfortable with certain worship expressions based on our "home patterns" of energy. Some of us will literally, neuromuscularly, resonate with grandeur, others with meditative silence, others with celebrative and interactive worship, and still others with pulsing, driving rhythms. Because our reactions arise from our bodies, they feel so completely "normal" to us that we cannot imagine others feel differently. That which isn't comfortable to us feels "foreign" and not at all about "the holy." Then we tend to make value judgments about it for all others.

See thinklikeafilmmaker for a deeper look at the Primal Patterns.

> *If we hear comments about particular music or forms of worship being "bad," can we offer a discussion about how our very physiology (our bodies) tend to create our opinions about what is "right?" Can we begin to see that what is "right" and "holy" may be a "different right" for someone else? How can we extend radical hospitality to each other?*

Reactions to change may be psychological ("what lies beneath"). Just like the horror flick called *What Lies Beneath*, when things "lurk" under the surface such as unresolved grief and tensions within the community, they often become like unwanted ghosts that are hard to pin down but then get played out in conflict about worship. I said this earlier in this chapter, but it bears repeating. Conflict over worship is sometimes not really about worship, so doing our homework to try to get to the bottom of it is important. Uncomfortable situations can occur when worship change *unearths larger issues*. Those candlesticks endowed with the memorial plaque commemorating Aunt Betty (stalwart saint of the church) become much more than candlesticks. They become a symbol of what was, and changing them out for something else for a Sunday or series can all of a sudden create an unanticipated intensity. A change in the order of worship can take on more anxiety than an earthquake because it may mirror what is already being experienced by some in the church— things are shifting, seemingly out of our control. Questions for reflection on this could include:

> *When an uncomfortable situation arises "about" worship, can we dig a bit deeper to see what underlying "dis-ease" this symptom may be pointing to? Could it be that through the lens of this problem, we might hit on a spiritual issue that could help transform us and move us toward more health and wholeness?*

Finally, **reactions to change may be political (power-plays based on the need for control).** What?! Politics? In church?! Well... ahem... yes. Politics happen when "birds of a feather flock together" and begin to voice complaints or opinions that they hope will sway others to their point of view. In my experience with churches in conflict over worship, again, the deeper issue at hand is based in fear of losing something. Let me use an example of what has become a flashpoint of controversy in many churches over the last couple of decades—screens installed in the sanctuary. I was called to consult with a church that was in just such a conflict. The screen for a new contemporary service had been installed in such a way that when it was in the "up" position, it was hidden and you couldn't even tell it was there. Terrific! But when it was down, it covered a beautiful stained-glass "rose" window. The people who were upset with this never attended the contemporary service, so they were never in worship when the screen was down. But just the *idea* that it was covering this window in the "other" service was a matter of huge controversy and literally beginning to split the church. When I came to do the Friday night session with "both sides," I had the screen down with a digital photograph of the window projected onto it. It took the group a full thirty minutes to realize that it was a photo of the window and not the window itself! This opened up a conversation about what was *really* going on—a fear held by the "traditional" crowd that their church as they knew it was slipping away into something they could not recognize. They felt out of control, and their human nature was to try to exert control in order to feel safe again. Those who were excited about new forms of worship felt rejected by the conflict, and so their own strong reactions were based in feeling hurt—their very deep human need for acceptance and belonging was injured. No wonder everyone was feeling so awful!

We spent time talking about these things, and I invited the "traditionalists" to share what they knew about *all* the beautiful artwork in the sanctuary with those who were newer in the church and had never heard the stories or the symbolic significance behind the windows. As a result, the folks in the contemporary service decided to utilize digital technology as I had done and feature various aspects of the windows on the screens as backdrops and even as featured images at times. And miracle-of-miracles, this led to an idea to use close-ups of the symbols as inspiration for a worship series, which led to—you may have guessed it—the screens coming down occasionally in the traditional service as well to utilize in beautiful, artful, and profound ways! What a gift.

Unfortunately, however, there are times when I have used a brutal phrase to describe the reactions of some people to a situation of conflict—"they hold the entire church hostage." I don't like to use that phrase, and I rarely use it, but sometimes it is the truth. There are times when fear, control, a lack of compassion, and an inability to see a different perspective keep the whole system from moving forward.

When conflict arises, is it possible to reframe the conversations beyond the stuck position of "this way" or "that way" into a more creative and life-giving, healing alternative? Can we steer the conversation away from "I think…" to "I feel…" in order to get at our human condition and the "buttons" that are getting pushed? What are the consequences of our conflicts for the health of the whole church?

One of the most popular questions in my workshops over the years has been, "How do we implement change in worship without making anybody mad?" The answer? "You don't." I'm sorry, I don't have a magic formula for making change easy. Change is difficult for almost all of us, and when it comes to changes to worship, nerves that we didn't even know we had get touched. We have to keep talking about our relationship with change out loud and affirming our diversity as God-given. We have to teach tools for grasping why we are diverse. We have to extend the idea that part of the call to "radical hospitality" is to accept that some moments in worship won't be "our cup of tea"—and that's all right. Like the weather in the Midwest, where I grew up, just wait a minute, it will change. A community devoted to diverse expression allows the story, the message, to take us on the ebbs and flows and ups and downs and highs and lows of dynamic storytelling and expressive praise and prayer. And we must keep our focus on the point of it all—the mission of worship—which is not to make everyone happy, but to facilitate the worship of God and the building up of the Body of Christ so that we might "go and do likewise" in the world.

When two or three are gathered, there *will* be diversity. Fact of life. I want to plant a seed that might reframe your own fear of facing diverse opinions in the congregation: *If we do not witness various perspectives within a community, it is direct evidence of domination by a few.* Let's celebrate if we are, indeed, in the midst of conversations (no matter how difficult) about worship—and I'm not talking about "conversations" that involve gripe sessions in the parking lot or anonymous letters to the pastor. Here are my best pointers about dealing in a healthy way with "the politics of change."

- Learn together—excerpt things from this book in your newsletter or blog, and plan a study based on the book with your whole congregation, not just the worship team.

- Listen together—share stories with each other about transformative worship experiences that are unforgettable in which the Spirit moved in powerful ways.

- Cultivate a culture of radical hospitality—extend hospitality to the stranger, those whose experience of worship is different from ours, and offer thanksgiving for the diverse ways God comes to each person.

- Clarify the mission of worship together—keep before the community the point of it all, taking the love and justice of the Gospel we experience in our worship and sharing it with the world in which we live each day.

- Don't always ask for permission—sometimes we make a bigger deal out of something that must be experienced first in order to be accepted. But make sure that new and unfamiliar experiences and worship expressions are done with excellence, filled with the Spirit, grounded in God's Word, and introduced in a meaningful way that points us toward our discipleship in Jesus, not just doing something we're doing because it is the new and groovy thing to do.

- Take incremental steps—just because you got a lot of new ideas from this book, do not do fifty new things in worship next Sunday—if you do, don't blame me! But also offer alternative experiences occasionally for those who are yearning for big leaps, not baby steps.

- Get people involved in the worship design process—this is a faithful thing to do so the people themselves are truly engaging in the "work of the people" and take ownership of knowing about and crafting worship.

THE WORSHIP TEAM REVIEW

It is important for the worship team to evaluate their work on a regular basis. But that review should *not* focus just on the complaints and reactions from particular people. When I'm working in a one-on-one consultation, I take notice of how much time the team spends on saying, "Oh my, so-and-so would have a cow if we do that!" or "So-and-so said …" When I hear a lot of this, I know the group has some codependent tendencies. And as the saying goes, "It takes one to know one." My own history of codependent behavior has made me especially attuned to the dangers of people-pleasing. I have seen pastors and staff become paralyzed about making any change at all because they fear the reactions of a few people. While it is important to work incrementally and do everything in our power to ground changes in good theological, historical, and biblical connections and to educate the congregation along the way, we also cannot become enslaved by our own fear of perceived reactions. In my experience, we can wrongly predict reactions, making up scenarios in our heads based only on fear, convincing ourselves to simply stop trying.

The review of the team should also not rely solely on whether or not we are doing it "like everyone else" or whether we can afford the latest techniques and technology. Roger Ebert was adamant that movie reviews should be relative—should take context into consideration.

He reviewed films keeping the genre in mind and how it fulfilled its particular purpose. He could give an epic film a "thumbs down" and a more simply-made movie a "thumbs up" because he was looking past the "bells and whistles" to other, more important criteria.[152] So how do we evaluate our worship as a team?

I didn't choose to use *Under the Tuscan Sun* as the case study for my research because it is the greatest movie of all time. Critics were divided over it, in fact. It is rare that we will ever create worship that touches everyone equally. And being "perfect" in our design and execution is even more rare, perhaps impossible, and actually not the point. I chose *Under the Tuscan Sun* because it so effectively communicates, through all the art forms utilized in filmmaking, themes and symbols of love, brokenness, family, home, justice, transition, new life, and resurrected hope. It even has scenes that reminded me of "sacramental" living, like the birth of a baby welcomed into the world and joyous scenes of table fellowship that featured the healing power of breaking bread together. When I speak of this film in my workshops, people who have seen it get a glint in their eye, and heads begin to nod in fond remembrance of their experience of it. Just like a moment in worship that was meaningful and memorable, even though they might not recall specific details of the movie, most still recall a visceral connection to the story and its messages. We all know how a film that has not been lauded by the critics can sometimes still be a box-office hit. The criteria for judging worship is not always about whether or not everything went off without a hitch; it's about whether the message was offered in an unforgettable way. Details will fade away, but a powerful message that has formed us lives in us and with us in our own life stories.

I'm not saying that we need not review and evaluate the details. You've heard me say throughout this book that paying attention to details in our preparation is important to keep the people's focus on the message, not the form. If any one of the artists involved in the film does not come through in their job, it can affect the whole. Details do matter. But what I am suggesting is that there are some criteria that can help us look at the "whole" picture more effectively. No matter what size or style of worship, I have found all churches can move to a higher or deeper level of engagement with these five basics for meaningful and memorable worship:

1. **Create intentional spiritual journeys**—does the worship series hold together in a cohesive way that deepens engagement with the overarching message over time? Have we created connections to the message throughout the series but also allowed each worship experience to stand on its own, making visitors and those who can't come every Sunday feel welcome and part of the journey? Have we connected the series theme to other aspects of our life together such as mission and education?

2. **Engage the congregation**—have we provided significant opportunities for the people to participate as fully as they are able, and are those opportunities adaptable and inclusive for all ages and abilities? Are we leading as strongly as we can so that the people can participate confidently? Are there many opportunities for leadership by a variety of people? Have the people been engaged in a visceral way, embodying the message in their responsive actions?

3. **Be sensory-rich in communicating the message**—are we honoring the diversity of ways that people take in information and express themselves by offering the message through all the senses? What categories of the Multiple Intelligences (see Chapter One) do we need to enhance? Are all the ritual artists working collaboratively so that each art form is often layered with other art forms? Are symbols powerfully communicated through sight and sound and action?

4. **Offer deeply spiritual leadership**—are leaders getting to worship fully even as they lead worship through spiritual practices that prepare and ground them? Have we "set the stage" for the message through threshold moments that provide a framework for our experience? Are verbal transitions more than simply perfunctory instructions about "what's next," or are they helping to guide and engage the congregation in their work of worship?

5. **Let it flow**—have we done the work of attending to the flow of worship, to transitions and energy dynamics? Does the worship feel like a journey from beginning to end rather than pieces cobbled together? Are we attentive and open to what the Spirit's movement in the congregation might reveal in the moment of worship that could change "the plan" in small or significant ways?

These five basics are what I teach in my Worship Design Studio 6-week webinar trainings called "Reboot Your Worship." In developing the training, I asked myself, "What are the basic things that worship teams could pay attention to that would effect immediate change for the better in their worship?" After several sessions of this training in the last couple of years, the response from hundreds of participants is that utilizing these basics as a lens for evaluation is very effective. As you can tell (unless you are reading the last chapter first), these basics are based on my research into effectively communicating the story through sensory-rich worship design. I am grateful for the work of filmmakers that has taught me so much about bringing stories to life. I pray you are inspired as well and that your work to proclaim the message of love and justice will result in unforgettable messages that change lives and change our world.

ENDNOTES

1 Cecil Williams, *I'm Alive: An Autobiography* (Harper & Row, 1980).

2 Abigail Wright, from her lecture "Think Like a Filmmaker," https://vimeo.com/134990548.

3 Rob Webber, *Visual Leadership: The Church Leader as ImageSmith* (Abingdon Press, 2002), 159.

4 Tex Sample, *Powerful Persuasion: Multimedia Witness in Christian Worship* (Abingdon Press, 2005).

5 Abigail Wright, "Think Like a Filmmaker."

6 Jon Boorstin, *Making Movies Work: Thinking Like a Filmmaker* (Silman-James Press, 1995), 8.

7 Academy of Achievement, https://www.youtube.com/watch?v=kBN9jpooZoM.

8 Martin Scorsese, *The Century of Cinema: A Personal Journey,* 1996 as cited in Clive Marsh, *Cinema and Sentiment: Film's Challenge to Theology,* (Paternoster Press, 2005), 2.

9 Marsh, *Cinema and Sentiment,* 9.

10 For more on the connection of memory, emotion, and story as it applies to ministry, see David Hogue, *Remembering the Future, Imagining the Past,* (Wipf & Stock Publishers, 2009).

11 Howard Gardner, *Frames of Mind: The Theory of Multiple Intelligences,* 3rd ed. (Basic Books, 2011).

12 Marsh, *Cinema and Sentiment,* 85.

13 Allen Palmer, "Why We Need Stories (in 3 words or less)," http://www.crackingyarns.com.au/2014/05/25/why-we-need-stories/.

14 Allen Palmer, "My philosophy (or why people go to the movies)," http://www.crackingyarns.com.au/about-2/my-film-philosophy/.

15 Allen Palmer, "How to Write a Logline," http://www.crackingyarns.com.au/2010/03/25/the-most-important-27-words-a-screenwriter-will-ever-write/.

16 Audrey Wells, from the director's commentary, *Under the Tuscan Sun* (Touchstone Pictures, 2003).

17 Personal interview, September, 2014.

18 Interview, Academy of Achievement, https://www.youtube.com/watch?v=XOxItKRzPOY.

19 Audrey Wells, director's commentary, *Under the Tuscan Sun.*

20 *Ibid.*

21 Nel Paul, PCC Cinema Program and Silver, Alain and Ward, Elizabeth, *The Film Director's Team* (Slman-James Press., 2nd ed., 1992).

22 For instance, see http://mentalfloss.com/article/59548/12-stories-behind-film-production-nightmares.

23 Edictive, "4 Weaknesses of Film Development Teams," http://edictive.com/blog/4-reasons-for-the-weakness-of-film-development-teams/.

24 Boorstin, *Making Movies Work,* 16–17.

25 Rainer Volp, "Space as Text: The Problem of Hermeneutics in Church Architecture," in *Studia Liturgica* 24 (1994), 171.

26 Chris Allen Tant, "Filmmaking Techniques, Art Direction and Resourcefulness," https://www.youtube.com/watch?v=U_4C8TozdhA.

27 James F. White, *Introduction to Christian Worship*, rev. ed. (Nashville: Abingdon Press, 1990), 89.

28 Fr. Richard S. Vosko, "Introduction," in Michael J. Crosbie, *Architecture for the Gods* (New York: Watson-Guptill Publications, 2000), 8.

29 Crosbie, *Architecture for the Gods*, 76.

30 *Ibid.,* 56, 144.

31 *Ibid.,* 26, 76.

32 *Ibid.,* 98. 128.

33 Janet Goodridge, *Rhythm and Timing of Movement in Performance: Drama, Dance and Ceremony* (London: Jessica Kingsley Publishers, 1999), 166.

34 Chelsea Wald, "Spaces of Worship," in *Science and Spirit Magazine* as cited at http://www.science-spirit.org/articles/newsoverview.cfm.

35 Nancy Chinn, *Spaces for Spirit: Adorning the Church* (Chicago: Liturgy Training Publications, 1998), 22.

36 Kendra Cherry, "Color Psychology: How Colors Impact Moods, Feelings and Behaviors," https://www.verywell.com/color-psychology-2795824

37 Maura Yost, http://www.creativebehavior.com/index.php?PID=42. For more on theories of color see Betty Edwards, *Color by Betty Edwards: Mastering the Art of Mixing Colors*, (New York: Penguin Group, 2004).

38 Chinn, *Spaces for Spirit*, 18–31.

39 Michael Rizzo, *The Art Direction Handbook,* (Focal Press, 2014).

40 "The craft of art direction — conversation with Judy Rhee" from *Pushing Pixels,* http://www.pushing-pixels.org/2012/09/07/the-craft-of-art-direction-conversation-with-judy-rhee.html.

41 Ricouer, Paul. "Metaphor and Philosophical Discourse." *The Rule of Metaphor: Multidisciplinary Studies of the Creation of Meaning in Language.* Translated by Robert Czerny with Kathleen McLaughlin and John Costello, (University of Toronto Press, 1977), 257–313.

42 Mary Collins, *Contemplative Participation* (Collegeville: The Liturgical Press, 1990), 40.

43 Rizzo, *The Art Direction Handbook,* 109.

44 Mark Pierson, *The Art of Curating Worship: Reshaping the Role of Worship Leader,* (Augsburg Fortress Press, 2010), 135.

45 See Kim Miller's stage designs at http://redesigningworship.com/category/ginghamsburg-worship/.

46 See examples of stage designs at http://www.churchstagedesignideas.com.

47 Personal interview with Ted Lyddon Hatten, January 2016.

48 *Ibid.*

49 Allen Palmer, from "Cracking Yarns," http://www.crackingyarns.com.au/2013/12/05/great-endings-7-want-a-massive-high-first-youll-need-a-shattering-low/.

50 Don E. Saliers, *Worship Come to Its Senses,* (Abingdon Press, 1996).

51 Don E. Saliers, *Worship as Theology: Foretaste of Glory Divine* (Abingdon Press, 1994), 152.

52 *Ibid.,* 141.

53 Boorstin, 50–51.

54 Marlene LeFever, *Learning Styles: Reaching Everyone God Gave You,* (David C. Cook, 2011).

55 Boorstin, *Making Movies Work,* 51.

56 This song, by Richard Bruxvoort-Colligan, can be found at http://www.psalmimmersion.com/#!psalm-65/airrp

57 For a wonderful book that will help you learn the structure of many prayer forms, see Ruth Duck, *Finding Words for Worship: A Guide for Leaders* (Westminster John Knox Press, 1995).

58 I highly recommend utilizing Pat Schneider's techniques for group writing sessions that nurture creativity, and therefore the soul, *Writing Alone and With Others* (Oxford University Press, 2003).

59 Garrison Keillor, *The Wittenburg Door* (San Diego: Dec/Jan, 1984/85).

60 Michael Hauge, "Story Structure: The 5 Key Turning Points of All Successful Screenplays," http://www.storymastery.com/story/screenplay-structure-five-key-turning-points-successful-scripts/.

61 Nick Morgan, "The Kinesthetic Speaker: Putting Action into Words," *Harvard Business Review* (April 2001), 113.

62 *Ibid.,* 113–114.

63 Jana Childers, *Performing the Word: Preaching as Theatre* (Nashville: Abingdon Press, 1998).

64 Albert Mehrabian, *Silent Messages: Implicit Communication of Emotions and Attitudes* (Belmont: Wadsworth Publishing, 1971), 43–44 as cited in Childers, *Performing the Word*, 57.

65 Childers, *Performing the Word*, 74.

66 Anecdotal. Boorstin says something similar: "No ten minutes should go by anywhere in the film without an event that radically changes the course of the action." Boorstin, 52.

67 Robert Jourdain, *Music, the Brain and Ecstasy: How Music Captures our Imagination,* (New York: HarperCollins, 1997), 305–308.

68 Janalea Hoffman, *Rhythmic Medicine: Music With a Purpose* (Leawood: Jamillan Press, 1995), 2–3.

69 Theo Van Leeuwen, *Speech, Music, Sound* (London: Macmillan Press, Ltd., 1999), 103–104, 140–141.

70 *Ibid.,* 106, 205.

71 Roy A. Prendergast: "The Aesthetics of Film Music," in *A Neglected Art: A Critical Study of Music in Film* (New York: New York University Press, 1977), 213–245.

72 *Ibid.*

73 Boorstin, *Making Movies Work,* 100–101.

74 Jourdain, *Music, the Brain and Ecstasy,* 301–3014.

75 Prendergast, "The Aesthetics of Film Music."

76 Jim Ellis, "Tips on Scoring for Film and Television," https://www.youtube.com/watch?v=o0zd5wt6v84.

77 As quoted in Prendergast, "The Aesthetics of Film Music."

78 *Ibid.*

79 Ellis, "Tips on Scoring for Film and Television."

80 Boorstin, *Making Movies Work,* 42.

81 www.giftsofthedarkwood.com

82 "You Are Mine," words by David Haas, The Faith We Sing (Abingdon Press, 2000), 2218.

83 Boorstin, *Making Movies Work,* 45.

84 Prendergast: "The Aesthetics of Film Music."

85 "Bordwell & Thompson's Terminology" as cited at http://www.filmsound.org/filmart/bordwell2.htm. Edited excerpts from David Bordwell and Kristin Thompson. "Sound in Cinema," in *Film Art: An Introduction* (Columbus: McGraw Hill Humanities Publishers, 2003).

86 Robert L. Mott, *Nine Components of Sound* as cited at http://filmsound.org/articles/ninecomponents/9components.htm.

87 Bruce Morrill, "Liturgical Music: Bodies Proclaiming and Responding to the Word of God," *Worship* 74, no. 1 (Jan 2000), 27–28. This article also appears in Morrill, ed. *Bodies of Worship*, 157–172. Morrill describes Alfred A. Tomatis' research in neurophysiology

which claims that through the "medulla (or brainstem) the auditory nerve connects the ear with all of the body's muscles, with the vagus nerve connecting the inner ear with all the major organs. The ear's vestibular function thereby influences ocular, labial, and other facial muscles, affecting such activities as seeing and eating… The ear functions, to speak metaphorically, as the gateway of stimulation or "charge" to the brain."

88 *Ibid.,* 32–33.

89 *Ibid.,* 36.

90 Van Leeuwen, *Speech, Music, Sound,* 103–104, 140–141, 205.

91 *Ibid.,* 103–104, 140–141.

92 Morrill, "Liturgical Music," 26.

93 Boorstin, *Making Movies Work,* 22.

94 *Ibid.,* 91.

95 Stephen Proctor, *Guidebook for Visual Worship,* download at http://illuminate.us/shop/a-guidebook-for-visual-worship/.

96 *Ibid.*

97 *Ibid.*

98 Eileen Crowley, *Liturgical Art for a Media Culture,* (Liturgical Press, 2007), 8. See this resource for an introduction to the history of media art.

99 See rosebrand.com for any of these alternative projection solutions.

100 I highly recommend downloading Stephen Proctor's *Guidebook for Visual Worship* at http://illuminate.us/shop/a-guidebook-for-visual-worship/ for a good starting place for details such as font size, style, color, slide transition times, etc.

101 See more about Camron's work at www.visualworshiper.com.

102 The Work of the People website, www.theworkofthepeople.com.

103 Duarte website, http://www.duarte.com/services/.

104 Nancy Duarte, "The secret structure of great talks," TedxEast, https://www.ted.com/talks/nancy_duarte_the_secret_structure_of_great_talks.

105 Nancy Duarte, http://www.duarte.com/how-to-think-like-a-film-maker-when-using-powerpoint/.

106 Camron Ware, as cited in Proctor, *Guidelines,* 8.

107 Proctor, *Guidelines,* 9.

108 Steven Ascher and Edward Pincus, *The Filmmaker's Handbook: A Comprehensive Guide for the Digital Age,* (Penguin Group, 1999), 214.

109 Boorstin, *Making Movies Work,* 91–92.

110 Ascher and Pincus, *The Filmmaker's Handbook,* 304.

111 Tomlinson Holman, "Roles of Sound," http://www.filmsound.org/articles/roles_of_sound.htm.

112 David Sonnenschein, *Sound Design: The Expressive Power of Music, Voice, and Sound Effects in Cinema,* (Michael Wiese Productions, 2001), 23–24.

113 *Ibid.,* 55.

114 *Ibid.,* 71.

115 Margaret Taylor, "A History of Symbolic Movement in Worship," in Doug Adams and Diane Apostolos-Cappadona, eds. *Dance as Religious Studies* (New York: The Crossroads Publishing Company, 1990), 29.

116 Winifred Whelan, "Bodily Knowing: Implications for Liturgy and Religious Education," *Religious Education* Vol. 36, no. 2 (Spring, 1983), 276.

117 James White, *Protestant Worship: Traditions in Transition* (Louisville: Westminster/John Knox Press, 1989), 152.

118 *Ibid.,* 152.

119 William H. McNeill, *Keeping Together in Time: Dance and Drill in Human History* (Cambridge: Harvard University Press, 1995), 99–100. See also White, *Protestant*

Worship regarding the history of expressions of worship among Anabaptist, Frontier, and Pentecostal traditions.

120 For a review of literature on the body in religion (at least before 1990), see Lawrence E. Sullivan, "Body Works: Knowledge of the Body in the Study of Religion," *History of Religions* 30, no. 1 (1990), 86–99. Catherine Bell gives a more brief overview in *Ritual Theory, Ritual Practice* (Oxford: Oxford University Press, 1992), 94–98.

121 Antonio Damasio, *Descartes Error: Emotion, Reason, and the Human Brain* (New York: HarperCollins Publishers, 1994), 173–175.

122 Clive Marsh, *Cinema and Sentiment,* 100–101.

123 Boorstin, *Making Movies Work*, 65–66.

124 *Ibid.,* 76.

125 *Ibid.,* 121.

126 Judith Weston, *The Film Director's Intuition: Script Analysis and Rehearsal Techniques* (Michael Wiese Productions. Kindle Edition.), Kindle Locations 5089–5094.

127 "I Was There to Hear Your Borning Cry," © 1985 words and music by John Ylvisaker.

128 Marjorie Procter-Smith, *In Her Own Rite: Constructing Feminist Liturgical Tradition* (Nashville: Abingdon Press, 1990).

129 Tex Sample, *Powerful Persuasion,* 123.

130 Recorded interview with Martha Graham, https://www.youtube.com/watch?v= xgf3xgbKYko.

131 See Ray G. Birdwhistell, *Introduction to Kinesics: An Annotated System for Analysis of Body Motion and Gesture* (Louisville: University of Louisville Press, 1952) and *Kinesics and Context* (Philadelphia: University of Pennsylvania Press, 1970).

132 Morgan, "The Kinesthetic Speaker," 115.

133 *Ibid.,* 116.

134 *Ibid.,* 117. Italics mine.

135 Weston, *The Film Director's Intuition,* Kindle Locations 5822–5823.

136 Jana Childers, *Performing the Word: Preaching as Theatre* (Nashville: Abingdon Press, 1998), 111–112.

137 *Ibid.,* 112. See also Charles L. Bartow, *Effective Speech Communication in Leading Worship* (Nashville: Abingdon Press, 1988), 25–26. Bartow speaks of the "interpretive dynamic" of speech in worship—"because speech in worship is not in any way mechanical... We need to 'live into' what we speak. We need to be grasped by the intellectual and emotional content of the call or confession and to manifest at the same time, in words, vocal tone, posture, facial expression, and gesture what has grasped us."

138 *Ibid.,* 112.

139 *Ibid.,* 49.

140 Mark Burrows, *Children First: Worshiping with the Family of God,* (Abingdon Press, 2010).

141 Boorstin, *Making Movies Work,* 82, 85.

142 Audrey Wells. director's commentary, *Under the Tuscan Sun.*

143 Interview featured at FilmSkills.com, https://www.youtube.com/watch?v=Xm4rvPMsN Jo&index=19&list=PLTQtyhf0KOJw8XCFrJUPw2-vbMV6ad3od

144 Summary description, https://www.youtube.com/watch?v=Xm4rvPMsNJo&index=19 &list=PLTQtyhf0KOJw8XCFrJUPw2-vbMV6ad3od

145 Boorstin, *Making Movies Work,* 56.

146 Ascher and Pincus, *The Filmmaker's Handbook,* 346–347.

147 Boorstin, *Making Movies Work,* 48.

148 *Ibid.,* 47.

149 Weston, *The Film Director's Intuition, Kindle Locations 5182–5183.*

150 Boorstin, *Making Movies Work,* 128–129.

151 Roger Ebert: *Life Itself,* (Life Itself, LLC, 2014).

152 *Ibid.*

INDEX

Expand Your Training

More Ways to Learn from Dr. Marcia McFee

Think Like a Filmmaker Live Q&A Webinars

Get clarity and personal advice just by logging onto a webinar! Once a month you can join Dr. McFee live to ask any questions about the book and/or worship at your church! It's a FREE virtual consult. Sign up at www.thinklikeafilmmaker.com.

> *"I want to express my sincere thanks and joy for your webinar. I enjoyed every minute and I actually took great notes! It was wonderful!"* —*Georgia, director of music*

Worship Design Studio

The book is just the tip of the iceberg when it comes to great training at your fingertips. Become part of the community of hundreds of churches that have a yearly subscription to Dr. McFee's coaching website that includes a vast collection of articles, webinars, resources, video sessions and almost ten years of worship series ideas! Use the promo code TLAF for an instant discount at checkout! Find out more at www.worshipdesignstudio.com.

> *"Our worship has been SOOOOO blessed by the Worship Design Studio's amazing resources! I'm grateful for all the talent you share with the series and planning—it makes my job less stressful when the mechanics and admin of running a church intrude, as they regularly do, on my worship planning and creativity time."* —*Mel, WDS subscriber*

Worship Design Studio Planning Retreats

What if you could go on a retreat and come home having discerned worship themes for the upcoming year with a worship expert as your guide? Join Dr. McFee at her late summer/early fall retreats in various places around the country to jumpstart you and your team for an amazing year of worship! Registration information in the Calendar link at www.marciamcfee.com.

> *"Quick affirmation—the planning retreat has made a tremendous difference in worship already. I have fleshed out the year thanks to your modeling how to make the lectionary work in series!! Thank you for letting God use you and your team!"* —Hillary, planning retreat participant

Continuing Education Retreats

Need to turbo-boost your worship design skills? Dr. McFee holds 5-day continuing education and spiritual renewal retreats that will heighten and deepen your leadership and get you on track for a production schedule that will free your time and your creativity. See www.marciamcfee.com for more information.

> *"Oh. My. Gosh. This was absolutely THE best workshop ever... ever. The caliber of what you presented and how you presented it, your methodology of teaching and sharing information, always affirming and invitational. I will be absorbing for quite a while."* —Pamela, retreat participant

Worship Design Studio Experience—Video Series

Wish you could bring your whole team to a retreat but can't find it in the budget this year? Get a virtual training experience through this video series filmed with a live audience! In over 16 hours of curriculum, see the concepts in this book come alive. Find more information at www.thinklikeafilmmaker.com.

"I want to tell you how much I loved your workshops! The majority of the congregation is elderly and not in favor of most changes, but after getting inspiration from you, my worship committee decided to forge ahead and see what happens… and we are getting positive feedback! Thank you again for the energy and new vision you have given us." —Linda, workshop participant

Keynotes and Workshops

Because Dr. McFee's live presentations are as inspirational as they are informational, she is a sought-after speaker. She is available for keynote addresses at your denominational event as well as one-day workshops designed specifically for worship arts teams from churches in a region. Fill out the contact form at www.marciamcfee.com.

"Thank you so much for your stunning plenary presentation at our conference last week. We not only learned from your example, it was a time of worship for us. That doesn't happen often in plenary addresses, so it is a rare and deeply treasured moment. We are all deeply grateful." —Deborah, executive director, international music organization

Church Consultations

For more focused and personal help, a variety of options are available for church consultations online or in person with Dr. McFee or a Worship Design Studio Associate. Contact us at www.marciamcfee.com for details.

"The week has been an almost constant source of individual comments regarding the whole of your visit here. This place is abuzz with excitement as the result of the weekend. We were blessed and doubly blessed." —Tom, pastor

Worship Design Studio Academy

Do you feel called to ministry as a worship designer, series team leader, director of worship arts, or consultant? The Worship Design Studio Academy will be receiving applications for our in-depth training program soon. Go to www.marciamcfee.com to contact us and let us know of your interest (seminary credit available).

> *"I have been digging deeply into the topic of worship for the past 10 years or so. This is undoubtedly the best practical guide for assessing 'what is, what can be, and how to get there' that I have seen. I am sure that I will be using this information in great detail throughout the application portion of my thesis."* —Brenda, doctoral student

Made in the USA
Lexington, KY
21 June 2016